Alan Palmer has a first-class honours degree in modern history from Oxford and was elected a Fellow of the Royal Society of Literature in 1980. He is the critically-acclaimed author of some 35 histories and biographies that include *Frederick the Great*, *Bismarck*, *The Decline and Fall of the Ottoman Empire*, *Twilight of the Hapsburgs* and *Victory 1918*. His *Napoleon in Russia* was Antonia Fraser's choice as a *Sunday Times* Book of the Year, of which she wrote: 'A fine piece of narrative history, a combination of suspense and scholarship.'

The SALIENT

YPRES, 1914–18

ALAN PALMER

CONSTABLE • LONDON

To Charmain and Christopher Johnson
in gratitude and with deep affection

CONSTABLE

First published in Great Britain in 2007 by Constable,
an imprint of Constable & Robinson Ltd

This edition published in 2016 by Constable

Copyright © Alan Palmer, 2007

3 5 7 9 10 8 6 4

The moral right of the author has been asserted.

A CIP catalogue record for this book
is available from the British Library.

ISBN: 978-1-4721-2480-7

Printed and bound in Great Britain by Clays Ltd, St Ives plc

Papers used by Constable are from well-managed forests
and other responsible sources.

MIX
Paper from
responsible sources
FSC® C104740

Constable
An imprint of
Little, Brown Book Group
Carmelite House
50 Victoria Embankment
London EC4Y 0DZ

An Hachette UK Company
www.hachette.co.uk

www.littlebrown.co.uk

CONTENTS

LIST OF ILLUSTRATIONS

The 2nd battalion, Scots Guard of the 7th Division nearing Ypres,
14 October 1914
(*Negative Q. 57189 courtesy of the Imperial War Museum, London*)

Survivors of the London Scottish after the Battle of Messines, 31 October
1914
(*Negative Q. 60737 courtesy of the Imperial War Museum, London*)

The 2nd battalion of the Royal Warwickshire Regiment aboard buses at
the height of First Ypres, 6 November 1914
(*Negative Q. 57328 courtesy of the Imperial War Museum, London*)

Christmas Truce, 1914: German soldiers greet British soldiers in no man's
land on Boxing Day
(*Negative HU35801 courtesy of the Imperial War Museum, London*)

The comforts of a German officer's dug-out, April 1915
(*Negative Q. 51067 courtesy of the Imperial War Museum, London*)

Soldiers of the East Surrey Regiment in the trenches, 11 June 1917
(*Negative Q. 2315 courtesy of the Imperial War Museum, London*)

A stretcher party on the second day of Passchendaele, August 1917
(*Negative Q. 5935 courtesy of the Imperial War Museum, London*)

Kaiser Wilhelm with Crown Prince Rupprecht of Bavaria, June 1918
(*Negative Q. 23728 courtesy of the Imperial War Museum, London*)

Australian infantry passing the ruins of Cloth Hall in Ypres, 25 October
1917
(*Negative E (AUS). 1171 courtesy of the Imperial War Museum, London*)

ACKNOWLEDGEMENTS

It is a pleasure to acknowledge the help I received from many different sources during the years spent writing *The Salient*. I am grateful to the staffs of the London Library, the Bodleian Library and the Oxfordshire County Libraries for their ready assistance. Sir Martin Gilbert – a friend ever since I had the good fortune to teach him in the Highgate School sixth form – shared with me some of his deep knowledge of both world wars. Dr Christopher Dowling, another one-time pupil, and his wife, Angela Godwin, welcomed me to the Imperial War Museum, where I also benefited from the guidance of Hilary Roberts of the photographic archive. Clare and Robert Brown encouraged me, as so often in recent years. On particular points, I am indebted to my niece Catherine Clarke and to Marsali Dening, whose father served with the Australian 14th Infantry Battalion. I much appreciate the loan of material from Michael Millard, including his father's unpublished recollections of Nieuport Bains before 1914 and of Third Ypres. At Ieper, Genevra Charnley was an informative guide to modern developments, and I thank the management and staff of the Ariane Hotel for their help and solicitude during my recent visits.

Anyone reading the reference notes and bibliography will realize the heavy debt I owe to the many detailed studies published in the last quarter of a century as well as to earlier official histories and memoirs. As it has proved impossible to trace all copyright holders, the author and publisher apologize to those whom they have not been able to contact. Every effort will be made in any future edition to rectify previous omissions. Max Arthur's *Forgotten Voices of the Great War* and Lyn Macdonald's *1914* and her *1914–1918: Voices and Images of the Great War* have been of particular value. So, too, were the many works written or edited by Malcolm Brown of the Imperial War Museum. He also wrote an informative introduction to the highly entertaining facsimile edition of *The Wipers Times* published by Little Books Ltd in 2006. Ian Beckett's invaluable *Ypres: The First Battle, 1914* includes the vivid letter by Captain (later Lieutenant-Colonel) Dillon (on pp. 68–9) from the Imperial War Museum archive. Gary Sheffield and John Bourne's edition of *The Haig Diaries* supplements Robert Blake's no less valuable earlier collection of Haig's private papers. Herbert Sulzbach's *With the German Guns* is a particularly stimulating personal narrative of a young German officer's experience. The Battleground Europe series published by Leo Cooper always made rewarding reading, especially Peter Oldham's *Messines Ridge* and Nigel Cave's *Sanctuary Wood and Hooge* as well as his summaries of Passchendaele, Polygon Wood and Hill 60. Peter Liddle's compendium *Passchendaele in Perspective* includes several contributions from which, as the reference notes show, I have profited greatly. Gavin Roynon's edition of the Crofton diaries, *Massacre of the Innocents*, is particularly attractive and well produced. Major and Mrs Holt's *The Ypres Salient* remains indispensable. It is far more than a guidebook.

Constable and Robinson have shown great patience in awaiting completion of a book delayed for two years by health problems and I much appreciate their understanding. With gratitude I recall the enthusiasm Carol O'Brien showed for the project when it was first mooted. Subsequently, I have benefited from the refreshing suggestions and eagle eye of my copy editor, Helen Armitage, as well as from Claudia Dyer's guidance at Constable and Robinson.

The Salient could not have been written without the support I received from Christopher Johnson and his wife, Charmian Hearne. I have enjoyed their hospitality and the fun of their young family time and time again. Christopher has been my computer mentor and, to my delight, found time to drive me to Ieper in 2001, 2005 and 2006 for research visits, his camera and notebook at the ready. With great pleasure I dedicate this book to them both.

Alan Palmer, February 2007

AUTHOR'S NOTE

In rendering measurements of distance and weight I have followed practices common during the First World War. Distances therefore appear in yards and miles. Readers accustomed to thinking metrically may find it useful to refer to the table featured below. Measurements of volume and weight are given as metric for German and French guns and shells i.e. France's famous 75 mm field gun but in traditional imperial units for British weapons i.e. the British 18-pounder field gun.

	Imperial	Metric
Distance	1 inch	25.4mm
	1 foot (12 inches)	304.8mm
	1 yard (3 feet)	0.9 metres
	10 yards	9.1 metres
	100 yards	91.4 metres
	1 mile (1,760 yards)	1.6 km
	10 miles	16.1 km
	100 miles	160.9 km
	500 miles	804.6 km
Weight	1 lb	0.5 kg
	1 stone (14 lb)	6.3 kg

Alternative Place Names

Place names are shown as they appear on the official war office maps. Many names in modern guidebooks and on all signposts are in Flemish. Ypres, for example, is now known as Ieper. A list of alternative place names is therefore printed here.

1914–18 place names	Modern Flemish/Dutch place names
Boesinghe	Boezinghe
Cloth Hall	Lakenhalle
Courtrai	Kortrijk
Dickebusch	Dikkebus
Dixmude	Diksmuide
Furnes	Verne
Gheluvelt	Geluveld
La Panne	De Panne
Lille (France)	Rijsel
Louvain	Leuven
Menin	Menen
Menin Gate	Menenpoort
Messines	Mesen
Mons	Bergen
Mount Kemmel	Kemmelberg
Nieuport	Nieuwpoort
Passchendaele	Passendale
Poperinghe	Poperinge
Roulers	Roeselare
St Eloi	Sint Elooi
St Julien	Sint Juliaan
Wytschaete	Wijtschate
Ypres	Ieper
Yser (river)	Ijzer

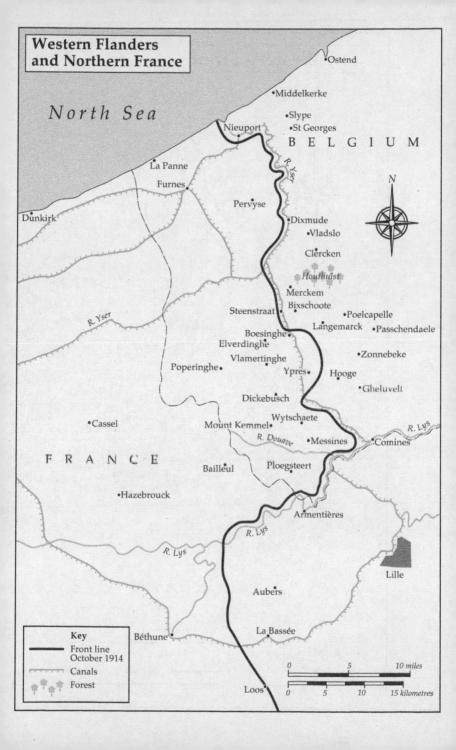

Western Flanders and Northern France

North Sea

B E L G I U M

F R A N C E

•Ostend

•Middelkerke

•Slype
•St Georges

Nieuport•

•R. Yser

La Panne•

Furnes•

Dunkirk•

Pervyse•

•Dixmude

•Vladslo

•Clercken

Houthulst

•Merckem

•Bixschoote

Steenstraat•

•Poelcapelle

Langemarck•

•Passchendaele

R. Yser

Boesinghe•

Elverdinghe•

Vlamertinghe•

•Zonnebeke

Poperinghe•

Ypres•

Hooge•

•Gheluvelt

Dickebusch•

Wytschaete•

Cassel•

Mount Kemmel•

R. Douave

•Messines

R. Lys

•Comines

Bailleul•

Ploegsteert•

•Hazebrouck

•Armentières

R. Lys

Lille

R. Lys

Aubers•

•La Bassée

Béthune•

N

Key

— Front line
    October 1914

Canals

Forest

Loos•

0		5		10 miles

| 0 | 5 | 10 | 15 kilometres |

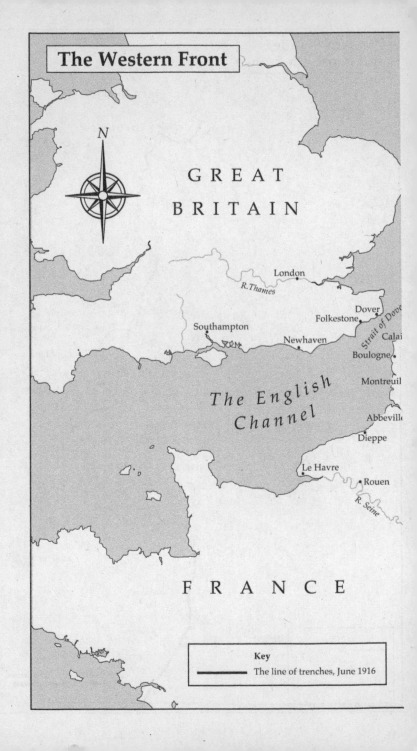

The Western Front

N

GREAT
BRITAIN

London
R. Thames

Dover
Folkestone
Southampton
Newhaven
Strait of Dover
Calai
Boulogne

Montreuil

The English
Channel

Abbeville

Dieppe

Le Havre
Rouen

R. Seine

FRANCE

Key
—— The line of trenches, June 1916

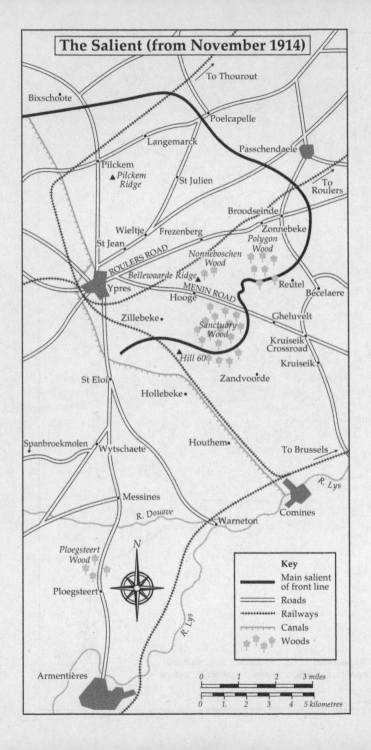

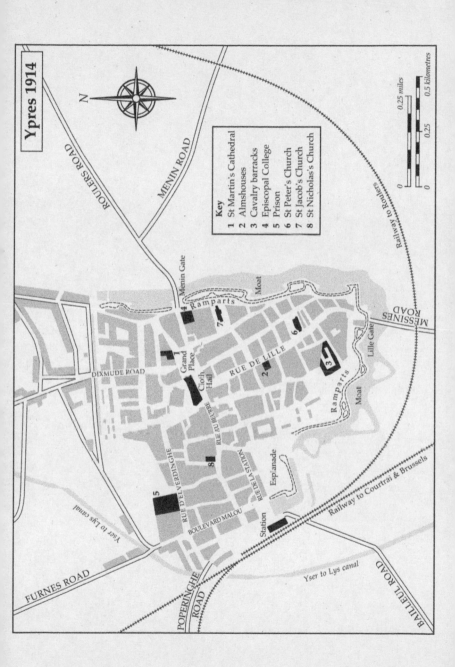

Ypres 1914

N

Key
1 St Martin's Cathedral
2 Almshouses
3 Cavalry barracks
4 Episcopal College
5 Prison
6 St Peter's Church
7 St Jacob's Church
8 St Nicholas's Church

0   0.25   0.5 kilometres
0   0.25 miles

ROULERS ROAD
MENIN ROAD
Railway to Roulers
MESSINES ROAD
Menin Gate
Ramparts
Moat
Lille Gate
Ramparts
Moat
RUE DE LILLE
DIXMUDE ROAD
Grand Place
Cloth Hall
RUE AU BEURRE
RUE DE LA STATION
RUE D'ELVERDINGHE
BOULEVARD MALOU
Esplanade
Station
Yser to Lys canal
Railway to Courtrai & Brussels
FURNES ROAD
POPERINGHE ROAD
Yser to Lys canal
BAILLEUL ROAD

PROLOGUE: CRUCIBLE OF WAR

Ypres is unique in British folk memory. Like Agincourt, Trafalgar and Waterloo it is a name to stir patriotic pride, though for different reasons and remembered in a different way. They were victories of a single day, celebrated in modern times by films and, at appropriate anniversaries, by the waving of flags and firework displays. By contrast, the struggle in Flanders is commemorated every evening by a simple ceremony in Ypres itself when the haunting sound of six bugles echoes the Last Post down silenced streets from under the arch of the Menin Gate.

Ypres was a defensive victory won by endurance and dogged determination in a series of battles, not by the master-stroke of one feat of arms. Although the first hours of the Somme brought heavier casualties than on any morning at Ypres, the fighting in Flanders became the longest campaign in modern British history and the costliest in lives. The first battle, at the onset of winter in 1914, destroyed the core of Britain's old professional army and exposed the realities of total war to volunteers who, less than a year back in time, never imagined they would find themselves on a battlefield. Between October 1914 and October 1918 seven soldiers from King George V's armies perished in the Salient for every hour the fighting continued. Tens of thousands more who returned home bore for the rest of their days the physical and mental wounds of their ordeal. Ninety years after Passchendaele, Ypres remains a national legend hallowed by mass sacrifice.

The Salient, the 35-mile bulge in the Western Front that covered Ypres, was the sector of line closest to England's shores; at least one officer is known to have downed a mug of breakfast tea in the trenches and dined that evening at his London club. With the return of peace, visitors from Britain began to travel again to Flanders, modern pilgrims to a town whose mediaeval splendour lay in ruins. At first they were advised to take the 61-mile sea voyage from Dover to Ostend aboard a Belgian steamer. Soon, however, they had the option of sailings by night to Zeebrugge from Hull or from Harwich.

I remember all the excitement of that Continental Train from Liverpool Street station to the coast and a night crossing from Parkeston Quay, Harwich, made shortly before my seventh birthday. My father had served in Egypt and Salonika not on the Western Front, but two of his brothers fought in Flanders (and survived). From Heist, where we were spending a holiday beside the sea, my parents took me on a trip to Ypres. I have a faint memory of the Flanders tower at Dixmude (by then Diksmuide), the original IJzertoren, a Celtic-style cross dedicated to the Flemish war dead. More sharply I recall trenches on Hill 60, a British tank preserved in Ypres, the pristine whiteness of the Menin Gate and watching work on restoring the Cloth Hall, with the belfry encased in scaffolding and walls that still – in 1933 – looked like a line of broken tooth stumps. This holiday fired a liking for Belgium and an admiration for its peoples I have retained all my life.

Since 1994, visitors are more likely to come by Channel Tunnel train and car than by sea, though there are still night sailings from Hull to Zeebrugge, while from Dover ferries cross to Calais and hydrofoils to Ostend. Young people – a little older than I was seven decades ago – take guided school trips to the Salient, seeing for themselves the contours of battle and the awesome cemeteries. They scramble into trenches preserved in Sanctuary Wood, peer into bunkers, stand beside mine craters, cast their eyes over guns, shells and helmets in local collections. At the In Flanders Fields Museum, on the upper floor of the restored Cloth Hall, computer technology enables them to trace the fate of individual soldiers and some civilians who stayed on, too. They hear the sounds of battle, and even the night sky is re-created for them. Educationally this is an excellent venture. The museum does not glorify war: it honours sacrifice by a sombre realism that is in keeping with modern Ieper's role as an international Town of Peace.

In its darkest years Ypres was of course an international Town of War, and since the early 1920s pilgrims have come from many

lands other than the United Kingdom. Cemeteries on both sides of
the Belgian-French frontier contain the graves of Americans,
Australians, Belgians, Canadians, Chinese, French, Indians, Irish,
Newfoundlanders, New Zealanders, Portuguese, South Africans
and soldiers from the islands of the West Indies. 'Ypern' also
became a name of sorrow and pride beyond the Rhine: over
100,000 soldiers of the German army lie buried in Flanders, more
men than the Treaty of Versailles allowed the post-war German
armed forces, the Reichswehr, to maintain. When in 2005 I saw for
the first time the *Grieving Parents* monument at Vladslo, sculpted by
Käthe Kollwitz, a Berlin mother mourning a son of 18, I was
moved by her artistry and deeply pacifist sincerity. Her two
kneeling figures must surely be the most poignant evocation of
family suffering in any war cemetery.

It was with some hesitation that I decided to write a book about the
Salient. At heart I have long been an 'Easterner', particularly
interested in the history of central Europe, the Balkans and the
Ottoman Empire, rather than a 'Westerner'. Moreover, there have
recently been so many fine compilations based on diaries, letters
and sound-recorded reminiscence that it seemed doubtful if anything further could be said about the fighting in Flanders. I found
from conversation that many younger people, stimulated by these
books and by television, were seeking to put their newly found
sympathy with the men in the trenches into a wider context. They
were asking questions often pondered in my mind. How did the
episodes of which they had read relate to policies and plans shaped
in the preceding years of fragile peace? Why in 1914 did Ypres, of
all Belgian's half-forgotten historic cities, become a crucible of war?
Was there an alternative grand strategy, to avoid what Winston
Churchill called 'chewing on the barbed wire of Flanders'? Should
the Salient have been abandoned for a shorter, more defensible
line? Were conditions for the German soldiery as bad as for the
British? And how far did the Great War in Flanders shape the
subsequent history of both Belgium and Europe? I decided to
attempt a book that would seek answers to these questions and
others as well.

The Salient therefore draws on published sources that range from
the journals of leading statesmen and military commanders down to

the diaries and letters and oral reminiscence of the 'other ranks' in the trenches. At times the book necessarily goes well beyond specifically military history, and it covers far more than the 400 square miles of salient shown on the maps. It looks also at Mons, the Marne, the Aisne and Antwerp, and treats fighting down the Yser to the sea as integral to the better known events around Ypres itself.

The narrative is not confined to the four years of the Great War. It goes back in time, for the dead hands of a German field marshal and a Belgian general helped determine strategy in the first two months of the conflict, and it is impossible to ignore lessons learnt by the French in 1870 or for the British Expeditionary Force (BEF), more recently on the South African veldt. My account continues beyond the Armistice, with a chapter on the aftermath of the long campaign during the inter-war years and ends with what is essentially an epilogue looking at the events of 1940, for they provide both continuity with and a contrast to the earlier clash of arms. Almost a century later, grievances raised in the Yser 'trenches of death' still find an echo in Belgium's current political controversies.

Fashions change in historical writing and prejudices with them. Although I hope to do justice to other peoples, inevitably I write as an Englishman, born into a generation that respected tradition and authority, though not uncritically. I am not prepared to look for 'bunglers' or 'cowards'. As for my heroes and heroines, they are not always mentioned by name. They abound in collective memory, serving in the trenches or in hospitals behind the lines, challenging death in single combat in the skies and, in their thousands, waiting anxiously at home for news week after week, in pride and in dread. All honour to them.

2

'UNEQUALLED IN GRANDEUR'

Five days after Britain went to war with Germany in 1914 a special Sunday edition of *The Times* included a full-page map of the North Sea and its shores, showing likely objectives in the coming clash of arms. West of the German frontier are names already in the news on other pages, the Belgian towns of Liège, Dinant, Namur. The cities of Brussels, Ghent, Bruges and Antwerp are on the map and so along the coast is Ostend, the port from where steamships had crossed regularly to Dover since 1847, with the fastest of the day's three services now enabling a traveller to reach London in six hours. Yet the choice of Belgian place-names seems haphazard, prompted perhaps by holiday familiarity or business links. In western Flanders, Nieuport is there, at the mouth of the River Yser. It was not a fashionable resort like Ostend although Nieuport Bains, a long beach north of the old town, offered golden sands, a casino-kursaal, tennis courts and a golf course in the making. Just 7 miles inland, Dixmude is also marked, a market town with a steady ongoing trade in cheap butter across to Kent. But southeast of Dixmude, down to the frontier with France, the map shows no names at all.

The region formed a shallow saucer, rimmed with ridges. It was crossed by canals, streams ('beeks') and two rivers, the Yser, flowing down to the sea for 50 miles from the chalky downland of Artois, and the 90-mile long Lys, a tributary of Belgium's principal river, the Scheldt. There were numerous scattered villages, clumps of woodland, a few nineteenth-century chateaux and occasional farms with thick hedges marking the boundaries of their largely open fields. On slightly rising ground in the centre of the saucer a slumbering town with Gothic spires and towers presided benignly

over the formless landscape. Nothing newsworthy had happened
there since Napoleon passed through more than a hundred years
ago: why include it on any map of likely battlefields? Ypres was
duly left off the map. So for that matter, 160 miles beyond the
Flanders frontier, was Verdun.[1]

Earlier cartographers would never have omitted Ypres. Long
before the coming of printing and the first newssheets the town
was a coveted prize, with a golden age back in the thirteenth
century. Some 40,000 people are thought to have lived there in
1260 when it was the centre of the Flemish wool trade and famous
across Europe for its cloth fair. At Nieuport ships from England and
the Hanse Baltic ports entered the river, making their way up-
stream to the centre of the town, some unloading their cargoes at a
covered quay within the Cloth Hall itself.

Despite plague and pestilence in 1318 and the migration of
many weavers to healthier towns the merchants continued to
prosper, their wealth arousing the envy of neighbours. Foreign
soldiery came, first the French, and then in the summer of 1383
an English army, led by Sir Henry Despenser, bishop of Norwich,
and allied to Ypres's trade competitors in Ghent. Technically the
English were Crusaders, assured by the Church of remission of
their sins for supporting an enterprise pledged to defeat French
schismatics loyal to the rival pope in Avignon. In practice they
were a rabble bent on loot and backed by a parliament with
trading interests at stake. Nieuport, Dixmude and several villages
were sacked; Ypres was invested. 'A great machine . . . called the
Gun of Canterbury' lobbed missiles at the defenders, the chroni-
cler Henry Knighton records.[2] But the town held out. After three
months of desultory campaigning, dust on the horizon gave
warning that a French relief force was approaching, and Bishop
Despenser broke off the siege. The Norwich Crusaders, their
numbers depleted by mass desertion, headed home. They sacked
Gravelines as they went, leaving their allies from Ghent to fend
for themselves. The English soldiery's earliest expedition to
Flanders was far from glorious.

For three centuries, war swept western Flanders with weary
regularity. Even in Tudor times the Belgian lands were already
dubbed 'the cockpit of Europe'. Ypres was frequently besieged.

Dutch rebels and their Spanish masters took control. So, too, did both Catholics and Huguenots during the French Wars of Religion. Commercial life remained vibrant, despite a fall in population, and, as in the Dutch cities further north, burgher pride was manifested in civic splendour: the Nieuwerke, built 1620–23, gave the east side of the Cloth Hall an elegant façade above a vaulted gallery. Ypres became a prime objective of Louis XIV's armies and was invested on four more occasions, assisted in 1658 by an English contingent, dispatched by Lord Protector Cromwell. Twenty years later the town finally succumbed to a sustained French assault.

During the next decade King Louis's renowned military engineer, Marshal Vauban, transformed Ypres into a pivotal fortress in a defensive chain that covered his citadel at Lille and ran from Dunkirk on the coast through Menin, Tournai and Maubeuge across to Dinant, on the Meuse. Ypres was fortified too hurriedly to rate as a Vauban masterpiece, but earthen ramparts strengthened by brick served as a protective perimeter; work began on linked canals to improve communications and, with a moat beside the ramparts, act as a defensive water barrier. Twice during the War of the Spanish Succession (1701–14) the Duke of Marlborough proposed to his allies that the British should lay siege to Ypres and oust the French. He was persuaded instead to deploy his armies further to the east, winning Ramillies on the first occasion and, on the second, the costly victory at Malplaquet, outside Mons.[3]

Ypres became a southwestern outpost of the Austrian Netherlands in 1713, but France continued to covet the region, which passed under direct rule from Paris in 1794, after the Revolution. Twenty years later, on the downfall of Napoleon, the peace treaty restored the old frontier, 12 miles to the south. West Flanders, with eight other Belgian provinces, was incorporated in the United Kingdom of the Netherlands.

For exactly a hundred years no foreign invader disturbed life in Ypres. When the Belgian people gained their independence from their northern neighbours in 1830, there was a brief incursion of Dutch troops into the provinces of Limburg and Liège, but no alarms troubled the south or west of the country. In April 1839 the Great Powers – Britain, France, Prussia, Austria and Russia – signed

the Treaty of London collectively guaranteeing Belgium's independence so long as the kingdom remained a 'perpetually neutral
state'. The combatants in the Franco-Prussian War of 1870 respected this undertaking. For the first time in six centuries the
Belgian people could stand aside from a major conflict in western
Europe. In the Ardennes they heard the ominous iteration of guns
from Sedan and kept a cautious watch along the frontier with
France, but the victorious Germans thrust forward to invest Paris,
and the fighting receded without any breach of neutrality. The
Belgians marvelled at their good fortune. Successive governments
through the last decades of the century shaped policy to make
certain it was retained.

In 1914, Ypres was still modestly prosperous, though the population was less than 19,000. The street names were in French, for it
remained the language of government, business and higher education, but the Flemish dialect of Dutch was in common usage, and
the village place-names sounded Dutch. The town was not
industrialized. A few small factories continued to turn out linen
and cotton fabrics. There were soap works and a bakery proud of its
gingerbread. A brewery flourished in one of the fourteenth-
century houses south of the cathedral; hops had been grown
around neighbouring Poperinghe for many centuries; it appears
to be from there that the plant was brought to Kent before the
Reformation. There were fields of sugar beet and turnips; rich
pasture sustained good healthy cows. Along the Menin Road
tobacco was cultivated, the leaves hanging down to dry in the
autumn from beams in farmhouse lofts or in the better-built
outhouses. As across so much of Flanders, lace-making provided
work at home for wives and daughters, with the local embroidery
as intricate in style as the tracery above the doors of the older
buildings. On Saturdays the Grand Place served as the Grote Markt,
with stalls that specialized in dairy produce, particularly butter, but
the family farms barely provided enough work for the younger
men except in harvest time. Some found jobs some 20 miles away
in the industrial complex around Lille, then France's fifth-largest
city.[4]

Vauban's ramparts were demilitarized in the middle of the
nineteenth century, giving the townsfolk a pleasant elevated

promenade: the Lille Gate was preserved, but the Menin Gate became little more than a passage leading to a causeway across the moat; a pair of decorative stone lions were left sleepily on guard. There was, however, still a military presence in the city. The Belgian army's cavalry school was at Ypres, with barracks near the Lille Gate and practice jumps in a secluded exercise arena out at Polygon Wood, 3 to 4 miles to the east. There the horsemen prepared for international shows and for the 1912 Olympics at Stockholm, in which Belgium won an equestrian bronze medal. As in most European countries, the cavalry constituted an élite, for there were little more than 300 cavalry officers in the whole army, and the school's commandant was highly respected by the citizenry. Few lads from Ypres served in the ranks of the cavalry, but since 1910, all 18-year-old men across Belgium had been conscripted into the army for 'personal service' of at least 20 months. They received their military training at Antwerp or with a garrison away from their town of birth.

Except on market day little broke the silence of Ypres's streets, apart from the clatter of hooves on the cobbles and the bells from St Martin's Cathedral or one of the old parish churches – St Peter's, St Jacob's, St Nicholas's. A carillon, too, rang out from the belfry of the Cloth Hall, for so long the pride of the city. The hall was the largest secular building of Gothic Europe, with a southern façade over 400 feet in length, a belfry 230 feet high, and conical corner-turrets at each end of the north and south fronts. The building of what originally served as a hall for the Drapers' Guild began in 1201 and was completed slightly more than a hundred years later; the ravages of a damp climate ate into the stonework and took a toll of the sculpted figures of the counts of Flanders, who for centuries looked down on the Grand Place from the façade. Careful craftsmanship, including 44 new statues to replace the counts, restored the Hall's full glory in the 1850s and 1860s. A visitor from England, the architect George Gilbert Scott, was impressed by its grandeur and the pre-war Baedeker guidebook suggests that the Cloth Hall inspired the successful design he submitted for the Rathaus in Hamburg. Anyone in London who walks from the British Library towards King's Cross may see the influence of Ypres in the clock-tower and frontage of Scott's Terminus Hotel at St Pancras Station.

In an increasingly sceptical age, Ypres remained assertively
Roman Catholic, honouring Our Lady of Thuyne as patron
saint, for she was credited with saving the weavers and their
families from the wrath and rapine of the Norwich Crusaders.
Not every bishop had been passively obedient. In the early
seventeenth century Cornelius Jansen, who was buried in the
cathedral cloisters, famously challenged Jesuit assumptions over
the teaching of St Augustine. But Jansenism was soon stamped
out in the province of its birth, though it survived around
Utrecht in the Netherlands. Religious conformity prevailed. In
1914 there were several convent schools in or around the town,
serving comfortably bourgeois Belgian families who could not
quite afford to send their daughters to Bruges or across to
England. Irish Benedictines first came when Vauban was putting
the defences in order, and they had been teaching in the town for
more than 200 years. With a medieval cathedral, almshouses, an
episcopal college and swans serenely paddling on the moat
beneath the ramparts, Ypres possessed the enchantment of a
small English city, Wells or Ripon perhaps.

Some of the older families had ambitions for their home town.
Over the previous 30 years the western quarter of Ypres had
benefited from far-sighted planning. The seven roads that radiated
to all points of the compass and had brought prosperity in the
city's golden age were given *pavé* surfaces and, in many places, the
shade of an avenue of poplars or willows. The canal that ran
northwards to join the Yser (itself canalized), south of Dixmude,
was modernized and so too was the canal that met the River Lys
at Comines.

In the city itself the architect Jules Coomans was entrusted with a
major restoration and development project, nearing completion in
the summer of 1914. A new redbrick railway station, with
wrought-iron stanchions supporting a long canopy over the platform, was opened in 1900; trains ran several times a day to Courtrai
and Brussels. Visitors stepped out of the Gare, crossed the grandly
named Boulevard de la Station and Boulevard Malou (renamed
Maloulan) and followed an esplanade lined with young trees to the
historic centre. Jules Malou, the local worthy whom the street
honoured, had been a Catholic Party deputy in the Brussels
parliament and finance minister in four governments. The land-

scaping was his brainchild, but Coomans's plans were backed by Malou's successor, Jules Vandenpeereboom, who was minister of post and railways in all five governments between 1884 and 1899 and briefly prime minister.[5] The burghers thought highly of the Vandenpeereboom family; a statue of Jules's father, Burgomaster Alphonse, was placed between the Cloth Hall and the cathedral in 1892. The head and shoulders of the statue, carefully restored after the years of bombardment, survive on the site today.

The Vandenpeerebooms were firm believers in the value of railways to the community; their enterprise served town and province well. 'The first view of Ypres as one approaches it by the railway from Courtrai is most engaging, the gentle hill . . . being crowned with an architectural group unequalled in Belgium for grandeur,' wrote the London ecclesiologist Francis Bumpus six years before the coming of the war, lavishing praise on the country's 'admirable railway system'.[6] If he consulted the current edition of Baedeker's *Belgium and Holland*, Bumpus will have found there a section specifically headed 'The Railways of S.W. Flanders'. Travellers were warned that the line served 'so many stations that the speed of the trains is extremely slow'; the 35-mile journey from Ostend took from two hours to two and a quarter.[7] But as the roads were much poorer than in neighbouring France, resort was often made to trams and light railways. By 1914 trams were running along the Menin Road from Ypres and out towards Bailleul.

In southern and central Belgium the density of railway track was as high as anywhere in Europe, with the hub of the system around Antwerp and Malines rather than Brussels. The pattern, established some fifty years before Francis Bumpus's visit, was dictated by economic needs, but inevitably it acquired military significance, particularly the line from Antwerp running through Hasselt to Liège, Namur and Dinant. Jules Vandenpeereboom had looked forward to the day when the railways he advocated for West Flanders would attract tourists to Ypres as an alternative to the medieval delights of Bruges and Ghent. Instead his railways, too, were to serve a military purpose, helping shape the strategy of four years of war: the line westwards through Poperinghe went on to cross the frontier and join the main French network at Hazebrouck, a junction for the Channel ports of Dunkirk, Calais and

Boulogne. Along the routes that converged on Ypres almost every village had a station, or at least a tram halt, some with names that became terribly familiar in the months ahead: Hooge, Langemarck, Poelcapelle, Gheluvelt, Zonnebeke, Passchendaele. Even so, the existing lines proved insufficient to meet the needs of the allied armies, and, by 1917, 1,000 miles of light railway or standard-gauge track supplemented the system.[8]

One point on a stretch of railway south of Ypres acquired strategic importance out of all proportion to its natural character. Between 3 and 4 miles to the southeast the line to Comines ran through a cutting, from which the spoil had been used to create an artificial hill, 200 feet above sea level. Over several decades trees shot up in the fertile soil, and shrubs and rambling wild flowers made the mound an attractive spot, known locally as La Côte des Amants; it was popular with summer-evening strollers. By spring 1915, La Côte had become Hill 60 on British war maps, though still with a 'Lovers Lane' marked in English beside the railway. The hill was a key position to both the allies and the invader. The struggle for control of the knoll that the navvies had made raged for almost four years, with battles fought above and below ground, for sappers tunnelled into the foundations to plant mines that exploded with devastating effect. When peace returned, Hill 60 – like Passchendaele or forts Vaux and Douaumont at Verdun – remained enshrined in collective memory as a symbol of resolute resistance and valour.

All that suffering lay in a future that was fortunately unimaginable at high summer in 1914, when the long days remained as gloriously sunny in Flanders as across the Channel. News of the assassination of Archduke Franz Ferdinand and his wife by a Pan-Serb terrorist in Sarajevo on 28 June stirred sympathy for Austria in Ypres and all the Catholic regions of the country, but Balkan issues were of scant concern to Belgium as a whole and Bosnia seemed far away. Even when, a month later, the resultant Austro-Serbian crisis caused the rival Great Powers to mobilize, there was little alarm in Brussels and even less in West Flanders. The first talks between the Belgian general staff and the ministry of posts and railways over a possible mobilization came as late as 29 July, only four days before the kaiser's envoy in Brussels demanded free passage for German troops to invade France.[9] The ultimatum surprised and shocked Flemings and French-speaking Walloons alike, but the refusal of King Albert to bow to the German demands won warm support across the kingdom. As dawn broke on Tuesday, 4 August, a proud people stood to arms.

3

PLANS AND ILLUSIONS

M ost Belgians took it for granted that their country would soon again enjoy peace. For three weeks the Belgian general staff published stirring communiqués, puffed with complacency. Although there was shock at reports of the arbitrary execution of civilians as alleged *francs-tireurs* and by the punishment burning of Louvain, war still seemed far away from Ypres, and for two months daily life continued uneventfully. The cavalry left their barracks for the Front. Reservists responded to the call to the colours, among them some of the mounted gendarmerie. They were joined by hundreds of volunteers from the city and neighbouring villages in a burst of patriotic enthusiasm that swept the country. There were fewer trains, but the trams kept running. The harvest was gathered in and schools reopened, though the convents received fewer boarding pupils. In the Grand Place the belfry of the Cloth Hall remained hidden behind wooden scaffolding in the hope that the craftsmen would soon be back, chipping away at the grime of 70 years to complete Coomans's restoration project in time to impress another flock of visitors next summer. At first the invasion of their country made little difference to the townsfolk of Ypres.

They were not the only people sustained by confident optimism. Across Europe political observers assumed the war would be brief. During 99 years since Waterloo 14 conflicts had been fought on the continent: none dragged on for more than 15 months. Most were far shorter: even the greatest of them, the Franco-Prussian War of 1870, lasted only 185 days. Why should this latest clash of arms break the pattern? For more than ten years trade rivalry, colonial ambition and the encouragement of national pride in order to silence domestic disquiet threatened an end to the long peace.

Diplomacy defused successive crises, but their frequency weakened international trust; a war became increasingly probable. When it came, after the Sarajevo murders, the immediate cause was a failure to prevent the chronic tension between Austria-Hungary and Serbia escalating into a confrontation of rival alliances, German-Austrian and Franco-Russian.

By now the economies of the powers were so interdependent that it was thought no government would risk ruin by commitment to a long war over a cause of little concern to Europe as a whole. When Kaiser Wilhelm assured his guards they would be home before the leaves fell, few Germans doubted their sovereign's word. In Paris newly enlisted students thought they would be away for 'two months, maybe three', while some undergraduates from Oxford and Cambridge who volunteered in early August felt certain they would be back in college by the start of term in October.[1]

This belief in a short, mobile war shaped the plans of the main belligerents. German strategy was based on a modified form of the 'great memorandum' completed by Field Marshal Count von Schlieffen in December 1905, on the eve of his retirement as chief of the general staff. He proposed a scythe-like sweep, in which 59 German divisions would wheel through Holland, Flanders and Artois to envelop Paris from the West within 39 days of mobilization and drive the exhausted French back on to a smaller army invading from Lorraine.[2] A demoralized France would then, it was assumed, sue for peace. Without support from their ally in the West, the Russians too would soon crumble.

Schlieffen's successor, Field Marshal Helmuth von Moltke 'the Younger' – nephew and namesake of the architect of victory in Bismarck's wars – drastically revised this grand design. He favoured a broad arrow thrust, swinging southwards down an arc west of Brussels but east of Ghent and Lille, ignoring both West Flanders and the Channel coast. Paris would still, he hoped, be invested within six weeks and France knocked out of the war, with her army crushed in a decisive pincer battle on the upper Marne. The size of the invasion force was increased from 53 divisions, as proposed by Schlieffen, to 55, and between 4 and 17 August 1914 four armies, totalling 940,000 men, poured across Germany's 83-mile frontier with Belgium in fulfilment of the plan.[3]

To some extent, French strategy played into Moltke's hands. In April 1913, General Joseph Joffre, chief of the French general staff for the past two years, presented Plan 17 to the council of national defence in Paris. Earlier proposals had assumed France would at first stay on the defensive, parrying an expected German attack from Lorraine and Alsace before launching a counter-offensive once the French fortresses of Verdun, Toul and Épinal blunted the on-slaught. Plan 17 – operative from May 1914 – allowed France to take the initiative earlier, as soon as mobilization was complete. The plan would carry the war eastwards towards the Rhine – and therefore by mischance away from the regions most threatened by the modified Schlieffen Plan. Five French armies were poised to invade Germany, three along a front southwards from Verdun to the Vosges, a fourth in reserve on the upper Marne and a fifth covering the Ardennes, with Thionville as the objective.

For several years intelligence reports of German map exercises had indicated Berlin's interest in the Belgian Ardennes but not in any region beyond the Meuse or the Sambre. Joffre personally thought a German invasion of Belgium unlikely, if only from fear that violation of the kingdom's neutrality would bring Britain into the war. If he were wrong, the Fifth Army would move north into the Belgian province of Luxembourg and, with support from the reserve Fourth Army, threaten the flank of any German force engaging the Belgian forts of Liège and Dinant. Plan 17 did not, however, assign any French corps to cover the 120 miles of Belgian frontier from Mézières to the sea, the very sector soon to stand in the path of General von Kluck's First Army. Joffre and his staff hoped that should war come to this region the gap would be plugged by the limited resources of the Belgian army and by a British expeditionary force concentrated along the Sambre, around the historic fortress of Maubeuge. But the council of national defence in Paris could never be certain *les Tommies* would be in the fighting line beside *les poilus*.[4]

Unlike Germany and France, Great Britain had developed no master-plan. For half a century successive governments avoided long-term European commitments; a deep reluctance to shed the fading splendour of isolation lingered at Westminster. Anglo-French relations in 1914 were based on the Entente Cordiale, established ten years previously when a formal Convention settled outstanding colonial disputes, including the rivalry over mastery in Egypt and the Sudan that had brought the two countries to the verge of war as recently as 1898. The Entente stopped a long way short of formal alliance. So too did the complementary Anglo-Russian Convention of 1907, by which agreement was reached over policy towards Persia, Tibet and Afghanistan. It was mistrust of Kaiser Wilhelm II's naval ambitions and in particular the rapid creation of a formidable High Seas Fleet that drew Britain closer to France and Russia and away from Germany, her traditional friend in Europe.

During the cycle of international crises over Morocco and the Balkans that threatened peace between 1906 and 1913, Sir Edward Grey, the foreign secretary, tended to collaborate with his two Entente partners in opposition to the Central Powers (Germany and Austria-Hungary), but the British government remained free either to engage in war or to stand aside. Legally, even the obligations of the famous undertaking to uphold Belgian neutrality were not binding on any one power alone but on all five signatories of the 1839 Treaty of London acting collectively. Yet cautiously, and without the knowledge of parliament or the full cabinet, links were established between senior officers in London and Paris. With the approval of the prime minister, the foreign secretary and the secretary of state for war, Anglo-French military conversations were held intermittently for more than eight years before the coming of the war.[5]

An informal, exploratory meeting of policy makers, held as early as 12 January 1906, determined the scope of the talks and gave warning of departmental conflicts ahead. 'It was settled between the Military Officers', the director of naval intelligence, Admiral Ottley, informed the first sea lord, 'that in the event of our being forced into war (by a German violation of Belgian neutrality or otherwise) our proper course would be to land our Military forces at the nearest French ports, Calais, Boulogne, Dieppe and Havre. About 100,000 British troops and 42,000 horses would be available. The entire British Army might be on French soil on the 14th day.'[6] The navy, however, favoured the traditional war strategy of blockade and amphibious operations rather than the dispatch of an expeditionary force across the Channel.

The foreign secretary sought to allay Admiralty fears of pre-cipitate commitment by the War Office: 'We haven't *promised* any help,' Grey explained three days after Ottley's report, 'but it is quite right that our Naval and Military Authorities should discuss the question in this way with the French and be prepared to give an answer when they are asked, or rather if they are asked.'[7] The 'navalists' were not convinced. They recognized, however, the need to deny Germany control of the North Sea coast from the Scheldt estuary to the Channel ports. To keep hold of Antwerp, Ostend and the new port of Zeebrugge made better strategic sense than commitment to a sector of a battle line deep inside France, they argued.

Many senior army officers – including the designated comman-der of the proposed expeditionary force, General Sir John French – also preferred bases in Belgium rather than close dependence on France. General French was in favour of establishing direct contact with the Belgian high command, independent of the ongoing Anglo-French talks. In early spring 1906 seven confidential meetings duly took place between General Ducarne, chief of the Belgian general staff, and the military attaché in Brussels, Lieutenant-Colonel Barnardiston. 'A satisfactory general agree-ment' was reached 'on a joint line of action', the attaché reported optimistically to London; detailed proposals set out ways to trans-port an expeditionary force from French ports to meet a German thrust towards Antwerp or through the Ardennes.[8] Ducarne, however, spoke largely for himself. His political masters feared any revelation of military consultation with Britain might com-promise Belgium's neutral status and provoke Germany.

During the next six years no attempt was made to develop these plans or to follow up the secret talks. By 1912 when, again on General French's initiative, a new military attaché sought to revive them, he found the Belgians unresponsive: colonial disputes in Africa had left them highly suspicious of British intentions. The war minister in Brussels even gave a warning that 'uninvited saviours of Belgian independence' would be fired upon. From October 1912 a division was stationed at Ghent, ready to augment the defences of Antwerp or, if necessary, repel a landing on the North Sea coast.[9]

Meanwhile the Anglo-French military conversations made slow progress, not least because the Admiralty retained greater influence

than the War Office in shaping imperial strategy. Closer co-
operation came with the appointment in August 1910 of the
Camberley Staff College commandant, Brigadier-General Henry
Wilson, as director of military operations (DMO). Wilson, a
Francophile since boyhood, was an Ulsterman who spoke French
well. While at Camberley he spent several holidays bicycling in
northeastern France near the German and Belgian frontiers, and
became so close a family friend of Ferdinand Foch, the rising star
among France's generals, that Foch invited him to his daughter's
wedding. At the height of the Agadir crisis with Germany in 1911,
Wilson crossed to Paris where, on his own initiative, he had talks
with General Dubail, acting chief of the French general staff.
Brigadier-General Wilson had no specific authority to speak for
the war secretary, or indeed for anyone else, and yet on 20 July the
two generals signed a memorandum of momentous importance.
They recommended that should France and Britain find themselves
allied in war against Germany, six regular divisions of the British
army – 110,000 men – and a division of cavalry would cross the
Channel to concentrate within a fortnight of mobilization in the
Arras–Cambrai–St Quentin area. General Joffre, who took office as
chief of the French general staff eight days later, accepted the
Dubail–Wilson memorandum as a working agreement, although
he recognized that it was never a firm commitment. The British
government 'wanted to make no engagement in writing', Joffre
explained to the council of national defence in 1913, while Plan 17
was under discussion: 'We shall therefore show prudence and not
depend on English forces in our operational projects.' [10]

On 23 August 1911, barely five weeks after Wilson's meeting
with Dubail, the British prime minister, Herbert Asquith, convened a meeting of the Committee of Imperial Defence (CID) to
consider strategy 'in the event of intervention' in a war between
France and Germany.[11] Wilson, a gifted lecturer with a persuasive
tongue, had an opportunity to expound his ideas, helped by maps
of Belgium and northern France that he had hung on the walls. He
surprised the service chiefs and the five cabinet ministers present by
working his way through a timetable that set out arrangements to
transport troops to Le Havre and Rouen and on by rail to
Maubeuge in great detail; allowance was even made for a ten-
minute coffee break at Amiens. His proposals were challenged by

Admiral of the Fleet Sir Arthur Wilson VC, the first sea lord, one of the few Crimean War veterans still on active service. Naval strategy, Sir Arthur explained, was based on the need to safeguard supply lines and defend the United Kingdom from invasion; the Admiralty had given no thought to sustaining an army on the continent; he personally assumed that earlier proposals to send an expeditionary force to France had been abandoned. The cabinet ministers, who included the future war leaders Lloyd George and Churchill, were more impressed by the brigadier-general's mastery of detail than the admiral of the fleet's generalized concepts. Captain Maurice Hankey, at the age of 34 beginning a long term as head of the CID secretariat, was by conviction a 'navalist', for he had been commissioned in the Royal Marines, but after writing up the minutes of the meeting even he was 'reluctantly driven to admit that the Senior Service . . . had sustained a severe defeat'.[12]

Over the next three years the navy continued to press for an essentially maritime grand strategy. Wilson remained the most articulate member of the CID. At times a combination of enthusiasm and self-esteem led him to give the French an impression that the War Office, Admiralty and cabinet agreed with him. Perhaps he believed it himself. He was mistaken. Traditionalists in both services mistrusted the continental commitment. Increasingly they came to mistrust Wilson personally too. He gained a reputation for intrigue, heightened by his closeness to Unionist politicians at a time when the Liberal government was seeking passage of a contentious Irish Home Rule Bill. As an Ulsterman himself, he warmly backed the dissidents in the Curragh incident of March 1914, when senior Protestant officers stationed at the Curragh in Dublin threatened to resign their commissions rather than march north to impose Irish Home Rule on Ulster. But so long as there was a possibility of Britain entering the war as an ally of France, Wilson's understanding of Joffre's needs made him irreplaceable as DMO. He was promoted major-general in November 1913, a few months after General French received the baton of a field marshal.[13]

Neither the British people nor their political leaders gave close attention to Europe's problems at high summer 1914. There was concern over the danger of civil war in Ireland but not over the implications of Austria-Hungary's quarrel with Serbia. It was not until the late afternoon of Friday, 24 July, at the end of a long discussion on Ulster, that the cabinet turned to foreign affairs for the first time since the murder of Archduke Franz Ferdinand, 26 days previously. Grey read out the terms of the Austrian note to Serbia, newly received in London: Vienna demanded official condemnation of pan-Serb propaganda and the participation of Austro-Hungarian officers in interrogating and punishing Serbian officials who had connived at terrorist activity. That evening, writing to Venetia Stanley, the young woman whose friendship he deeply cherished, the prime minister deplored the 'bullying and humiliating ultimatum'. With the casualness of a detached observer of events he then added: 'We are within measurable, or imaginable, distance of a real Armageddon . . . Happily there seems to be no reason why we should be anything more than spectators.'[14]

Over the weekend the newspapers in London, Edinburgh and Manchester were not unsympathetic to Austria, and the general editorial tone showed restraint. The peak of the holiday season was at hand, and both the papers and weekly magazines continued to advertise excursions across the Channel. The first Monday in August would be the last official bank holiday before Christmas: Londoners were offered a day trip from Charing Cross station to Calais and back for 11 shillings and 6 pence or, an even better bargain, to Boulogne for 10 shillings (in today's currency 50p, though by present value the equivalent of about £20). Despite the news from Vienna and Belgrade, there was no sense of imminent doom at Westminster. Arthur Balfour, the former Unionist prime minister, saw no reason to change plans for an Austrian holiday at Gastein; he did not cancel his train reservations until the following Wednesday. On Saturday (25th) the foreign secretary went fly-fishing in Hampshire, as was his habit at weekends, but he was back at his desk next afternoon, pressing for a four-power conference. Winston Churchill, the first lord of the Admiralty, spent Sunday morning on the beach at Cromer with his wife and their three children, though he too returned to London by train later in the day. Asquith relaxed at his Berkshire country home, enjoying a round of golf at Huntercombe. Once away from London, the crisis seemed remote: Asquith's Sunday letter to Venetia Stanley even conceded that 'on many points Austria has a good, and Servia a very bad, case.'[15]

By Tuesday morning (28th) the prospect for Grey's conference looked slim, however. Russian backing for Serbia and German encouragement of Austria made it impossible to localize the dispute, while the French alliance with Russia (of which the precise terms remained unknown) extended the confrontation to western Europe's borders. The tone of the British press hardened day by day. From Berlin came reports of mass patriotic demonstrations continuing well into the night, and, though as yet there was no call-up of German reservists, the regular army in the Rhineland was said to be on the alert.

Lord Kitchener, Britain's most illustrious serving soldier, home on leave from Egypt, had lunch with Churchill on that Tuesday. 'The Germans must inevitably march' through Belgium 'to invade France', Churchill predicted. Kitchener agreed with him. Both men thought it 'very unlikely' the Belgians would resist.[16] That view was widespread in London and in Paris. The Belgians were not rated a defiant people, like their Dutch neighbours. Germany was Belgium's closest trading partner, while there had been frequent tension between Brussels and Paris. Little was known of King Albert (who acceded aged 34 in December 1909) or his Bavarian-born queen, Elisabeth, named in honour of her aunt, the Empress–Queen of Austria-Hungary, who in 1898 was assassinated by an anarchist in Geneva. Intelligence reports suggested the Belgian field army was weak, six nominal divisions totalling 120,000 men. The army as a whole was undergoing thorough reorganization. It lacked social cohesion, for while the officers were francophone (French speaking), the rank and file were predominantly Flemish Dutch-speakers, with a low level of literacy. There was a shortage of heavy artillery and infantry regiments had barely a hundred machine-guns among them. Many of these new-fangled weapons were so cumbersome that on the march they were conveyed in dogcarts, like the milk delivery in Belgian towns. In London it was reckoned that, at best, the Belgians might check the Germans for a few days. More likely they would be granted free passage to invade France. No one anticipated that, as Churchill was to write, 'a week later every British heart would burn' with sympathy 'for little Belgium'.

As first lord, Churchill had a duty to make certain the Royal Navy was ready for war. A practice mobilization, proposed four months earlier, had brought the warships together at Spithead for a royal review in mid-July. Most reservists subsequently returned home, but the great capital ships were still off Portland. On Tuesday afternoon (28th) they were ordered secretly to their war-stations, confidently awaiting the early challenge of a new Trafalgar in the North Sea.[17]

Ready, too, were Britain's 'Saturday-afternoon soldiers'. The Territorial Force, created six years previously by transforming local volunteer battalions and locally raised yeomanry into a supplementary reserve administered by county associations under centralized War Office supervision, now numbered 268,777 officers and men.[18] In wartime, the force was expected to provide 14 infantry divisions and 14 brigades of mounted yeomanry, as well as companies of engineers, artillery batteries, and battalions of cyclists and railway workers; but the Territorials were raised for home defence not a continental war, and between 1910 and 1914 only 20,000 had volunteered to serve overseas. All were obliged to spend a fortnight each summer in camp, and by late July and August many were already under canvas.

The regular army, in the United Kingdom never more than 150,000 men, was puny in comparison with the conscript armies of the continent. In theory a British infantry division comprised 18,000 officers and men in three brigades, each divided into four battalions. A cavalry division was much smaller: some 9,300 officers and men with 9,800 horses in five brigades. Most divisions were well below strength when war was declared, but the War Office could count on rapid growth once mobilization brought the reservists back to their depots. One key division of the proposed expeditionary force was already on a war footing at Aldershot, where a test mobilization had long been planned for 27 July. Other army commands were put on defensive alert on the Wednesday (29th). With no publicity, Britain entered the 'Precautionary Period': preparations were completed for implementing emergency measures set out in a War Book compiled by Hankey and his secretariat over the previous four years. Slowly, and for the most part reluctantly, the British people acknowledged the imminence of war.[19]

Not so the government. Within the cabinet, Grey, Churchill, Lord Chancellor Haldane and Asquith himself were conscious of

Britain's moral obligation to assist France withstand a German attack. They were convinced a German military triumph would encroach on Britain's vital interests and ultimately threaten invasion. But there was a strongly non-interventionist peace party in the government, their views echoed by the Liberal press. As late as Saturday morning (1 August) the cabinet rejected proposals to give France an unequivocal assurance of British support. At a further three-hour meeting on Sunday afternoon, Grey won the backing of all but one of his colleagues for a pledge that the Royal Navy would protect the French Channel coast from German attack, but, despite the eight years of Anglo-French staff talks, Asquith would not risk widening cabinet splits by seeking approval to send an expeditionary force to fight in France.[20] Not until the small hours of Bank Holiday Monday (3 August) did he authorize full mobilization of the army, and the authorization did not reach the War Office until shortly before noon. By then Asquith knew that Germany had occupied the Grand Duchy of Luxembourg and presented an ultimatum in Brussels requiring, within 12 hours, an assurance of unimpeded progress for the German army through Belgium to invade France.

News that Belgium had rejected the ultimatum reached Downing Street soon after midday on 4 August, while the cabinet was in session. It was decisive in hardening the resolve of ministers to resist aggression: a call to arms to help Belgium fend off the bullying of a mighty neighbour carried a nobler ring than an appeal to stand by France, for so long suspect as an imperial rival and now allied to oppressive Tsarist Russia.[21] The British ultimatum, demanding that Germany respect Belgian neutrality, was sent even before King Albert sought military aid. At 11 p.m. on Tuesday, 4 August, 15 hours after the first invaders crossed the frontier, Britain joined France, Russia and Belgium at war with Germany.

The provisions of the War Book were put into effect with smooth efficiency. Soon reservists reporting for duty filled the barracks: 12 years earlier many were fighting in South Africa; within a fortnight they would form 60 per cent of the British Expeditionary Force (BEF) in France. Railway schedules were scrapped to provide hundreds of special trains, merchant ships taken over by the Admiralty, 250 of them within a few days, with many more to

follow when they had completed voyages to home ports. Requisitioning began: of buildings, of motor vehicles and, above all, of
horses. Up to 150,000 horses were seized, some arbitrarily from
farmers at harvest time and even from London cabbies dependent
on them for a livelihood.[22] Yet, despite this rigid fulfilment of
contingency planning, confusion remained at the highest level.
Since the Curragh incident in March, Asquith had taken over the
duties of secretary of state for war as well as serving as prime
minister. Such an arrangement could not continue once the
fighting began. A few hours before the ultimatum to Germany
expired, Asquith invited Field Marshal Lord Kitchener to serve as
war secretary, having plucked him from the Calais boat in Dover
harbour as he was about to set out for Cairo.[23]

To bring into a Liberal cabinet an awesome autocrat, Tory by
temperament and unversed in parliamentary ways, was – as Asquith
admitted to Venetia – 'a hazardous experiment'; it was forced on
him by newspaper clamour and prodding from the first lord of the
Admiralty.[24] Kitchener's presence might boost public confidence
in a hesitant government but, though his earliest acquaintance with
war was as a volunteer in the French army of 1871, his victories had
been won in Africa and his experience of supreme command
shaped in India. At 64, he was the average age of France's generals
but some ten years older than most senior British commanders. He
was out of touch with recent developments, undervaluing the
Territorials and knowing little about the conversations with
France. Moreover, to have a field marshal serving as war secretary
fettered Sir John French. There were moments during the following months when, to Sir John's chagrin, Kitchener behaved as if he
were a supreme commander.

One outstanding problem remained unresolved. Cabinet approval had still to be given for a continental commitment. Late on
the Wednesday afternoon (5th) Asquith presided over a council of
war at 10, Downing Street. Four cabinet ministers, three field
marshals (Kitchener, French and the octogenarian Lord Roberts),
an admiral and six generals sought answers to the most basic,
strategic questions posed by the coming of war: should an army
cross to France? If so, when and in what strength, and where should
the BEF concentrate?[25]

German guns were already shelling the forts of Liège when the council met, but reliable news was slow to reach London, and Asquith's opening remarks reflect the day's uncertainties. His admiration for King Albert's defiance of the invader was tinged with doubt over the effectiveness of the Belgian army, but there were reports that the Germans had crossed into the Dutch province of Limburg, raising the possibility that the Netherlands too would resist Germany; on 31 July, Dutch mobilization had preceded Belgian by five and a half hours. As both banks of the lower Scheldt are in Holland, Dutch entry into the war would make access to the great port of Antwerp easier.[26]

When Sir John French, as commander-designate of the BEF, addressed the council he summarized existing proposals for concentrating the force around Maubeuge and urged it be sent across the Channel as early as possible. Then, however, to Major-General Wilson's consternation, French resurrected a project he had advocated as long ago as 1906, the establishment of a base at Antwerp, capable of striking at the German right flank. This strategic deviation was at variance with all that had been agreed in the Anglo-French discussions. Lord Roberts supported French, but Churchill warned that the navy could not guarantee 'the sea communications of so large a force on the enemy side of the Straits of Dover'. When no confirmation came of the invasion of Limburg, the Antwerp option receded. But the attraction of a flanking manoeuvre across the open Flemish countryside retained its appeal for French. His military reputation rested on his enterprise as a cavalry commander in South Africa, saving Cape Colony from invasion and dashing to relieve Kimberley. He was a horseman of outstanding personal courage. By temperament he rejected all thought of static war.

Kitchener, not yet installed at the War Office, also wanted to see the BEF cross to France as soon as practicable. He had doubts over its size, however, and argued it would enjoy greater freedom of movement if centrally based on Amiens rather than accept narrow confinement within the Maubeuge sector. General Sir Douglas Haig, already certain to command I Corps of the BEF, thought the war would last 'many months, possibly years'. With reluctance he too accepted the need to send troops immediately to France, but he criticized the extent of the commitment proposed by the director of military operations. Haig wanted 'a considerable portion of

officers and NCOs . . . withdrawn from the Expeditionary Force'
and retained in England for several months in order to train a
powerful new army, a million strong.[27] Little was settled that
Wednesday, though offers of contingents from Australia, Canada
and New Zealand were welcomed and the Indian Army was asked
to dispatch a division to Egypt, as the forerunner of a much larger
force to fight in Europe.

By midday on Thursday (6th) the cabinet had at last agreed that
the BEF should leave for France, and a second council of war met
in the afternoon.[28] By now Kitchener was preparing for a conflict
that, as he warned startled cabinet colleagues, might last three years
or more: new armies of volunteers must be raised speedily, he
insisted. Within a few days he was appealing for 100,000 men aged
between 19 and 30 to enlist. A famous poster, with the field
marshal's forefinger pointing towards 'YOU' rammed home his
message. By the end of the week more than 7000 recruits were
answering Kitchener's call each day.[29] Officers and NCOs of
experience were needed to train them, as Haig had observed at
the first council of war.

During Thursday's meeting Kitchener cut the size of the BEF to
four infantry divisions rather than the six proposed in the Wilson–
Dubail memorandum. The cavalry division was, however, retained. A fifth infantry division would follow the vanguard, but
the sixth held back to augment home defence. The debate over the
relative merits of Amiens or Maubeuge as a base dragged on until
12 August when Kitchener reluctantly accepted the original
proposal of Maubeuge, after an emissary from Joffre emphasized
the need for the BEF to cover the upper Sambre as soon as
possible.[30]

The advance troops of the BEF embarked at Southampton on
Sunday (9th), to cross to Boulogne at night. Almost a thousand
special trains pulled into Southampton on a single day. By 17
August some 81,000 men and 30,000 horses had sailed for France,
landing at Le Havre and Rouen as well as at Boulogne. Most troops
left Southampton, but use was also made of Folkestone and
Newhaven while other contingents came from Bristol, Liverpool
and as far away as Dublin. Their ships met the main fleet of
transports in the Channel as they awaited escorts to crowded quays

in the French harbours. On 16 August transports and troopships made a record 137 crossings, safely and without serious incident.[31] Naval patrols sealed the shipping lane, ensuring there was no danger of interception by German warships. The sea was calm, the days hot and sun-drenched, the nights heavily humid. Some 15 years later Major-General Childs recalled his first evening ashore in Normandy, watching a blood-red sun sink into the Seine estuary while thunder rolled in ominously from the ocean.[32]

Field Marshal French crossed from Folkestone aboard the cruiser HMS *Sentinel* on Friday afternoon, 14 August. With him travelled his chief of staff, Major-General Sir Archibald Murray, together with General Wilson as Murray's deputy. Wilson's reputation for intrigue and 'unreliability' during the Curragh incident had denied him the more senior post for which as DMO he had hoped, but Murray's chronic ill-health was to give him considerable influence in the weeks ahead. For good or ill, Wilson was respected at headquarters as the one general who, it was believed, understood French military plans.[33] In the event, however, Wilson was slow to appreciate that the weight of the German attack had already made Joffre abandon his Plan 17 strategy of an advance in the east, choosing instead to concentrate all his forces on defence in the north.

The general instructions Sir John French received from the secretary of state for war lacked precision – inevitably, perhaps, since Kitchener had as yet not met Joffre and was understandably puzzled over his strategic objectives. Significantly, the only town mentioned by name was not Maubeuge but Amiens, 'the place of your assembly'. The field marshal commanding-in-chief (as French was styled) was ordered to exercise 'the greatest care towards a minimum of losses and wastage'; he should ensure his subordinates understood the need to avoid the 'risk of serious losses', unless the 'risk is authoritatively considered to be commensurate with the object in view'. As for Anglo-French relations in general, Kitchener emphasized that, 'While every effort must be made to coincide most sympathetically with the plans and wishes of our Ally . . . I wish you distinctly to understand that your command is an entirely independent one, and that you will in no case come in any sense under the orders of any Allied General.' Strangely, the French war minister was never informed of these instructions.

Throughout the first six months of the fighting around Ypres, Joffre therefore assumed Sir John had been told to follow his orders. It is curious that after eight years of Anglo–French staff talks so basic a question of high command remained unresolved.[34]

On his first evening in France, Sir John watched two infantry brigades settle into a forest of tents spread along the heights northeast of Boulogne, where Napoleon's army had massed ready to invade England. But if the column of the Grand Army above the tents evoked the past, the field marshal's second visit to his troops looked to the future. For, near Amiens next day, he inspected the first 'machines' of the Royal Flying Corps (RFC). No. 2 Squadron had flown down from Montrose in Scotland to join nos 3 and 4 squadrons on 12 August at the airfield above Dover's white cliffs. Next morning the three squadrons took off from Swingate Downs and crossed the Channel without mishap. French was much impressed by the efficient mobility of the RFC: it was only five years since Louis Blériot made his 31-mile pioneer flight from Sangatte to land bumpily near Dover castle.

No. 5 Squadron joined the aircraft already at Amiens later that Saturday. On Monday the whole flight reached a landing ground east of Maubeuge, and by Wednesday a Blériot of 3 Squadron and a BE2 of 4 Squadron were airborne over Belgium, seeking the enemy through lowering cloud, though without success. The embryonic RFC – numbering, in all, less than 2000 officers and men – was thus the first British unit to see service at the Front. Within a week 63 aircraft were supporting the BEF, all intended as reconnaissance eyes for troops on the ground, especially the gunners. As yet only a few senior officers perceived in these flimsy craft a deadly weapon of attack.[35]

The main body of the BEF travelled to the Maubeuge area aboard traditional French troop trains. Caterpillars of wooden carriages and trucks some 500 yards long wound slowly northwards beside fields rich with corn, though much was already harvested. The first phase of their journey, 55 miles from Le Havre to Rouen, took the first battalion of the Coldstream Guards four and a half hours overnight on Friday and Saturday. Five nights later a battery of the Royal Horse Artillery fared better, covering the full 170 miles from the Seine to the Belgian frontier in 24 hours, despite halts to water and feed the 228 horses that travelled with the guns.

Several units followed circuitous routes because of congestion on the French railways; the sappers of the 57th Field Company took six days to travel from Southampton to Rouen and on to the Mons area. Like their French comrades, the troops were generally carried in cattle trucks, stifling in August. Some preferred to stay with their guns and limbers in open wagons, but many were soon soaked by thunderstorms or caked with grime from the notoriously smoky locomotives.[36]

Senior officers made the journey in greater comfort. On 17 August, Haig, by now commander of I Corps of the BEF, arrived with his staff, without incident, at Le Cateau, where French established his General Headquarters (GHQ). The staff officers of II Corps were less fortunate: early that morning Major-General Grierson, their corps commander, suffered a fatal heart attack as the train approached Amiens. Grierson was a bon viveur of Falstaffian girth but high intelligence, widely respected, a loyal colleague of French and associated in planning the expeditionary force from its inception. His death was a serious blow to the BEF as a whole. He had studied the structure of the German army in detail and acquired a deeper understanding of Potsdam military mentality than any of his colleagues. Moreover, while I Corps's officers had worked with Haig at Aldershot, II Corps was a new creation, and French was counting on Grierson's experience to bind the staff speedily together.

As a successor to Grierson, Sir John asked for Major-General Plumer, whose skill at improvisation he had admired in South Africa. Instead, the autocratic Kitchener gave command of II Corps to Sir Horace Smith-Dorrien, a survivor of the Zulu War of 1879 and the most senior general in the British army. Unfortunately, Smith-Dorrien had long been on notoriously bad terms with Sir John French. No one was certain of the origins of their quarrel though it was exacerbated by Smith-Dorrien's forceful exposition of the need to accustom cavalry to serve as dismounted infantry.[37] To compound his problems, on this occasion Smith-Dorrien had no opportunity to get to know his staff before II Corps was thrown into battle.

But, as Sir John drove up to advanced headquarters at Bavai on 21 August, he was optimistic. Within 17 days of mobilization the BEF was in the line and on Belgian soil, though in the province of

Hainaut not Flanders. French's troops were fresh, keen and well trained, with a core of veterans, many of whom he remembered from South Africa. Their equipment was good, their marksmanship excellent: the Lee-Enfield Mark III rifle, introduced in 1907, was superior to the German Mauser, lighter and shorter, and with a 10-round magazine and a turned-down bolt handle that made rapid fire easier – '15 rounds a minute' was the norm. French's numbers were smaller than he wished, but the promised 5th Division was to cross the Channel at the weekend and would form the nucleus of a III Corps. I Corps and the cavalry brigades were deployed on a northwest-to-southeast axis from Mons down to the outer for-tifications of Maubeuge. II Corps was around Mons itself and for 15 miles westwards along the Canal du Centre to Condé, beyond the French frontier. 'I am quite satisfied with the situation. Concen-tration complete,' Sir John French wired Kitchener. Across south-ern Belgium on that evening 257 French and British battalions with 1120 guns faced 358 German battalions with 2164 guns assigned to their three invading armies.[38] Just 40 miles northwest of Mons, the rhythm of daily life continued undisturbed at Ypres.

4

THE MOBILE WAR

A traveller leaving Mons and following the N7 towards Soignies and Brussels will find beside the road, some 5 miles beyond the town, a memorial to the earliest encounter between the BEF and the Germans. It marks the place where at seven o'clock on the morning of Saturday, 22 August, Corporal Edward Thomas of the Royal Irish Dragoon Guards fired his rifle at four horsemen scouting ahead of General von Kluck's First Army and trotting cautiously towards the canal. The German patrol, surprised to find the BEF already in the line, turned back to rejoin their squadron. There followed a traditional cavalry charge, Captain Hornby leading two troops of horse forward with flashing sabres, in the spirit of Balaclava. Now, however, the dragoons sought not guns but men; they needed to discover more about the enemy facing them. Five wounded prisoners were captured and led back for questioning.[1]

Throughout Friday there had been rumours of Uhlans to the north of Mons, as Kluck's First Army wheeled southwards from Brussels, and the skirmish did not take Field Marshal French by surprise. He anticipated advancing towards Soignies along the Brussels road, engaging the flank of the First Army while, to the British right, the French Fifth Army (General Lanrezac) checked the German Second Army (General von Bulow) around Charleroi. His optimism was dented by news that the Fifth Army's counter-attacks had been repulsed but, even so, he remained confident. He did not know that the French had suffered heavy losses nor that Bulow's army was poised to take the last of the forts of Namur, commanding the Sambre and Meuse. His chief of intelligence, Colonel Macdonogh, warned French that a reconnaissance flight by the RFC had spotted a German corps well to the northwest of Mons, threatening to envelop the town. When Sir John received a request from the French to hold the Mons–Condé canal for 24 hours he assumed the Fifth Army was regrouping, and II Corps duly dug trenches, the first of hundreds hacked in Belgium by the British over the next four years.[2] Most trenches were to be cut across 'Flanders fields' or woodland, but these earliest defences in industrialized Hainaut had as a foreground a canal as wide as a cricket pitch with barges moored in slimy water and a backcloth of slag-heaps, factory chimneys and railway sidings. It was a familiar scene to sappers from the south Staffordshire Black Country.

The battle of Mons began in earnest soon after nine o'clock next day (23rd) when the ringing of bells summoning good Catholics to Mass on a wet and misty Sunday was blanketed by the sudden thunder of artillery and the whistle of shells. It was soon evident that the German guns had a greater range than the British 18-pounder. Yet the abiding memory for both armies was not of an artillery duel but of German infantry thrusting forward in tightly packed lines against rifle fire so rapid and accurate that it seemed they were facing nests of machine-guns.[3]

Rather curiously, French thought the early exchanges of fire were no more than preliminary skirmishes; he set out from Mons early to inspect a new brigade forming at Valenciennes and did not return to the Front until the early afternoon. By then there had been heavy fighting for four hours northeast of the town, where road and rail bridges spanned the canal between the villages of Nimy and Obourg. It was a day of valiant defiance that, by nightfall, cost the British 1,600 men dead or gravely wounded, heavy losses in the ranks of some of the army's most skilled professionals. Four Victoria Crosses – the first of the war – were earned on that Sunday: Lieutenant Dease (posthumously) and Private Godley of the Royal Fusiliers; Captain Wright and Lance Corporal Jarvis of the Royal Engineers.

Sir John French gave orders to strengthen the defences over-night, ready to meet new attacks on Monday. Shortly before midnight, however, he learnt with alarm that because the French Fifth Army had suffered such a series of defeats Lanrezac was already preparing to pull back from the frontier and head southwards. Hurriedly, French changed his plans: rather than risk isolation from

the Fifth Army, he ordered a general retreat towards Maubeuge to
begin at first light.[4]

In many respects the fighting around Mons anticipated early
battles in the Ypres salient. There, too, tightly packed German
infantry swept courageously forward against hastily dug trenches, to
be mown down by rapid rifle fire; their commanders seem to have
learnt nothing from the Mons experience. Around Ypres the
British had yet to find an effective response to the pounding of
artillery, while the 'field marshal commanding-in-chief' remained a
distant figure, unmethodical in his staff work, still buoyed up with
the prospect of smashing the German line and releasing the cavalry
to thrust deeply into Belgium. But industrialized Mons could never
have become a bastion of defence like Ypres. Although French
considered taking refuge within heavily fortified Maubeuge, he
wisely rejected the temptation, rightly suspecting the fortress lacked
the resources to withstand investment for more than a fortnight.[5]
Briefly he thought of falling back westward to cover Dunkirk and
Boulogne, but to do so would open a gap between the BEF and the
French for von Kluck to exploit. Instead, within 48 hours of
scrapping his plan to keep a foothold in Hainaut, Sir John informed
Kitchener he would retreat 'behind the Oise to reorganise and
refit'.[6] That was like quitting the Thames at Richmond to recover
beside the Severn at Worcester. In the event, the retreat to the
valley of the Marne became some 50 miles longer.

Harassed retreats followed eventually by advances and avenging
pursuits were not unknown to the British army, notably in the
Iberian Peninsula, but never before had the fortunes of war spun so
swiftly as in the four weeks after Mons. First the Germans and then,
briefly in September, the British and French believed final victory
was theirs for the taking; the illusion 'it will all be over by
Christmas' lingered into the autumn. For footsloggers in the
BEF, with some 100 lb of weight bearing down on their backs,
the cloudless, sultry days were long, the cobbled roads exhausting,
the Routes Nationales monotonously straight and endless. The first
battalion of the Gloucestershire Regiment marched 244 miles in 13
days, with only one of rest, and on two successive days covered
more than 20 miles. During the retreat the BEF's infantry had an
average of four hours rest in every 24 and the cavalry only three.[7]
Reminiscences decades later conjured up images of Belgian

refugees fleeing ahead of the enemy, with their possessions in dogcarts, blocking the roads and sometimes overspilling into the fields. Other memories recalled cut and bleeding feet, daily rations of tinned bully beef and biscuits, no cigarettes or tobacco and much less water than throats parched by sun and dust demanded.[8]

The retreat was not an extended route march: there were bridges to demolish, sudden shelling and skirmishes when German troops were unexpectedly encountered. On four occasions the skirmishing developed into battles. On 24 August the first battalion of the Cheshire Regiment suffered heavy losses in a delaying action at the village of Elongies: out of a battalion of 27 officers and 1,007 men, only five officers and 193 in the ranks survived unscathed. Two days later the Coldstream Guards fought off a surprise assault on the village of Landrecies, which Haig was visiting at the time. Further west, that same day, Smith-Dorrien committed the tired and battered II Corps to checking the momentum of the German advance at Le Cateau in a gallant action that made the government in London anxious and infuriated Sir John French; Le Cateau was more costly than Mons, incurring 7,800 casualties and the loss of 34 guns.[9] At Néry on 1 September the crack German 4th Cavalry Division, emerging from the mists of an autumn morning, surprised a battery of the Royal Horse Artillery: two 13-pounders were taken immediately, three more were soon out of action, but the last continued to defy the Germans for two hours, long enough for a counter-attack that inflicted such heavy losses on the cavalry division that it took no part in the battle of the Marne. Captain Bradbury, the officer in charge of the gun, was awarded the Victoria Cross posthumously; the two sergeants who survived, Dorrell and Nelson, were similarly honoured.[10]

It was a weary army that crossed the Marne on 5 September. Sir John French established headquarters at Melun, on the Seine, barely 25 miles east of central Paris. Despite reinforcement by the first division to arrive of the promised III Corps, the BEF was still short of men, horses and guns; for the first time, there was concern over the supply of shells. French continued to write and speak of the need to 'refit'. By now he was looking for 'recuperation' well south of the Seine; there was talk of developing La Rochelle as 'the place of assembly' to replace Amiens, with Le

Mans as an advanced base. In alarm, on 1 September, Kitchener crossed to Paris for urgent talks in an 18-hour visit. Much to French's indignation, the war secretary travelled in field marshal's uniform. He insisted that the BEF remain in the line, but ominously St Nazaire, on the Atlantic coast, Le Havre, on the Channel, as the principal supply port. Disembarkation at Boulogne was already suspended.[11]

On the day after Kitchener returned to London the French government left Paris for Bordeaux. France had lost more than 300,000 men killed, wounded or reported missing in the first month of war, far heavier casualties than in 1870, the campaign that gave both Joffre and Kitchener their baptism of fire. Joffre was no strategic genius, but he was imperturbable and resolutely defiant. Generals whom he considered had lost their nerve were dismissed: in the Fifth Army, Lanrezac made way for his I Corps commander, Franchet d'Esperey, who had checked the Germans at Guise with élan. General Gallieni, Joffre's one-time mentor, became military governor of Paris. General Foch was given command of a newly created Ninth Army.[12] The French railways hurried westward divisions no longer needed for the Lorraine offensive proposed in Plan 17 but by now aborted. Reinforcements were found elsewhere, too. Inactive troops keeping watch on the Italian and Spanish frontiers entrained for the north, as well as Algerians, Moroccans and Tunisians from Marseilles. Joffre was building up new armies for the counter-offensive he planned at the first opportunity.

Physically the Germans were as exhausted as the British and French; they had been marching for 33 days and suffered heavy casualties.[13] In Kluck's First Army, Captain Walter Bloem's Brandenburg Grenadiers covered 200 miles before they reached the Marne. Their 'heels, soles and toes' were inflamed, 'patches of skin rubbed off to the raw flesh'; many had 'uniforms in rags. They look like scarecrows and march with eyes closed,' he wrote.[14] Through field glasses, staff officers could see the skeletal ribs of the Eiffel Tower; on 3 September cavalry patrols entered a village 8 miles from the city boundary. They were elated. Paris seemed about to fall.

Across the Channel the early euphoria had by now given way to apprehension. The public was starved of the news it craved: what really was happening? Joffre allowed no war correspondents in 'the zone of the armies'; reporters who attempted to slip through the military police presence were arrested, even respected representatives of *The Times* and *Daily Mail* (both Northcliffe owned) and the *Daily Chronicle*, London's leading Liberal daily.[15] The papers relied on bland communiqués, tales from refugees and reports from neutral capitals, mainly of alleged atrocities. Kitchener sent Colonel Swinton, an inventive sapper officer and the ingenious author of uplifting tales of soldiering, to the Front as an official observer. His commissioned status allowed Swinton to circumvent the French ban, and he sent to London judiciously worded anonymous dispatches, widely syndicated. Their prevailing tone was patriotically optimistic. Other 'experts' were less reliable: a long resistance by the vaunted fortresses of Belgium and France was predicted; unfortunately, by the end of August six had already fallen.[16]

It had always been accepted there would be casualties in the BEF – that was the nature of war, as South Africa had shown: 21,942 soldiers failed to return from three years of fighting the Boers, 5,774 of them killed in battle. But no one foresaw the enormity of the mounting losses in the present conflict.[17] The first shock came on 30 August when Lord Northcliffe authorized a special Sunday edition of *The Times* that broke tradition by printing 'sensationalist' headlines on the front page. In what Asquith privately condemned as 'a most wicked' dispatch, a correspondent at Amiens depicted 'a retreating and broken army . . . battered with marching', and 'grievously injured' regiments 'with nearly all their officers' lost.[18] Within days the earliest casualty lists were published, with a bleak warning that others were soon to follow. A sense of 'my country really needs me' sent recruiting soaring: over the next 12 days 301,971 volunteers enlisted in the army, more than twice as many as over the four preceding weeks. The Press Bureau censors appear to have anticipated a patriotic response of this nature when they cleared the Amiens dispatch for publication.[19]

The impact of these terrible tidings on the older generation was sobering. Amid the idyllic peace of a Cornish cliff path above Polzeath, Laurence Binyon found a seat looking out to sea where, in 'proud thanksgiving,' he composed his elegy, 'For the Fallen'. The famous threnody, with its affirmation 'We will remember them' is now recognized as a tribute to all who were to die in the world wars and later conflicts, but it was written even before the horrors of battle were intensified by the barbed-wire stalemate of the trenches. The helmeted mud-caked veterans of 1917 whom we so often identify with the 'fallen' are outwardly as remote from Binyon's young men of 1914 – 'straight of limb, true of eye, steady and aglow' – as from the bowmen of Agincourt.[20]

The first editor to whom Binyon submitted 'For the Fallen' rejected the poem, and it did not appear in print until Monday, 21 September, in *The Times*. By then the tide of battle in France had turned, and the character of the war was changing dramatically. At the start of the month Joffre had the advantage of headquarters that were close to the battle line and, after the government's exodus to Bordeaux, free from interference by ministers. By contrast Moltke, chief of the German general staff, was 150 miles away in Luxembourg. He could only watch his plans unravel on wall maps in the cloakroom of a girls' school, the improvised operations room for Supreme Headquarters (Oberste Heeresleitung – OHL). Moltke was responsible for grand strategy on the Eastern Front as well as the Western and had already detached two corps from Kluck's army and sent them to East Prussia to stem a perceived Russian threat to Königsberg. Moreover, Moltke – cultured, sensitive, cello-playing, reflective – had no opportunity to keep his own counsel. Close on hand, in the German legation, Kaiser Wilhelm and his itinerant court were in residence; General von Falkenhayn, the Prussian war minister, accompanied his emperor. Under pressure, Moltke faltered. On 2 September he abandoned his modified Schlieffen Plan and improvised: Kluck was to give up any project for enveloping Paris by crossing the Seine to the west. Instead, he was to turn northeast of the capital and support Bulow's Second Army in echelon, crossing the Marne's tributaries, the Grand and Petit Morin, and driving a wedge between the BEF and Franchet d'Esperey's Fifth Army.[21]

This was a risky manoeuvre, though one that Kluck anticipated. His First Army would engage the Fifth Army but expose the right flank to Gallieni and the recently constituted French Sixth Army, while Foch and the Ninth Army threatened the left. Joffre, able to identify the new deployment through the novelty of aerial reconnaissance, alerted Franchet who, in co-ordination with General

Wilson, planned a joint Anglo-French attack to open at 6 a.m. on 6 September.[22] Kluck, however, struck first, some 18 hours ahead of Franchet, while the Sixth Army was completing its preparations and with the BEF still 10 miles behind the proposed starting line. The fighting became so intense that on Monday, 7 September, Gallieni commandeered a fleet of Parisian taxis and buses to rush three battalions of reinforcements to the battle, which reached its climax next day 'in a swelter of tropical heat' along the Marne valley.[23] The outcome was still uncertain.

Next morning Bulow found he was losing touch with Kluck. He feared that Foch and the BEF would encircle his Second Army, which had suffered heavy losses. In alarm, he warned OHL that he was preparing to order the Second back to the right bank of the Marne. That evening an emissary from Moltke, Lieutenant-Colonel Hentsch, head of intelligence in Luxembourg, arrived at Bulow's headquarters in the village of Montmort with authority to recommend emergency measures. Bulow's pessimism convinced Hentsch of the need for realignment. But once the Second Army retired, Kluck and the First Army would have to retreat, too, or leave a gap open for French and British cavalry to advance northwards. On 9 September the weather broke, and rain poured down on congested roads. Confusion bordered on chaos; Hentsch, who set out from Montfort soon after dawn to drive to First Army headquarters at Mareuil, 50 miles to the west, did not arrive until midday. His fears were confirmed. As Moltke's spokesman, he asserted that he enjoyed plenipotentiary authority and compelled a reluctant Kluck to pull the First Army back to the River Aisne. By nightfall the Germans were in full retreat, to the surprised relief of the sorely pressed French armies and the BEF. On 11 September, when Moltke himself belatedly visited the battle zone, he ordered the new line north of the Aisne to be fortified and held.

Physically the strain brought Moltke close to collapse. Four days earlier he had written an abject letter of despair to his wife; a staff officer found him hunched over a table, his face tense and eyes tearful. It was a relief when, on the evening of 14 September, an emissary from the kaiser brought orders that he should report himself sick. Unobtrusively, General Erich von Falkenhayn took over as chief of the general staff while remaining Prussian minister of war.[24] News of Moltke's 'retirement for reasons of health' was kept from the German public until 3 November. Over the following days 33 lesser-known elderly generals were relieved of their commands and forced into retirement. Falkenhayn was a tougher character than his predecessor. He brought to the conduct of war the ruthless professionalism Bismarck had applied to statecraft.

'An incontestable victory', Foch reported to Joffre on the day Moltke visited the Front. In Paris, and to a lesser extent London, the optimism of the war's early days returned. Gallieni's legendary taxicabs were back on the boulevards, many proudly fluttering a tricolour flag. A few days later General Wilson, looking ahead with his French opposite number, General Berthelot, reckoned the allies would be on the Belgian–German frontier within a month, poised to advance to the Rhine. Berthelot, Joffre's deputy, thought Wilson unduly cautious: three weeks was his estimate.[25]

On paper, the cavalry's hour had come, for both the French and British commanders: '*En avant, soldats, pour la France,*' Franchet ordered; '*Vitesse, vitesse*', Foch urged on a cavalry division newly seconded to his Ninth Army.[26] Haig noted in his diary that he 'met 5 Cavalry Brigade moving at a walk'; he 'motored on' and caught up with their commanding officer, General Chetwoode. ' I explained to him', Haig wrote, 'that a little effort now might mean the ending of the war,' and the brigade 'trotted on'.[27]

Sir John French, who three weeks back confidently counted on a cavalry breakthrough at Mons, was by now less sanguine, acutely conscious of the weariness of both horses and riders. Moreover he personally knew the Aisne valley, where a limestone massif ran for some 25 miles (40 km) above the right bank of the broad river. A densely wooded ridge, 5 miles wide and 165 feet above river level, was bisected by the Chemin des Dames, the straight road westwards from Craonne to Juvigny laid by Louis XV's engineers to ease the buffeting of his daughters as carriages bore them from palace to hunting-lodge. Now the ridge and river, with the road some distance back, offered the Germans a natural defensive position, looking out over open country south of the Aisne, ill-suited for siting field guns. Even so, Joffre urged French, Franchet d'Esperey and Foch to press ahead and go for a breakthrough. On

the left of the line, between Soissons and Compiègne, the French
Sixth Army was to seek to turn the German flank.

Late on 12 September the 11th Infantry Brigade of III Corps
found the bridge over the Aisne at Venizel relatively intact. By
three o'clock next morning the brigade had secured a foothold
on the north bank. Despite having marched 30 miles through
heavy rain, the infantry successfully scaled the heights to reach the
crest of the ridge as a misty dawn broke, but resistance stiffened
during the day.[28] The Germans were able to use heavy mortars
and howitzers as field artillery, with devastating effect on the
troops below. Haig's I Corps took Bourg but ran into heavy and
sustained fire from entrenched positions on a wooded spur
beyond the town. To the east of Craonne, where the high
ground recedes, Franchet's Fifth Army made a spectacular advance northwards to the outskirts of Sissone, but French's hopes
of reaching Laon were frustrated.

French had foreseen that the Germans would resort to trench
warfare once they could take advantage of a natural obstacle and
end their retreat. To him the ominous novelty was entrenchment
in depth, for clefts in the rocky slopes enabled the first trenches to
be supported by second and third lines, placed in tiers. It was a
defensive development he would encounter with costly consequences in the year ahead.[29] For the moment, French persisted
with the assault on the German positions, ordering II and III Corps
to entrench if they gained a firm footing beyond the river, but he
was disturbed by the latest change of fortune. 'I think it is very
likely the enemy is making a determined stand on the Aisne,' he
noted in his diary on 14 September. This was an understatement.
As French's biographer Richard Holmes observes, 'The stand was
to last for four long years.'[30]

Falkenhayn was not content to remain on the defensive. Like
Joffre, he transferred troops no longer active along the Lorraine
frontier westwards, while he sought to wheel around his oppo-
nent's flank. The German Sixth Army, recently poised to attack
east of Verdun, was brought to a sector north of Compiègne,
though the redeployment took longer than Falkenhayn anticipated
because of damage and destruction of railway tracks in northern
France and southern Belgium. Increasingly, OHL was attracted to
the open countryside west of the battle zone of the past five weeks

and as yet untouched by the war, in places a corridor 100 miles wide. Falkenhayn began to hanker for another Schlieffenesque campaign: he would advance down the coast to Abbeville and on to Rouen and the lower Seine while, at the same time, going over to the offensive in Champagne in a new search for that elusive anvil on which the French armies would be broken. OHL was, of course, responsible for grand strategy on all the battle fronts but, provided Germany was safeguarded from a Russian invasion, Falkenhayn never doubted the key to final victory in the war lay in the West: France must be humbled and Britain isolated.[31] As a pointer to the new resolve to press ahead in the West, OHL left Luxembourg on 25 September for Mézières, across the French frontier. The supreme war lord and his miniature court came, too, with the kaiser accommodated in an industrialist's mansion at Charleville; but at least the width of the Meuse kept his sovereign away from the chief of staff.[32]

Joffre, too, looked to the corridor between the sea and the recent battlefields, though for different reasons. A swift enveloping north-northeast movement up the Oise could clear the enemy from two of France's productive agricultural *départements* or administrative divisions and recover a vital coal-mining area; the occupation of the militarily denuded coastal strip would establish links with the main Belgian army, which had fallen back on Antwerp. The 'Belgian option' retained a strong appeal in London and in BEF's head-quarters at Fère-en-Tardenois. French and Wilson, his acting deputy, thought similarly to Joffre. They were encouraged by a visit from Churchill, ever eager to safeguard the Channel ports. On 27 September, French requested Joffre 'to disengage us from our present position as soon as possible and put us on the left flank of the Allied forces'. A deployment of this character would give the cavalry an opportunity to harry the German flank, he empha-sized.[33] In many respects French was seeking to revert to the strategic role he envisaged for the BEF on the eve of Mons, before Lanrezac's withdrawal forced him to retreat. Joffre approved, though with reservations over the availability of transport.

There followed what is often labelled 'the Race for the Sea'. In reality it was a late starting race to exploit an open flank. On 6 October, Falkenhayn finally committed himself to an offensive in

Flanders. That Tuesday evening the first troops from III Corps left the Aisne, to move slowly and under cover of night towards Amiens and on to Abbeville and the roads into Flanders. It was another week before they crossed the Belgian frontier and sighted the towers of Ypres on the horizon.

5

ANTWERP AND BEYOND: 'A TRUER HELL'

While the French and the BEF were locked in battle with the Germans across northern France, the Belgians continued to resist the invaders on the right of their main line of advance. It was a familiar theatre of war. For centuries the search for ways to protect the rich trading cities of this largely open countryside had engaged the best military minds. At the height of Louis XIV's reign in the late seventeenth century Marshal Vauban was responsible for two chains of fortresses, primarily designed to defend the frontier of France. Although many of Vauban's bastions and casements were subsequently strengthened, successive modifications failed to keep pace with the growing destructive power of artillery. By the middle of the nineteenth century the newly independent kingdom needed a military engineer capable of designing forts that would withstand the impact of high-explosive shells fired from long-range guns. King Leopold I believed he had found Belgium's Vauban in Henri-Alexis Brialmont, a colonel from Limburg province.[1]

Brialmont, though a highly professional soldier, was also a prolific writer of books and pamphlets on colonial expansion and the need to develop overseas trade and a navy. It was appropriate he should be entrusted with modernizing the defences of Belgium's principal port and wealthiest city, Antwerp. Work began in 1854 on a ring of ten forts, 27 miles in circumference, with innovative armoured turrets to shield their guns. By the end of the decade Antwerp lay at the heart of a defensive complex as formidable as any in Europe. Bismarck's wars, and in particular the bombardment of Paris by Krupps' massive guns, soon outdated much of Brialmont's work, and in 1878 he began a more ambitious project, the construction of an outer perimeter line of 66 miles. Twenty new forts had armoured cupolas sunk into solid concrete; they were designed to withstand the heaviest shells that fell on Paris. Some forts were so extensive that they dominated the villages and meadows like castles. At Zwyndrecht, 3 miles east of the city, the fort straddled the Waasland railway to Ghent and was linked by a rampart to Fort Sainte Marie, several miles to the north. East and south of the city – by Brialmont's reckoning the most likely line of approach – ingeniously concealed redoubts strengthened the forts, their flanking guns covering the glacis to repel infantry assaults. In the late 1880s the most modern artillery was installed in the forts, guns of which to be proud, their black powder charges ready to propel shells to targets 5 miles distant. These vintage guns still armed the forts 25 years later.

From Antwerp, Brialmont turned his attention to Liège and Namur, two cities with rocky terrain better suited to the construction of defensive works than the heathland outside Antwerp. Six large pentagonal forts and six smaller triangular *fortins* or small forts protected Liège while, further up the Meuse, Namur lay within a tighter ring of nine forts. General Brialmont died in 1903 aged 82, but his advocacy of static defences continued to dominate Belgian staff work. By 1910 – the year of King Albert's accession – it was accepted that if war came, the government would find refuge in Antwerp, whether the invaders came from France or from Germany.[2]

When Albert appealed to Paris and London for military aid on 4 August 1914 a powerful German column was already across the frontier, moving forward to Liège. By the following morning the inner city was in German hands, but Brialmont's outer circle of defences continued to resist for a fortnight, only surrendering after General Ludendorff brought up heavy Krupps mortars and Austrian-built Skoda howitzers to pound the forts into submission. This protracted resistance delayed the full advance of the German First Army (Kluck), enabling five Belgian divisions to hold a line along the River Gette until 18 August, when they fell back northwards on Antwerp, the city in which Albert had already established his headquarters. The Belgian 4th Division supported the fortress garrison of Namur, where Brialmont's defences held out for four days before crumbling under bombardment from the heavy siege guns brought down the Meuse valley from Liège. After nightfall on 23 August the division slipped out from the German noose and headed south to the wooded hills around Mariembourg before striking westwards for the Channel coast. Eventually, a week after leaving Namur, the 4th Division – still 12,000 strong – reached the 'national redoubt'. By the beginning of September, Albert, who in accordance with the constitution was automatically commander-in-chief in wartime, had around him a field army of more than 90,000, together with some 70,000 troops manning Antwerp's fortresses.[3]

At GQG – Grand Quartier Général, the French GHQ – Joffre and the French command assumed that if the Belgian line along the River Geete became untenable, Albert would fall back through Brussels towards Oudenarde and Tournai, on the River Scheldt. There the Belgians would provide the left wing of a combined allied front. The king, however, thought otherwise. Throughout the war Albert remained stubbornly and proudly independent, deeply mistrustful of the French and with no intention of allowing GQG to dictate Belgian strategy. He stuck firmly to the Brialmont doctrine, refusing to budge from Antwerp, confident the redoubt could hold out long enough for the allies to gain a decisive victory in France and bring the war to an end.

Yet Albert was determined that Belgian arms should contribute to that victory: the field army was to harass the advancing Germans by a series of sorties against their flank. As early as 24 August – the first day of the retreat from Mons – Albert took the offensive, sending his best infantry regiments forward on a 20-mile front towards Malines. Concentrated fire by German field guns along the Malines–Louvain canal checked the incursion, and on 26 August Albert pulled back his troops to Antwerp. In a more ambitious second sortie a fortnight later six Belgian infantry divisions and a cavalry division sought to turn the German right flank and threaten both Louvain and Brussels. Some cavalry reached the outskirts of Louvain, but the two divisions at the centre of the 40-mile front met heavy resistance on the left bank of the River Dyle, and, on 13 September, Albert ordered a retreat to Brialmont's perimeter again. Although the venture left 8,000 men dead, wounded or captured, the two sorties showed the allies the potential value of continuing Belgium's armed resistance. All Albert sought in return was British and French support in maintaining the 50-mile corridor along the border with Dutch Zeeland and across Flanders to Ghent, Bruges and Ostend.[4]

With the French army reeling under the weight of the German assault, Joffre could spare no troops to help the Belgians, but Albert's reasoning made good sense in London. On 25 August, Captain Hankey, long an advocate of 'the Belgian option', suggested to Churchill that Royal Marines might be landed on the coast so as to pose an apparent threat to Kluck's western flank. The first lord welcomed Hankey's proposal, as too did Kitchener, provided the operation did not divert men or material earmarked for the army in France. Three battalions of marines were put ashore at Ostend on 27–28 August, with orders from Churchill to 'occupy the town' and 'be ostentatious', as if 'to cover the debarkation of a Division of the Army'. There was to be no advance inland, but 'reconnaissances of cyclists' might 'push out . . . to Bruges, Thourout and Dixmude'.[5]

The 3,000 marines were never intended to remain in Belgium. Their task was to attract the attention of the enemy, and on 31 August they were withdrawn without firing a shot, their mission accomplished. For the presence in Flanders of foreign troops in an unfamiliar uniform was soon known in Amsterdam and, as Churchill hoped, the report duly reached German intelligence. At the same time tales of a Russian army, at least 80,000 strong, landing at Aberdeen and Liverpool were current across England and Scotland; the fanciful conjured up Cossacks allegedly 'stamping snow off their boots' as they boarded trains to be whisked to Dover or Harwich for the crossing to Belgium. The rumour, which the authorities did nothing to discourage, received verisimilitude by an unexplained 17-hour delay on the Liverpool to Euston railway on 27 August, the day the first marines went ashore at Ostend. Americans caught up in the railway chaos as they headed for the transatlantic liners at Liverpool sailed for home excited by tales of the phantom army. By the following Friday (4 September) the *New York Times* was splashing news of the Russian expeditionary force across its front page, above dispatches from beleaguered Paris.[6] At OHL, Moltke's staff remained sceptical, but they were puzzled by the persistence of reports from so many different sources. The threat posed by Ostend as a base well behind German lines and the possibility of a Russian presence in Flanders influenced Moltke's decision to pull back from the Marne and helped determine Falkenhayn's later strategy.[7]

Churchill, with his deep sense of history, continued to emphasize to his cabinet colleagues the importance of Antwerp and the Flanders littoral. Grey, however, declined to press the Dutch to allow British warships passage up the Scheldt to Antwerp, and Kitchener was reluctant to divert troops earmarked for the BEF in France.[8] But, as first lord of the Admiralty, Churchill held departmental responsibility for the Royal Naval Air Service (RNAS), and at the end of August he authorized Commander Charles Samson to convert a temporary airfield at Dunkirk into an RNAS base. A few days later Churchill himself visited Samson's base, the first in a series of six crossings he made to France and Belgium before the end of the year.

Within a week Samson was assigned not only three squadrons of aircraft but 60 motor cars as well: all were protected by armour plating; most armed with a Maxim machine-gun. Although the main task of the RNAS was to attack zeppelins and aircraft that threatened London, the planes bombed German troops and positions as deep into France as Cambrai; their pilots became the first English aviators familiar with the topography of the Lys basin and the River Yser. Close co-operation between the aircraft and the improvised armoured cars allowed Samson's 'Dunkirk Circus' to reconnoitre the Franco-Belgian border as far south as Cassel, where an advanced base was established, and Armentières.[9]

Churchill gradually built up the strength of what was still on paper an RNAS commitment. Six aircraft flew to Antwerp to support the Belgians when it became clear the Germans would soon turn their attention to the city; two planes even raided the zeppelin base at Düsseldorf on 22 September, though without causing serious damage. In Dunkirk itself Samson's force was augmented by a brigade of almost 3,000 Royal Marines, commanded by Major-General Archibald Paris, and also – with Kitchener's approval – by 450 men from the Queen's Own Oxfordshire Hussars, a Yeomanry regiment that included Major Jack Churchill, the first lord's brother; it became the first Territorial unit to see active service abroad. Between 60 and 100 London buses were commandeered (along with their drivers) and attached

to the Marine Brigade.[10] Samson's armoured cars, a flight of
aeroplanes and the Marine Brigade moved forward to an advanced
base at Cassel, showing the flag briefly in several towns – including
Ypres – in the hope that the Germans would believe a sizeable
expedition had already crossed to Flanders. The Oxfordshire
Yeomanry remained in the Dunkirk area, later moving inland
to St Omer. At Westminster there was a growing feeling that,
while the BEF attacked German positions on the slopes above the
Aisne, Churchill was mustering an expeditionary force of his own
along the Franco-Belgian border. Soon 'Winston's little army', as
Asquith dubbed it in a letter to Venetia Stanley, would grow even
bigger.[11]

On the evening of 24 September, Joffre telegraphed King Albert
urging him to order a third sortie, towards Brussels. Reluctantly the
king sought to find physically fit regiments to mount an attack but
General Hans von Beseler, the German commander, struck first,
employing the formidable artillery that had levelled the defences of
Liège six weeks previously. His command was a scratch force: a
Marine Division and five divisions of the III Reserve Corps
comprised the infantry; his striking power came from 173 heavy
guns, massed south-southeast of the city astride the railway and
roads to Malines and Brussels. The artillery included both Krupps
15-cm howitzers and the massive Skoda heavyweights, manned by
Austrian gunners.

The siege of Antwerp began in earnest on 28 September. Soon
after midnight shells began to rain down on four forts, 12 miles from
the centre. Two of the forts, Liezele and Breendonck, stood up well
to the bombardment, holding out for nearly a week, but Waelhem
and Wavre Ste Catherine were under repair and fared badly. Within
half an hour of the initial assault the magazine blew up at Waelhem,
and a fault in the concrete at Wavre enabled the first shell that hit
the cupola to pierce a vault, from which fumes began to choke the
gunners. On 30 September persistently accurate shellfire led to the
collapse of a cupola at Fort Lierre; three days later the casement
caved in at neighbouring Kessel. In the smaller redoubts the gunners
were both outranged and at a disadvantage, for their powder
emitted plumes of black smoke, revealing the sites of concealed
emplacements. At Duffel the black plumes brought a concentrated

response from German field guns, the shells soon destroying the redoubt. Cautiously, Beseler's infantry moved forward in the afternoon of 1 October: the bombardment had opened a gap in the defensive line east of Wavre, but there remained the River Nethe to cross and beyond it, almost 10 miles to the north, Brialmont's inner ring of forts. Still further north were the old fortifications of the historic city, with a deep fosse and walls strong enough a century back to let French war minister Lazare Carnot defy the allied armies for several weeks as the Napoleonic Wars drew to a close. Antwerp remained a hard nut to crack, not a shrivelled apple to be shaken to the ground by the rolling thunder of distant guns. As late as 1 October, *The Times*, underestimating the destructive power of the Krupps heavyweights and Skoda howitzers, could still write confidently of the city's impregnability.[12]

General von Beseler had two major concerns. Did he possess enough shells to sustain a long bombardment? Could he bring the Belgian defenders to their knees before British or French reinforcements arrived in strength and exposed the weakness of his infantry? Fortunately for him Joffre's staff were preoccupied with the uncertainties of the Marne and the Aisne, while the British response during September remained slow and confused: Belgium received only six naval guns and gun-crew, six anti-aircraft pom-poms, an armoured train and the morale-boosting activities of the RNAS planes.

Churchill wanted to give more support, but he was hampered by the vulnerability of the Antwerp–Ghent–Ostend corridor to German cavalry attack and by the refusal of the Foreign Office to countenance violations of the Scheldt Convention, the guarantee of Dutch sovereignty over the lower waters of the river.[13] Kitchener was fully aware of the value of Antwerp to the allies: the Belgian presence was a constant threat to the German line of advance and the airfields around the town less than 100 miles from the German border; but he stopped short of reassigning battalions intended for the proposed 7th Division and urgently needed by Sir John French.[14] Ironically, French would have welcomed closer contact between the BEF and the Belgians. Even so he was opposed to the dispatch of any British force to bolster the inner defences of Antwerp. 'Putting mobile troops *inside* a fortress' was folly, he insisted.[15]

Late in the evening of Friday, 2 October, the Foreign Office received a telegram from the British minister ('ambassador') with a warning from the Belgian prime minister, Broqueville, that the government would be forced to leave for Ostend next morning; it seemed unlikely the army would continue to resist once the king and his ministers had gone.[16] Confirmation of the loss of two forts and three redoubts had thrown Broqueville's colleagues into panic;[17] some 60,000 Germans were said to be closing in on the city. Asquith was in Wales that evening, but in his absence Grey, Churchill and Kitchener responded swiftly: General Paris's Marine Brigade, already back in Dunkirk from Cassel, was ordered to head for Antwerp; preparations began to ship General Capper's 7th Division – 8,000 well-trained infantry, with cavalry support – to Ostend and Zeebrugge. With Kitchener's backing, Churchill and his principal naval adviser set out immediately for Flanders to co-ordinate operations and, in Churchill's phrase, 'brace . . . the Belgians . . . to their task'.[18] Joffre, too, responded to the grave news, though without enthusiasm: he promised the dispatch of a Territorial division and a regiment of marine fusiliers. By Sunday morning (4 October) Kitchener could assure the Belgians they might count on the coming of 53,000 allied troops. As yet, however, no more than 2,000 Royal Marines had reached the city, most aboard double-decker buses from the streets of London.

Churchill spent Sunday and much of Monday watching the marines in action against Beseler's infantry in the streets of Lierre, a historic small town 6 miles from the city centre. On Monday morning Asquith received a telegram from him offering to resign office if he were given command of the British forces in Antwerp. Although Kitchener was prepared to commission Churchill a lieutenant-general, Asquith summoned the first lord back to his responsibilities at the Admiralty. Sir Henry Rawlinson, a general whose solid qualities Kitchener rated highly, was on his way from the Aisne to command an Antwerp Expeditionary Force of 40,000 men that would include the 7th Division.[19] Rawlinson reached Antwerp on Monday evening. Capper's troops, delayed by problems of disembarkation at Zeebrugge on 6–7 October could not progress further north than Bruges before Antwerp fell.

The Royal Marines did, however, receive reinforcement next morning. Six weeks previously Churchill had gained cabinet approval for 'surplus' naval officers and ratings to be formed into a Royal Naval Division (RND), a force in which he took great interest, commissioning several young and enthusiastic volunteers known to him personally. 'Churchill's Pets', as the division was inevitably called, were spared tedious weeks of basic training. On the Sunday that their progenitor was in Antwerp, two brigades of the RND – 8,000 men – embarked at Dover. Among the officers were Asquith's son, Arthur, who had joined the division three days previously, and the poet Rupert Brooke, with a week in khaki behind him. The RND was delayed at Dunkirk and did not enter Antwerp until after dawn on Tuesday (6 October). They were at once deployed in the trenches around the old Fort 7, near Vieux-Dieu, 6 miles from the city.[20]

The soldier–sailors arrived too late to support a Belgian counter-attack. On Monday evening Churchill and Rawlinson attended a meeting of the Belgian supreme council of war (conseil supérieur de guerre), the third held that critical day (5 October). They found King Albert resolute and the garrison commander General Deguise defiant, but the field-army leaders were unsure of their exhausted troops and the government ministers demoralized. It seemed unlikely the 7th Division or the promised French marine fusiliers would reach Antwerp before German cavalry cut the artery to the coast. The council agreed that the British marines and the RND would help the Belgian 2nd Division hold the inner forts while the rest of the field army withdrew across the Scheldt. Churchill visited the RND and the Royal Marine Brigade in their trenches before obeying Asquith's order. Reluctantly he returned to London four days after setting out. King Albert left Antwerp on Tuesday afternoon (7 October) on horseback, with Queen Elisabeth in a car, frequently stopping to encourage the weary Belgian infantry, giving them cigarettes as they paused. As commander-in-chief, he maintained close contact with Joffre and General Rawlinson during the three-day journey to Ostend. He refused Joffre's request for the Belgians to head for Ghent, a city he felt already doomed. Instead he sought the greater security of the coast, where he counted on support from the Royal Navy.[21] That night the German bombardment spread to the inner city, the first shell falling close to the cathedral (as at Verdun 16 months later).

After two days of heavy bombardment, General Paris believed

the surrender of the city imminent. He ordered the RND out of the trenches after nightfall on 8 October. The 'sailors in khaki' and three battalions of the Royal Marine Brigade crossed a pontoon bridge over the Scheldt and began a 25-mile march to St Gilles-Waes and the railway to Bruges. Rupert Brooke's letters give a vivid impression of the confused impact made by the fighting for Antwerp on a 27-year-old Cambridge Apostle, once the colour sergeant of Rugby School's cadet corps. The oil tanks at Hoboken blazed behind them, 'hills and spires of flame . . . a Dantesque Hell', wrote Brooke a few days later. Carcasses of horses and cows sizzled in the heat. But beyond the river, Brooke continued, 'I saw what was a truer Hell. Thousands of refugees, their goods on barrows and hand-carts and perambulators and wagons, moving with infinite slowness out into the night, two unending lines of them, the old men mostly weeping, the women with hard drawn faces, the children playing or crying or sleeping. That's what Belgium is now; the country where three civilians have been killed to every one soldier . . . I can only marvel at human endurance.'[22]

Winding trails of refugees became a common sight in Flanders that autumn. A quarter of a million civilians fled Greater Antwerp during the German assault, some along the route Brooke followed, others crossing into Holland, the wealthiest able to make their way down the Scheldt to Flushing and the North Sea. Fishing boats with Ostend registration markings were soon moored at Ramsgate and Folkestone. As many as 100,000 Belgian refugees reached England during the next two months. Not all were made welcome when they settled in close-knit communities suspicious of outsiders.[23]

Battle casualties for the RND were relatively small: seven officers and 50 ratings killed in action, three officers and 135 ratings seriously wounded; but five officers and 931 ratings were taken prisoner. The 2nd Naval Brigade – in which Brooke was serving – reached Ostend by train without incident and was back in England six days after leaving Dover. Some battalions of the 1st Naval Brigade marched to St Nicholas, to board cattle trucks for a hazardous journey under German fire to Ghent. The remaining three battalions, and some of the Royal Marines, were less fortunate: the German advance cut off almost 1,500 men, who were forced to cross the frontier and accept internment in Holland. The week-long expedition thus reduced the RND by some 28 per cent of its strength; later in the war the division, fully trained and equipped, was to fight with distinction, notably at Gallipoli and on the Somme.[24]

On the evening of Friday, 9 October, German patrols entered Antwerp, and the city surrendered. The last Belgian troops withdrew that night. On Saturday afternoon in Fort Sainte Marie, across the Scheldt from the docks, General Deguise surrendered his sword to a Colonel von Kleitz. Only the fort commander, a sergeant and a private accompanied their general. Deguise explained to Kleitz that of 400 men in the fort's garrison, these were all who remained with him. 'The German colonel very politely refrained from any comment,' Deguise recalls. It is an affecting scene; but might the general have prolonged resistance significantly longer? Could he have left Sainte Marie to continue the fight from one of the northeastern forts, as yet beyond the range of Beseler's guns?[25] At least five of Brialmont's forts surrendered intact, as inviolate as their later descendants, the cupolas of the Maginot Line, in June 1940.

In retrospect the Antwerp rescue bid seems the first bungled sideshow of the war: too little attempted, too late and too slowly. It was not, however, a total failure. The grandiose 'expeditionary force' gave the allies five vital days to consolidate their position in western Flanders and cover the approaches to Dunkirk, Calais and Boulogne. Little more could have been expected of it. Only with Dutch collaboration and the opening of the Scheldt to British warships and transports might Antwerp have been maintained as a forward base. Even so, the power of the enemy's siege-train and the U-boat threat to communications must soon have made the allied position there untenable. The 'national redoubt' could delay a conqueror: it could not defeat him.

The fall of Antwerp was a victory that boosted German morale. A fortnight previously Kaiser Wilhelm was 'very depressed . . . and pessimistic', while OHL feared that 'a serious sortie from Antwerp' might cause the loss of Brussels, so denuded of troops was Beseler's corps. Now at Wilhelm's headquarters in Charleville there was champagne 'for the first time since we left Berlin'. Along the Aisne the sound of cheers and patriotic singing from across the lines intrigued the British rearguard: 'A German victory?', Captain Paterson of the South Wales Borderers speculated on 10 October. An American reporter, Alexander Powell, witnessed the victory parade, a march past through the city centre that lasted five hours; what especially caught his eye were the colour of the uniforms – Prussian grey, Bavarian dark blue, Saxon light blue and, unexpectedly, Austrian gunners in 'a beautiful silver grey'.[26]

Berlin's newspapers celebrated the taking of Antwerp for several days, seeing in it a greater triumph of German arms than the occupation of the first enemy capital seven weeks previously: surely this time there would be no further resistance from the Belgians? Press photographers remained at the ready in the fallen city; they had a reward of a sort. Among trophies captured were several of Churchill's commandeered London buses. Seven Germans clambered aboard a double-decker in the heart of Antwerp and posed for the camera. Along the top deck a billboard still advertised the play in which Gerald du Maurier would be appearing that night at Wyndham's Theatre. Inappropriately it was entitled *Diplomacy*.[27]

6

ARMIES IN COLLISION

The full reality of war struck Ypres on 7 October 1914, the day Churchill arrived back in London from his Antwerp venture. Early that Wednesday afternoon about a dozen shells from German field guns heralded the approach of cavalry and an infantry battalion with cyclists down the Menin Road. The townsfolk were not surprised. As at Mons in August, tales of Uhlans on reconnaissance patrol had come in from neighbouring villages during recent days, for Falkenhayn was deploying his 4th Cavalry Corps northwards in a sweep to cut off French or British forces heading for the Flanders coastal plain. Most of the Germans who entered Ypres soon left, making for the railway junction at Hazebrouck across the French border, but several hundred remained in the town, resting horses overnight and awaiting clarification of their orders. Meanwhile they replenished supplies by the simplest of methods, confiscation. A levy of 65,000 francs (£2,700 – some £54,000 by today's values) was removed from the municipal coffers as a guarantee of the citizens' good behaviour. Individual shops suffered: a jeweller in the rue au Beurre, the road out of the Grand Place towards the station esplanade, lost watches worth more than £1,000; drapers subsequently complained of suits, trousers and underwear purloined; the post office till was rifled, though it yielded little.[1] There were no atrocities or acts of punitive vandalism, but the townsfolk viewed the future with apprehension. A long occupation seemed likely; the nearest allied troops were some 20 miles away and as yet only in small numbers.

Falkenhayn, however, was a cautious commander. His Cavalry Corps, roaming large stretches of the Flanders plain, had become dangerously detached from the main German Sixth Army, attacking down a long front from Armentières southwards to Arras. Already Bailleul and the approaches to Hazebrouck were proving more stoutly defended than the towns of Belgian Flanders; British troops had been identified at Abbeville and were heading for the region in great numbers; Indian regiments were known to have come ashore at Marseilles in the last week of September and entrained for the north; from intelligence reports Falkenhayn learnt that the 7th Division was disembarking at Zeebrugge and could soon strike at his rear. On 8 October he decided to pull back his cavalry, rather than risk their being trapped by British forces converging on West Flanders from opposite directions. The cavalry would be absorbed in a new Fourth Army, forming in Germany. Flanders, he believed, merited a more systematically planned and executed offensive. After destroying Ypres's telegraph system, the invaders withdrew. Thereafter, for the duration of the war, the only Germans to enter Ypres came as prisoners, often wounded and needing emergency treatment at improvised hospitals.[2]

The British arrived next Wednesday morning, 14 October, at nine o'clock. First down the road from Roulers came dragoons in the 6th Cavalry Brigade of IV Corps, as Sir Henry Rawlinson's Antwerp Expeditionary Force had been renamed when integrated in the BEF three days earlier. After a week of autumn sunshine the weather broke on the previous evening, and they were greeted by steady rain, an ominous augury for the months ahead. The brigade – together with the Life Guards and Royal Horse Guards (the Blues) of the 7th Cavalry Brigade and supporting artillery and field engineers – formed General Byng's Cavalry Division and had ridden from Bruges through Thourout and Roulers, covering the Belgian field army as it withdrew to re-form at Nieuport, where sluice-gates and locks held back the sea from the Yser flat lands. The main body of IV Corps comprised Capper's 7th Division, which fell back from Ghent and Bruges through Aeltre and Thielt and, on the previous evening, had linked up with Byng's cavalry at Roulers, a linen town with more inhabitants than Ypres but not deemed defensible.

Throughout the morning the 7th Division filed into Ypres: almost 18,000 men had disembarked at Zeebrugge on 6 October. By midday, as the clouds lifted, and the rain relented, the Grand Place was packed with some of the finest troops in the regular

British army: Grenadier Guards, Scots Guards, Gordon Highlanders, Green Howards, Royal Scots Fusiliers, Royal Welch
Fusiliers and the Rifle Brigade among them. There were battalions
from the Royal Warwickshire, Bedfordshire, South Staffordshire
and Wiltshire regiments, together with the Northumberland
Hussars, a yeomanry regiment providing 7th Division's cavalry
squadron.

Eight of Capper's 12 battalions had been serving overseas when
war was declared and were brought hurriedly home from South
Africa, Egypt, Malta and Gibraltar, in some instances well ahead of
their equipment. Kitchener retained the remaining four battalions
of the 7th Division when the BEF crossed to France, partly as a
safeguard against invasion but also to help train his 'New Armies'.
Many of the men thronging the centre of Ypres had fought in the
Boer War. All except the yeomanry were professionals, sharing the
confidence and superb marksmanship shown by I and II Corps at
Mons nine weeks previously.[3]

As yet Capper's men had seen little fighting, although Byng's
cavalry clashed several times with patrols on the march southwards
from Bruges. 'We are getting fed up with all this waiting, and all are
anxious to get in action,' Gunner Burrows of the Royal Field
Artillery noted in his diary next day.[4] Sir John French, with his
distaste for fortress inactivity, had every intention of capitalizing on
the division's eagerness and mobility. The commander-in-chief
had conferred with General Foch at the weekend and agreed with
him on a general strategy of counter-offensive, a grand design for
rolling back the invader from the lower Yser and upper Lys to the
Belgian heartland.

French required Rawlinson to push forward and establish a line
from the ridge west of Roulers to Menin, with Courtrai, Oudenarde and Brussels as ultimate objectives. Allenby's Cavalry Division was at that moment consolidating its hold on the rising ground
west of Messines, and Sir John anticipated that II Corps and III
Corps would support the main French attack to recapture Lille by
extending the line southwards through Armentières, Neuve Chapelle and La Bassée. Haig's I Corps, the last to be relieved by the
French on the Aisne, would then give support to Rawlinson and
possibly to the Belgians around Nieuport and Dixmude, but it was
not expected to reach the Ypres region for another three days.[5]

Less than 18 hours after entering Ypres, Capper and Byng were
on the move out again, the cavalry trotting cautiously over cobbles
made slippery by rain and persistent mist, the humbler work horses
hauling 18-pounders towards the eastern hillocks that form the rim
of the Ypres saucer. Behind trudged the infantry, passing forlorn
columns of refugees seeking safety in the west and often blocking
the road. To Capper's left were French Territorials, shipped from
Le Havre to Dunkirk to help plug the gap between the BEF and
the Belgians along the upper Yser. From the south came the sound
of heavy firing: II Corps was heavily engaged west of La Bassée and
III Corps around Armentières (with a gravely wounded Lieutenant
Bernard Montgomery among the casualties at Méteren, some 9
miles southwest of Ypres). [6]

Towards Roulers and Menin there was no sign of the enemy;
Samson's armoured cars, reconnoitring well ahead of the 7th
Division, reached the outskirts of Menin itself unchallenged. Most
of the division spent two nights in the fields or found cover in the
clusters of farm buildings or small villages. On Friday afternoon (16
October) the Life Guards and the Blues – the Household Brigade
that in peace formed the sovereign's ceremonial escort – found
billets in a larger village on a ridge 300 feet above sea level and a
little over 7 miles from Ypres. The village bore a name that as yet
meant nothing to the British army: Passchendaele. There the
brigade remained for two nights. [7] It formed a vantage point
commanding the countryside from Roulers in the east to Kemmel
(a 'mount' 520 feet above sea level) and, below it, a ridge between
Wytschaete, at 260 feet, and Messines, slightly more than 5 miles
south of Ypres.

Sir Henry Rawlinson's orders for Sunday, 18 October, were to
push forward on Menin. He was, however, suspicious of German
troops reported moving westwards from Brussels to Courtrai and,
to Sir John French's anger, postponed the attack, pending reports
from reconnaissance patrols. [8] But before dawn on Monday, Capper's division moved down into the plain and on towards Menin
while the French cavalry descended in force on Roulers. At first all
seemed to go well. Soon, however, IV Corps encountered much
greater resistance than had seemed likely on the Sunday. Heavy
cloud ruled out aerial reconnaissance until mid-morning, but when
the planes were eventually airborne the RFC reported columns of

men, horses and guns on the plain west of Courtrai. They threatened to cut the Menin Road and to mount a full-scale assault on Ypres itself. Rawlinson at once ordered Capper's advance troops to pull back, much to the frustration of the Royal Welch Fusiliers who were within 2 miles of Menin town.[9]

Byng's cavalry brigades took up positions between Zandvoorde and the Kruiseik crossroads, on the Menin Road, and then along the paved road that followed the ridge for 5 miles to Passchendaele. There, as dusk fell, the villagers could see the flames of Roulers lighting the night sky, the town fired by a bombardment that forced a brigade of French cavalry to withdraw.[10] Sadly, families packed clothes and blankets on to dogcarts and prepared to swell the trail of refugees, some farmers making sure their family had a cow with them. Next day – Tuesday, 20 October – the remaining British troops pulled out of Passchendaele and down the ridge to join the defensive concentration in the plain, where trenches were being dug. Thus, almost haphazardly and as a temporary expedient, the Ypres Salient began to take shape. The trenches were not, as yet, a systematic network like the German experiment above the Aisne. They were primitive improvisations, often hardly more than a sandbagged ditch at the edge of a sodden field of beet or turnips

Sir John French remained wedded to the idea of an offensive. On Monday evening the commander-in-chief received Haig at GHQ and ordered him to press forward, capture Bruges, 'defeat the enemy and drive him on Ghent'. Confidently, French assured Haig that 'he estimated the Enemy's strength on the front Ostend to Menin at about one corps, not more'.[11] This was an extraordinary miscalculation, flying in the face of intelligence reports. In reality Falkenhayn had already concentrated a force twice that size and more troops were on their way by train from Munich, Augsburg, Stuttgart and Dresden.

The grey columns that the RFC observers sighted west of Courtrai on Monday were the main body of the new Fourth Army, essential to realizing the hopes Falkenhayn continued to cherish of early victory in the West. The army, commanded by Albrecht, Duke of Württemberg, comprised five reserve corps, four of them newly raised, hurriedly trained and short of equipment; the other corps was formed by Beseler's victorious troops from Antwerp, who took Zeebrugge on 14 October and Ostend a day later. There were 130 infantry and rifle battalions in the German Fourth Army and 20 cavalry squadrons, but its strength lay in guns, for the artillery was supplemented by 16 heavy mortars that had bombarded Antwerp. The official history of the campaign shows the army had no less than 176 medium or heavy guns.[12] Even without this intimidating assembly of fire-power the Germans were far stronger than their opponents. Together with the re-formed Sixth Army south of the French border – five corps under Rupprecht, Crown Prince of Bavaria – they went into battle with twice as many infantry divisions in Flanders as the allies and could count on five more corps arriving before the end of the month.

Falkenhayn's neo-Schlieffen Plan envisaged an advance by the Fourth Army down the coast 'to cut off the fortresses [sic] of Dunkirk and Calais' and sever links with England while the Sixth Army would break through in the centre around Arras.[13] It was essential for him to launch the Flanders offensive with an assault on the left of the allied line; on Saturday, 17 October, German artillery shelled Nieuport while Beseler's cavalry reconnoitred the canalized Yserlee as far south as Dixmude, some 12 miles inland.

The allies, too, attached great importance to the lower Yser. This was the region in which King Albert was seeking to restore order and fighting efficiency in regiments that had completed the demoralizing retreat from Antwerp. It was also a sector of great interest to General Foch: he saw the Dixmude–Ypres line as the springboard for a manoeuvre that would turn the German right flank by swinging across to Courtrai, on the River Lys 20 miles to the northeast, with the BEF pressing ahead to Ghent. As early as 13 October, King Albert issued a stirring proclamation calling on the army to uphold 'our national honour . . . Let anyone who talks of retreat be deemed a traitor to his country,' he declared. Over the following days Albert impressed on his five divisional commanders his determination to resist the German onslaught: any general whose men fell back would be instantly dismissed; officers claiming to be sick would face court martial. Marksmen were placed behind the lines with orders to shoot any men who abandoned their posts in panic.[14]

Albert set up his headquarters at Furnes, 5 miles behind the Front, although he made his home, with Queen Elisabeth and their three children, at the Villa Maskens on the edge of the dunes at La

Panne. The Belgian 2nd Division was concentrated close to Nieuport, the 1st around Schoorbakke; the 3rd held at first in reserve at Lampernisse; the 4th straddled the Yser from Tervaete down to Dixmude, while the 5th and 6th were thinly disposed for 8 miles along the canalized Yserlee from Dixmude as far as Boesinghe, a village some 3 to 4 miles north of Ypres. On mobilization in August the Belgian field army had numbered 117,000 men. Now less than half of that number was in the line along the Yser, with the certainty of heavy casualties when the fighting was resumed with full intensity.

In talks with Foch the king emphasized that Belgium was waging war as an associated power; the army would remain an independent, unified force under his command. He agreed, however, to co-operate with the French, establishing a similar relationship to that of the commander-in-chief of the BEF. Foch promised support and on 22 October a special army group, General d'Urbal's Détachement d'armée de Belgique (DAB) came into being. It eventually comprised four full-strength corps and two cavalry corps and was committed to close collaboration with the Belgians. On 23 October the vanguard of the DAB, General Grossetti's 42nd Division, reinforced the defenders of Nieuport.

One French unit was already assisting the Belgians when the German guns first opened up along the Yser. The 6,000 French Marine Fusiliers, originally assigned for the defence of Antwerp but slow to move north, were officially attached to the Belgian army on 13 October and covered the approaches to Dixmude. The marines came from Brittany. Like Churchill's Naval Divisions they were surplus seamen, with little training in land warfare, but their enterprise, ingenuity and collective courage compensated for the lack of fighting experience ashore. Their commander, Rear-Admiral Pierre Ronarc'h was also a Breton, a torpedo specialist. He had, however, seen service ashore in China 14 years earlier with the French contingent of the international force sent to relieve the Peking legations in the Boxer Rising. It was in the same expedition that Major von Falkenhayn, accompanying the much larger German contingent, gained his reputation for ruthlessness.[15]

For many years British studies of the Ypres campaign tended to ignore the early fighting along the canalized river, at best treating it as a separate 'Battle of the Yser', more often dismissing it in two or three sentences. It was left to Professor Strachan in 2001 to emphasize that 'the crisis on the Yser was part of a larger encounter battle, pivoting on the city of Ypres', a battle in which 'Dixmude, tenaciously held by the French marines, became the key to the movements of both sides.'[16] What happened along the river from Nieuport to Dixmude determined the strategic character of First Ypres and the fate of the BEF. Had the Germans broken through at this point it would have been impossible to hold the city or sustain British armies in Flanders. For the Germans to have faltered and fallen back would have brought Foch's grand design closer to fulfilment.

The region was ill suited for battle. This was land wrested from the sea, criss-crossed by canals and ditches and permeated by constant dampness, with water never far below the surface of the polders. The Yser estuary, running for a mile and a half down to the sea beyond Nieuport, is flanked by sand dunes that offered some protection to troops sheltering from German shelling; they continue along the coast through La Panne and on to the outskirts of Dunkirk. Inland the Yser was backed by an embankment 10 feet high, carrying the railway to Ypres and as straight as a yardrule. But there were six bends along the canalized river between Nieuport and Dixmude, so that in places the embankment stood more than 2 miles back from the river. During the fourth week of October these dank, mist-covered fields, oozing mud with every step, formed a fragile crucible for the fiercest fighting on the most northern sector of the whole Western Front.

The main German attack on the Yser began on 18 October, the Sunday on which Capper's 7th Division and the Household Brigade moved cautiously forward along the Menin Road. The Belgians and the Marine Fusiliers offered fierce resistance during the first four days, throwing back assaults on Dixmude, but they were gradually forced to abandon outposts east of Nieuport town, despite the courage of the 14th Regiment of the Line, who lost no less than 900 men. A Royal Navy flotilla, commanded by Rear-Admiral Hood (who had accompanied Churchill to Antwerp), stood off shore and began responding to the German bombard-ment on the Sunday morning.

Allied naval participation in the battle continued for 11 days. At the peak of operations on 24 October the flotilla comprised 15 Royal Navy warships, headed by two ageing cruisers, two new shallow-draught monitors with howitzers and 6-inch guns and eight destroyers, together with five French destroyers. On 25 October the 15-year-old battleship HMS *Venerable* augmented the strength of the flotilla, broadsides from her 12-inch guns inflicting heavy casualties on Beseler's infantry at a time when the Belgian artillery was becoming ominously short of shells.[17] After a week's continuous fighting, the Belgians were forced back to the railway embankment, though tenaciously holding on to Dixmude, and the Germans seemed poised to complete a break-through. Before the war Dixmude was an attractive pocket-size Bruges. Some 15 assaults were launched against the town during 24 October, leaving it ablaze and in ruins by the next morning. Nieuport, too, was again constantly shelled.

There remained one other natural defensive weapon. The proposal to create a sea-water barrier to halt the Fourth Army has been variously attributed to Foch, two Belgian generals, the chief lock-keeper at Nieuport and King Albert himself; perhaps it sprang from a common historical recollection of Dutch resistance to imperial Spain. To be effective the flooding needed high tides, winds from the northeast and the ability of the lock-keepers to man the sluices despite frequent shelling. On 23 October, Albert ordered his sappers to seal off 22 culverts under the embankment, preparatory to flooding the fields and villages east of the railway.

Simply to open the sluice gates at Nieuport was out of the question. To do so would put at risk the allied forces locked in battle across the low-lying fields. Controlled inundation was essential, and the work had to be done at night in order to take the Germans by surprise. Hendrik Gheeraert, who had spent all his life working the canals, was the only person who knew where the cranks for operating the sluices were stored. In collaboration with two lock-keepers, Karel-Louis Kogge and Feman Umé, Gheeraert set about controlling the inrush of water. On 26–27 October, Kogge sought to open the gates of the Furnes canal, the most seaward of three sluices at Nieuport (close to Belgium's most cherished oyster beds), but he could not shift them before the tide began to ebb. Next night Umé and Gheeraert had more success at

the Ypres canal and Comte canal locks, and by 29–30 October all
three sluices were open and under control. During the week the
tidal height increased day by day, to pass the 16-foot marker on the
night that the sluices were finally opened, when there was a full
moon. Very rightly, in Nieuport today, monuments and plaques
close to the magnificent equestrian statue of King Albert honour
the heroism of Gheeraert, his fellow lock-keepers and the Belgian
military engineers who assisted them.[18]

Poor weather and frequent sea-mists during this last week of
October gave greater cover as the operation continued, and at first
the Germans attributed the worsening conditions in the fields to
persistent rain. By 29 October, however, they perceived the threat
that endangered their advance. They captured the small town of
Pervyse, beyond the railway embankment, on that Thursday but
the rising waters soon forced them hurriedly to withdraw. Next
day, at Ramscapelle further north along the embankment, bugles
rang out to rally the Belgian and French infantry to mount one last,
stumbling, bayonet charge across the squelching clay and, as night
fell on Saturday, 31 October, they threw back Beseler's III Reserve
Corps. The Fourth Army's offensive 'to cut off the fortresses of
Dunkirk and Calais' was at an end.

The Marine Fusilier Brigade, strengthened by two battalions of
Senegalese and backed by Grossetti's 42nd Division moving up
from Furnes, still held Dixmude itself. For 11 more days the town
formed an outpost above the rising waters on the right bank of the
Yser, until the XXII Reserve Corps, commanded by Falkenhayn's
elder brother, Eugen, launched a powerful assault on 10 November, backed by heavy bombardment from massed field guns. By
nightfall Dixmude had fallen.[19]

Thereafter for three and a half years a muddy, yellow or green
moat over 20 miles long and from two to two and a half miles wide
separated the opposing armies. Occasionally the Germans raided
the sector facing Dixmude, using small boats or rafts and backed by
fire from grenade launchers and mortars. The Belgian defences on a
promontory across the Yser, a mile northwest of the ruined town,
were so exposed to bombardment and assault that they are singled
out today for remembrance as the 'Trenches of Death'. The black,
gold and red national flag flies proudly over them.

★   ★   ★

The battle for Dixmude coincided with the opening three weeks of First Ypres further south. It was on 21 October that the full force of the Fourth and Sixth German Armies was turned against the BEF and the French in front of Ypres, and for the first time the line of the Immortal Salient was clearly defined on the map. From Bixschoote a curved 36-mile front ran eastwards in a bulge through Langemarck, southeastwards down to Zandvoorde, curving round southwestwards between Hollebeke and Houthem, to straighten out along the Messines Ridge and then down to the French border east of Armentières.

For 'Wednesday 21 October' Haig's diary records a day of 'uncertainty, excitement and despairing messages'.[20] In seeking to fulfil French's order to 'defeat the enemy and drive him on Ghent', the British 2nd Division pressed on eastwards, with 'hard fighting and bayonet work', but the enemy seemed 'to have been advancing when our attack took place'. In the afternoon Rawlinson visited Haig's headquarters in the Hotel de la Châtelaine, to let him know that 'hostile infantry and guns' were heading for Ypres from another direction, south-southeast along both sides of the Comines canal. Soon there was more perplexing news for Haig. 'Now', he writes, 'without warning the French cavalry guarding our left flank is ordered to retire west of the [Dixmude–Ypres] canal' and confront a German division reported to be moving down from the north.[21] These laconic jottings go far to explain why First Ypres caused such devastation and cost so many lives. The commitment of Foch and French to a drive from the Yser northwards into central Belgium clashed with Falkenhayn's neo-Schlieffen project. The battle became a head-on collision between two armies set on the offensive.

Personally, Haig doubted the wisdom of pressing forward beyond the first objectives without careful reconnaissance. He was prepared to call a halt, at least temporarily. All, however, depended on the field marshal out at GHQ in St Omer, some 30 miles from Haig's hotel in the Grand Place. Sir John French was uneasy. The strain of adjusting his mind to a different concept of warfare was wearying him. He mistrusted Kitchener and was angered by the War Office's failure to respond to his pleas for more ammunition for his 18-pounders and howitzers. His mercurial temperament swung from over-confidence to depression and

back again in the course of a single day. He admitted that the
discovery of five German corps in a region where he thought there
was only one had come as 'a veritable bolt from the blue'.[22] Joffre,
visiting GHQ on that Wednesday morning, found French pressing
for work to begin on an entrenched camp at Boulogne capable of
sustaining the whole BEF should it be forced into retreat.

But the gloom soon passed, once Sir John's staff began to feed
him better news. The promise of an additional French corps in the
Ypres zone, reports of fresh troops arriving to build up III Corps
and the coming of the Lahore Division as vanguard of an Indian
Corps strengthened by battalions of Sherwood Foresters and the
Manchester Regiment, all lifted Sir John's spirits. That afternoon
he motored into Ypres and conferred with Haig, approving his
decision to delay the advance. Once back at GHQ, his orders
determined the tactics for the coming week: 'Action against enemy
will be continued tomorrow on general line now held, which will
be strongly entrenched.'[23] As on the day before Mons, French's
telegram to Kitchener that evening was an up-beat nightcap, 'In
my opinion the enemy are vigorously playing their last card, and I
am confident they will fail.'[24]

Throughout the next three days the Germans sought desperately
to break through to Ypres. More than 1,500 of them perished in
the meadows, copses and burning villages around Bixschoote and
Langemarck. Thousands more passed into captivity, among them
some 800 in one small village: Kortekeer on the Dixmude Road,
southeast of Bixschoote, was attacked at first light on 23 October
by five battalions of 2nd Brigade. Some 29 years later Lieutenant
Hyndson of the 1st Loyal North Lancashires recalled 'the glorious
sight of masses of grey-coated men standing up to surrender'.[25] The
abiding British memory of the three days' fighting was of blazing
villages, 'heavy rifle fire all round and heavy shelling' and of the
German infantry advancing line after line as steadily as on man-
oeuvres.[26]

Next day Captain Dillon of the Oxford and Buckinghamshire
Light Infantry wrote what Dr Ian Beckett rightly calls a 'graphic
account' of a German attack as seen from the parapet of his trench:
'A great grey mass of humanity was charging, running for all God
would let them straight on us not 50 yards off . . . Everybody's
nerves were pretty well on edge as I had warned them what to

expect and as I fired my rifle the rest all went off almost simultaneously.' The rapid fire halted the attack. 'A great moan' was heard and Dillon saw men 'with their arms and legs off trying to crawl away; others, who could not move gasping out their last moments with the cold night air biting into their broken bodies and the lurid red glare of a farmhouse showing up some clumps of grey devils killed by the men on my left further down. A weird awful sight!'[27]

One 'grey devil', who was in battle for the first time, was appalled by all he saw around him. 'Corpses, corpses, and more corpses, rubble, and the remains of villages', artilleryman Herbert Sulzbach noted: 'The bodies of friend and foe lie tumbled together . . . A dreadful night comes down on us. We have seen too many horrible things all at once, and the smell of the smoking ruins, the lowing of the deserted cattle, and the rattle of machine-gun fire make a very strong impression on us, barely twenty years old as we are, but these things also harden us up for what is going to come. We certainly did not want this war! We are only defending ourselves and our Germany against a world of enemies.'[28]

Langemarck was soon to become a German patriotic legend. A High Command communiqué, circulated to the press on 11 November, paid tribute to the heroism with which young volunteers 'surged forward against the front line of the enemy positions'[29] singing Deutschland über Alles or Die Wacht am Rhein. Particularly singled out for praise were the 204th and 206th Reserve Infantry regiments and the many student battalions, some formed around university fraternities. A German cavalry officer, Rudolf Binding, writing a fortnight before the communiqué was issued, reported: 'Our light infantry battalion, almost all Marburg students, have suffered terribly. In the next division just such young souls, the intellectual flower of Germany, went singing into an attack at Langemarck just as vain and just as costly.'[30] By Christmas the German public was calling the battle der Kindermord von Ypern ('the Massacre of the Innocents at Ypres'). In the 1930s, Nazi propaganda harnessed the legend, emphasizing the glory of sacrifice for the Fatherland rather than the tragic wastage of young lives. Inevitably, as with all Nazi manipulations of history, later scholars have subjected 'the myth' to close scrutiny, emphasizing in particular that older men returning to the colours considerably outnumbered the young.[31] But there is no reason to doubt the courage and patriotism of the youthful volunteers nor their resort to song at such a time; across the lines, the 2nd Royal Welch Fusiliers heartened their spirits on 28 October with 'Celtic harmonies and favourite hymns' during a pause in the week's heavy fighting.[32] Today at the entrance to Langemarck Cemetery a memorial room perpetuates the student 'innocents', their names carved on oak panels, the archway carrying the crests of their universities.

The British too suffered heavy losses during the three days of battle. In Haig's I Corps the 1st Division lost 1,006 men, and the 2nd Division was under constant bombardment. Capper's 7th Division (IV Corps), astride the Menin Road around Gheluvelt, lost 2829 officers and men while the survivors (as one was to write) were 'weary, unwashed, unshaven, short of sleep and sometimes of food'.[33] Rapid movements of individual units, doubts of identity in autumn mists or under the artificial fog of bursting German shells led to confusion and chaos. British, French and Germans all fell victims to what a modern, sanative euphemism calls 'friendly fire'. The full horror of war was unleashed on friend and foe and by friend and foe.

Just 12 miles south of the Langemarck–Bixschoote sector the battle for the Messines Ridge, which had been raging for nine days, also reached a new intensity on 21 October. Three crack German divisions of Rupprecht's Sixth Army sought to drive Allenby's two cavalry divisions back through the villages of Hollebeke and Wytschaete and into the small town of Messines, taking the ridge itself. The cavalry, fighting dismounted and in shallow trenches, survived heavy bombardment and stood firm, although the Germans took and briefly held Hollebeke.

After nightfall on 25 October the predominantly Bavarian infantry encountered a new enemy, Punjabi sepoys in the Ferozepore Brigade of the Baluchis Regiment defending Wytschaete. Next morning the Indians went over to the attack, fighting for the first time in Europe under conditions for which no amount of training on the subcontinent could have prepared them. At Messines Ridge, and later across the French border at Neuve Chapelle, they fought with courage and enterprise. Within a week of going into action, Sepoy Khudadad Khan won a Victoria Cross at Hollebeke when, although wounded, he continued to fire a machine-gun after his four companions had been killed. Indian casualties were high: more than a third of the Baluchis perished on the battlefield itself or were mortally wounded.

As early as the evening of 23 October, Falkenhayn was concerned at the failure to dent the allied line northeast of Ypres. He ordered XV Corps to 'march as quickly as possible' from the Aisne by way of Douai and Cambrai to Lille, intending to use the corps's two divisions to reinforce his northern flank.[34] Meanwhile the offensive would continue with unremitting intensity, taking advantage of German superiority in heavy artillery, with the strongest assault made against the weary 7th Division. The 2nd Border Regiment, entrenched on the edge of the woods around the hamlet of Kruiseik, suffered an incredible dawn-to-dusk bombardment throughout 24–26 October, shells falling at the rate of two a minute and causing, on average, 150 casualties a day. Small wonder that on Monday (26 October) an attack by 15 German infantry battalions forced their dazed neighbours, the 1st South Staffordshires, back along the Menin Road towards Ypres.[35] They were 'terror stricken men' of a 'fine . . . division', wrote Haig, who encountered them when he 'rode out about 3 p.m. to see what was going on.'[36] He strengthened the line with reinforcements from I Corps before the Germans could discover that the elusive breakthrough was almost theirs.

Next morning (Tuesday, 27 October) I Corps launched a series of counter-attacks, in a general move to press forward towards Roulers in partnership with the French IX Corps, whose immediate objective was the village of Poelcapelle, 2 miles east of Langemarck. Both armies were battle weary and little progress could be made.

Once the early mist cleared the 1st King's Royal Rifles attempted to seize a spur on the Passchendaele ridge at Keiberg, above Zonnebeke. It was a valiant but costly undertaking, in which the battalion lost five officers and 115 men. Among those mortally wounded by shrapnel that Tuesday was 23-year-old Lieutenant Prince Maurice of Battenberg, son of the widowed Princess Beatrice and youngest grandson of Queen Victoria. When Victoria's eldest grandson, Kaiser Wilhelm II, heard of his cousin's death he sent a message of condolence to the family using the Crown Princess of Sweden, another grandchild, as intermediary. Dynastic bonds were not yet severed by the mounting awfulness of the conflict.[37]

At OHL in Mézières on Monday evening Falkenhayn assessed reports of the three-day bombardment and, as so often in his years of command, was vexed by indecision. He had doubts over the plan he had begun to formulate four nights earlier. Was it a strategic error to assign reinforcements to the northeast of Ypres, where crack regiments of Haig's I Corps held in reserve could stiffen resistance? Was the enemy more vulnerable south of Ypres? On Tuesday morning he left Mézières and reached Sixth Army head-quarters at Douai by noon to confer with Crown Prince Rupprecht. The preliminary directive of 23 October was modified. A special task force of six divisions would be formed within the Sixth Army under the orders of General von Fabeck.

Back in Mézières that night Falkenhayn issued a new directive: 'The attack will be launched on 30 October in a northwesterly direction from the general line Wervicq to Deulemont . . . All available Sixth Army heavy artillery will move up in support of the breakthrough . . . Concerted action by Fourth and Sixth Armies is essential.' The character of the attack was to be unchanged: a preliminary 'bombardment with heaviest calibre weapons on Messines and Ploegsteert Wood' was recommended.[38]

The additional divisions gave Army Group Fabeck, backed by 260 heavy guns and field howitzers, a superiority of at least two to one between Gheluvelt and the Messines Ridge.[39] Fabeck, whose military career had so far remained unexceptional, was determined to seize the opportunity to stamp his name on history. In an order of the day, circulated on 29 October, he stressed the 'decisive importance' of a breakthrough: 'We must and shall therefore conquer . . . and strike the decisive blow against our most hated enemy,' he proclaimed. His men were assured they could win the glory of ending the war and thus 'settle for ever the struggle of centuries'.[40]

7

DAYS OF CRISIS

A long the Menin Road the early hours of 29 October were cold, dank and heavy with menace. On the previous afternoon an intercepted wireless message from German Fourth Army headquarters had given warning of an attack to be launched against Gheluvelt next morning. In churned-up fields a little over half a mile east of the village the first battalions of three regiments stood on the alert, Coldstream Guards and Black Watch in General Lomax's 1st Division north of the road and the Grenadier Guards of Capper's 7th Division (now administratively absorbed in Haig's I Corps) to the south. At times during the night the rattle of field guns and limbers clattering down *pavé* roads could be heard from well behind German lines. Each battalion had a nominal battle establishment of 1,007 men, but all three were considerably under strength, the troops weary and weakened by heavy fighting over the last three days. So too were other regiments held in reserve along the road towards Ypres, 5 miles away. Among them were the 1st Gloucesters and 1st Scots Guards. Most of the men bivouacked in the fields, with the more fortunate under shelter in farmsteads or barns.

Gheluvert was a straggling village typical of West Flanders with now deserted houses clustered around the church and reaching out north of the road towards a windmill and a chateau, by English reckoning a large manor house. West of the lane to the chateau was an orchard and behind it a copse. Further back still, almost a mile from the Menin Road and in the sector assigned to General Monro's 2nd Division, came the first clumps of Scotch firs in Polygon Wood. The trees were not as yet the sorrowful stumps that stand out so gauntly in the paintings of Paul Nash and the photographs of later years; the many copses on both sides of the Menin Road still provided cover for troops resting or cautiously moving forward. They were to need it in the coming days.

At half-past five on that Thursday morning, 80 minutes before dawn, the German guns opened up. A combination of smoke from high explosive and a rise in temperature intensified the morning mist. By six o'clock, when four battalions of Bavarian infantry attacked the Coldstream and the Black Watch the battlefield was shrouded in fog, visibility down to 40 yards. For I Corps the morning became disastrous. Everything went wrong. Contact between forward troops and reserves was hampered by the shelling, which brought down the 'air links', as telephone wires were widely called at the time. Messages had to be conveyed by 'runners' or mounted dispatch riders, exposed to enemy fire; many failed to get through. The fog made it hard for gunners to identify advancing infantry, often obscured by cottage walls and projecting farm buildings. Moreover, after a week of constantly renewed action, basic weapons needed cleaning, greasing or oiling. Two machine-guns, sited to command the Kruiseik crossroads east of the village and each capable of firing 500 rounds a minute, jammed in quick succession. Within an hour of the initial bombardment the Bavarians dented the line, taking prisoner two of the Coldstream's four companies and some 200 Black Watch. Four more battalions of Bavarians engaged the Grenadiers to the south of the crossroads, emerging from the mist about half-past seven and inflicting heavy casualties. So severe was the hand-to-hand fighting that, by dusk, only five Grenadier officers and less than 200 other ranks survived: 470 Grenadiers were lost during the day.[1]

Among German soldiers who received their baptism of fire along the Menin Road that morning was Adolf Hitler. Although an Austrian national, he had volunteered for service in the Bavarian army at the start of the war. His unit – the first battalion, Reserve Infantry Regiment 16, known as the 'List Regiment', from the name of its commanding colonel – reached Lille by train from Augsburg on 23 October and was hurriedly absorbed into Fabeck's Army Group. During the four days of fighting that began along the Menin Road, the List Regiment – 3,600 strong when it arrived in Flanders – lost 2,889 men. Not all fell to enemy fire: the Bavarians wore caps, rather than helmets, and in the smoke and fury of battle their Württemberger and Saxon comrades could not distinguish mud-spattered Bavarian uniforms from British khaki. Colonel List himself was killed by shellfire on the third day of the battle.[2]

A further wave of Bavarian attacks was launched south of Gheluvelt shortly before midday, after the fog had lifted and before rain clouds swept in. There was serious concern for the strain on the BEF's reserves, and reinforcements were hurried northwards. At the same time six German aircraft flew over the battlefield and on to Ypres itself. They threw down the first bombs to fall on the town, believing that reserve troops were already stationed within the walls, but it was Belgian civilians who suffered rather then the military. Increasingly during the following weeks Ypres became a target for aircraft and, far more seriously, artillery. That night the first heavy shells were fired into the town, with the route out towards Dixmude the main target. For the next month the German gunners sustained a systematic bombardment. At first the shells rained down on the bottleneck of roads leading to the two principal gates. After a few days they were falling on the centre, around the cathedral and Cloth Hall.[3]

By nightfall on 29 October the Bavarians held the Kruiseik crossroads and the slightly sloping plateau behind the village, a natural launching pad for further attacks. Sir John French was well satisfied with the general situation, although staggered by the mounting list of casualties as the reports came in to him. Late in the afternoon he met Foch at his headquarters in Cassel and welcomed an offer of support from the cuirassiers and dragoons in General Conneau's Cavalry Corps. Back at GHQ, Sir John sent off yet another confident telegram to Kitchener. He also ordered a resumption of counter-attacks in the north of the Salient next morning.[4]

The full weight of Fabeck's main assault fell on the tired defenders of the Menin Road on 30 October once the familiar early mist lifted. Around Zonnebeke the attack was contained, but at Gheluvelt the Bavarians took advantage of the higher ground won on the previous day to destroy Haig's latest line of trenches in a 75-minute bombardment. To the south, around Hollebeke, the 2nd Bavarian Corps broke through a weakly held line. No more than 1,500 lancers and dragoons, fighting dismounted, and 1,000 Indian infantry were spread over a three and a half mile front. They had only ten guns to support them. From Hollebeke the Bavarians were able to advance to the village of St Eloi, on the main road from Ypres to Armentières and Lille. At one point the Bavarians came within 3 miles of Ypres, but they did not consolidate these forward positions, apparently fearing they might soon be surrounded. Attempts by Allenby's cavalry to regain the lost ground and force the German 2nd Corps back to their overnight positions were abandoned, largely because of the need to counter a fresh German attack that threatened another breakthrough, further southwest. This time the objective was the ridge that ran for a mile and a half northeastwards from Messines to Wytschaete.[5]

Despite French's optimism General Foch had doubts over the BEF's ability to stem the series of sustained assaults. One of his ablest staff officers, Captain Édouard Réquin, had arrived in Ypres at mid-afternoon, in time to see the trail of improvised ambulances bringing casualties in from Hollebeke to fill the clearing stations and temporary hospitals within the town. Réquin's report to Foch was followed late in the evening by worrying signs that Fabeck was bringing up reserves from Comines to intensify the threat to Messines. The worsening news prompted Foch to drive the 13 miles from Cassel to British GHQ at St Omer soon after midnight and have Sir John roused from sleep for emergency discussions.

Foch's account of the meeting suggests the field marshal was close to panic but other reports, including the earliest French source, play down the sense of drama. There is, however, no doubt everyone present acknowledged that if the gap widened around Hollebeke it would be hard to prevent a decisive fracture of the line. To French's evident relief, Foch offered eight battalions and six batteries of field guns to strengthen the Hollebeke sector as well as reinforcements from Grossetti's 42nd Division to aid the defenders of St Eloi. Foch continued to discuss details of the new deployment with General Wilson until half-past two in the morning, long after French had retired to bed.[6]

While Foch and Wilson were in conference the last British reserves, both Territorial units, made ready for the Front. The Oxfordshire Yeomanry (1st Queen's Own Oxfordshire Hussars) set out from St Omer to cover 35 miles to the western edge of the Messines Ridge, with troopers in the saddle and senior officers in their private motor cars. The London Scottish (14th battalion, London Regiment), who reached Ypres during Thursday night's bombardment and spent Friday in reserve at Sanctuary Wood, were roused from billets in the town and set out before dawn, 750 grey kilted 'exiles' following their pipers up the 4-mile road to Wytschaete.

Persistent rain eased off during Friday evening, giving way to a warm and still night, deceptively peaceful through the small hours. Down in the trenches Allenby's forward troops could hear a German band playing Lehár and Strauss, the light music drifting incongruously over the churned-up wasteland from an officers' mess in a captured chateau. The Germans were confident. So certain was Falkenhayn of imminent victory that Kaiser Wilhelm travelled to Crown Prince Rupprecht's headquarters at Douai, going forward with him to the Ypres sector to witness the fighting in the trenches in anticipation of making a triumphant entry into the last of Belgium's historic cities.[7]

Battle resumed on Saturday (31 October) with another display of *Kindermord* patriotism. At half-past four bugle calls sent the 26th Württemberg Division forward against Indian troops from the Punjab and a battalion of the Inniskilling Fusiliers holding Messines. The 5th Dragoon Guards – in the 1st Cavalry Division – blunted the ferocity of this first assault at barricades thrown across the main crossroads, but later in the morning German Grenadiers, supported by a constant bombardment by heavy guns, broke into Messines from the north, and the cavalry and the fusiliers were forced back from the central square to the western fringe of the village, with behind them a sharp dip down into a valley through which meandered a small stream. Throughout the morning a desperate fight continued to hold the western side of the Wytschaete Road (now N365). By noon reinforcements were on hand to support the Inniskilling Fusiliers, including two battalions of Yorkshire Light Infantry and Scottish Borderers. Across the shallow valley the Oxfordshire Yeomanry waited with their horses ready to back up a cavalry counter-attack or aid General Hubert Gough's 2nd Cavalry Division who, dismounted, were holding on in Wytschaete itself.

By now the London Scottish, too, were waiting. They had reached a windmill on the edge of a copse south of Wytschaete and were eager to become the first Territorial infantry to go into action. Three months ago many were still working in City banks and offices, like 23-year-old Ronald Colman, who was to survive a serious wound that day and win film fame in the 1930s as Raffles and Rudolf Rassendyll. Also serving with the London Scottish was the screen's archetypal Sherlock Holmes, Basil Rathbone, who had married on leave in Chelsea four weeks previously. The London Scottish were, in some respects, precursors of the 'pals battalions' recruited for Kitchener's New Armies from among men who shared a common social, recreational or professional background. Before the war the 'Scottish' formed a clubable community of 'exiles' in the capital, enjoying Burns Nights and other national celebrations. They were best known as rugby players, with their club XVs respected for verve and audacity.[8]

Sadly, these qualities may well have contributed to the battalion's disastrous losses on 31 October, although there was also a weakness in the command structure and a consequent confusion over orders. The London Scottish should have gone forward to help the cavalry in small groups, cautiously crouched, scurrying to low trenches around a ruined farm hurriedly dug by sappers earlier in the battle. Instead, when early in the afternoon the Scottish at last went into the attack, they broke cover at the double, advancing uphill in good order like an extended three-quarter line and ran on beyond the farm, believing they were participants in a general counter-attack. Once atop the ridge, they became a tragically exposed target for the sweep of machine-guns, followed by shells from well-sited artillery. They suffered more than 300 casualties that day. Yet despite finding their outdated Lee-Metford rifles defective, the survivors of the initial charge joined the dismounted cavalry and continued to hold the trenches throughout the night, on one occasion in fierce hand-to-hand fighting against persistent Bavarian counter-attacks, made under cover of darkness.[9]

Messines and Wytschaete were of strategic importance to Germans and British alike, for the ridge commanded the southern approach to Ypres, but the decisive point of battle on 31 October lay some 5 miles southeast of the town along the Menin Road, where there had been such heavy fighting two days previously. Around Gheluvert the German bombardment began later than on the ridge, not until six in the morning. Five battalions of Lomax's 1st Division held a mile and a half of the line on either side of the road. To the west, the 2nd Welch Regiment repulsed the first attack and so, to the east, did the 1st Queens (West Surrey), but the Germans could not be prised from an orchard, where they continued to pin down a company of the 2nd King's Royal Rifle Corps (KRRC) throughout the morning. By eight o'clock, with the light rapidly improving, the heavy artillery intensified the bombardment, for the first time using observation balloons to ensure the guns were sighted on their precise targets; shells fell on the Welshmen's trenches east of Gheluvert church. So intense was their fire that some 20 shells exploded along a hundred yards of village street in a single minute. Here the dazed survivors of the onslaught could not prevent a breakthrough while, at the same time, the 1st Scots Guards and 1st South Wales Borderers were hard pressed in the grounds of Gheluvert chateau, their overnight headquarters.[10]

Soon after ten o'clock a third wave of German infantry swept into the attack. Seven fresh battalions advanced down both sides of the Menin Road, with three more battalions and the List Regiment in reserve, giving the German infantry a superiority of at least three to one. By now the five British battalions had suffered such heavy casualties that among them they could muster barely 1,000 men, one-fifth their theoretical strength. German artillery superiority at that moment cannot have been less than six to one. There was, however, a significant development during the day: the first high-explosive shells arrived from England; by the afternoon, they had reached selected batteries of field guns, previously restricted to firing shrapnel. But throughout the remaining days of battle the shortage of shells, both shrapnel and high explosive, remained a prime concern for French and his corps commanders.

As at Langemarck in the previous week, the Germans launched their assault with cheers and patriotic songs; the mood of exultation soon faded. Concentrated rifle fire from the KRRC checked the advance. Their corps commander, General von Deimling – soon himself to be wounded by shrapnel – assumed that nests of machine-gunners lay concealed behind the bushes and in the fallen masonry of ruined cottages. After an hour of intense exchanges of fire, Deimling ordered up two batteries of field guns. The delaying action gave the KRRC company commanders an opportunity to

begin an orderly withdrawal, but nothing could save Gheluvert. By
11.30 a.m. the village was in enemy hands, and the German heavy
guns began pounding the *pavé* surface of the road towards Ypres.
The British infantry took to the fields, seeking the cover of
primitive trenches and ditches. The retreating artillerymen made
every effort to save the 18-pounders with their six-horse teams but
found themselves exposed to the full blast of the bombardment:
'We pass through a perfect hail of shells up the Menin Road. Awful
time!', Gunner Burrows of the Royal Field Artillery noted in his
diary, lapsing into the present tense as he rekindled the stress of the
morning. 'How we got out of it is a mystery! Shells are bursting all
over the place. My off-horse is wounded and nearly drops down
with exhaustion . . . We go back a mile and stop in a field.'
Burrows counted himself lucky to survive: two officers, an NCO
and a gunner in his battery were killed, and several of the drivers
wounded.[11]

When Gheluvert fell, all the reserves of the 1st Division were
already in the line apart from two field companies of the Royal
Engineers and a company (250 men) of the Black Watch. General
Monro, commanding 2nd Division, had already agreed with
Lomax that if his 1st Division were sorely pressed he could call
on Monro's reserves for support. Shortly after midday Lomax rode
back from the front for a joint staff conference with Monro at
Hooge chateau, two and a half miles east of Ypres and recently
assigned by Haig to the two divisional staffs as a shared headquarters. Before leaving for Hooge, Lomax instructed Brigadier-
General Fitzclarence VC to call on help from the 2nd Worcesters,
on stand-by with the 2nd Division's reserves in Polygon Wood.

Shortly before one o'clock in the afternoon Major Edward
Hankey, acting battalion commander of the 2nd Worcesters, set
off from the wood with six other officers and 350 men, and orders
from the brigadier to launch a counter-attack to recover Gheluvert.
Fitzclarence accompanied the battalion for the first half a mile, as far
as the hamlet of Polderhoek. Between the hamlet and Gheluvert
chateau was largely open scrubland, broken by a stream and by a
cutting on the Ypres–Roulers railway, which was reached by a
quarter past one and gave the Worcesters relative protection from
the German shelling that began as soon as they broke cover. Even
so, the battalion suffered almost 100 casualties before storming into

Gheluvert chateau, where more than 1000 Bavarians were ransacking the house, too intent on a quest for liquor and loot to spot their attackers before they fell upon them. Two batteries of 60-pounders (howitzers) gave support to the Worcesters from the fields around Veldhoek, some 2,000 yards to the west, and by 2.30 in the afternoon much of Gheluvert was again in British hands. In one corner of the chateau grounds, Major Hankey found survivors of the Scots Guards and South Wales Borderers still holding out, almost six hours after their comrades were overwhelmed. To the major's surprise, the defenders were commanded by a near neighbour and fellow-rider to hounds, Colonel Leach. 'My God, fancy meeting you here!', Hankey exclaimed, as they shook hands. 'Thank God, you've come,' a weary Leach replied.[12]

Further back towards Ypres the road was blocked by motor vehicles, a long trail of wounded men in search of clearing stations and artillery horses terrified by the screaming shells that fell either among them or in the adjoining fields. Soon after one o'clock, Lomax, Monro and their staffs were still conferring at Hooge when two of the shells hit the chateau, one exploding above Monro's office. Lomax was gravely wounded, though his life lingered on for another 20 weeks; Monro was shaken and stunned but soon able to exercise command again. Five senior staff officers were killed outright and five more wounded, two of them mortally. For several hours the 1st Division had no commander: Haig appointed General Bulfin to take over from Lomax, but he was heavily engaged in the Comines canal sector, fighting around Zandvoorde and Hollebeke. In his absence General Landon took command.[13]

Haig's response to the successive crises on 31 October has been a subject of controversy.[14] Three days earlier he had moved his headquarters from the Hotel de la Châtelaine in the Grand Place to the White Chateau, yet another of the many nineteenth-century mansions off the Menin Road, less than a mile west of Hooge. About eight o'clock in the morning he rode some distance down the Menin Road with some of his staff to see if they could get a clearer understanding of the situation at Gheluvert but soon gave up the task and returned to the White Chateau. Throughout the morning his staff tried to piece together the sequence of events, for the most part relying on reports from runners, as the telegraph wires had been shot away. The confusion along the road intensified, with stragglers making their way westwards independently, often dazed and constantly under bombardment. Soon after midday Haig accepted that Gheluvert had fallen and feared that the 1st Division was broken. While Fitzclarence was improvising the Worcesters' counter-attack, Haig discussed with his staff a plan to fall back from the Salient and establish a new line on the traditional defences of Ypres, the ramparts and the Yserlee canal.[15] During the discussions he received news of the shells falling on Hooge chateau. He turned aside from future planning to deal not only with the crisis in command but also with reports of German gains at Zillebeke, where a Saxon regiment threatened an advance to cut the Menin Road from the southwest.

Shortly afterwards – apparently about two o'clock – the commander-in-chief arrived at the White Chateau. When Sir John saw the congestion on the Menin Road he left his car and threaded his way for half a mile through 'crowds of wounded [who] came limping as fast as they could go, all heading for Ypres'. He found Haig and his chief of staff 'white faced' and 'evidently confused' and was told: 'They have broken us right in and are pouring through the gap.' Haig wrote in his diary, 'Sir John was full of sympathy,' adding in a later version: 'No one could have been nicer at such a time of crisis'; but he had no reserves to plug that gap. After half an hour he left, intending to find Foch and seek French help yet again. Within minutes, Haig learnt of the Worcesters' success at Gheluvert and an aide-de-camp let Sir John know the good news before his car drove away. This sudden change of fortune lifted French's boyish spirits like the climax of an adventure story and left a deep impression: 'The Worcesters saved the Empire,' he was to tell Lord Selborne the following February.[16]

Yet so mercurial was Sir John's temperament that when half an hour later he met Foch at Vlamertinghe, the Frenchman thought him fatalistically depressed. According to Foch's 'shadow', Colonel Weygand, the field marshal said that if his surviving troops continued to fight 'there was nothing more he could do but go up and be killed with them'.[17] Foch dismissed such talk: Sir John should think of winning, not dying. He deplored any proposal to fall back on the inner defences of Ypres: to ease pressure on the British he would order the French infantry to counter-attack next day on either side of the harassed 1st Division. Jointly the two commanders prepared a directive for Haig: he was not to retire, though he might adjust the line, specifically around Zonnebeke; the 2nd Division should keep in close contact with the French IX Corps commander, General Dubois (who was present during the discussions). 'It is of the *utmost* importance to hold the ground you are now on,' Sir John insisted in a separate personal message to Haig.[18]

While Foch and French were conferring at Vlamertinghe, Haig again rode up the Menin Road, this time to Veldhoek, accompanied by his senior staff. He wished 'to see if I could do anything to organize stragglers and push them forward to check Enemy', he explains in his diary. At that moment he was still contemplating retirement on Ypres: the men were worn out with constant fighting by day and trench-digging at night; two brigadiers warned him that if the Germans made 'a push at any point' they had doubts of 'our men being able to hold on'.[19] Haig scrupulously sought to follow the Vlamertinghe directives that he must have found awaiting him on return to the White Chateau. Reluctantly, however, he decided Gheluvelt must be abandoned, despite the sacrifice of so many lives in the morning and the afternoon's counter attack. The village was now too exposed, in danger of another German thrust from the south that would trap its new defenders. As soon as night descended on the fields around Gheluvert, the troops were moved stealthily to a new line on rising ground slightly more than 600 yards to the west.[20]

By their long and courageous defiance of Fabeck's massed battalions Haig's men had achieved all he could have asked of them. Today a memorial plaque on the wall of the base of a long-disused windmill pays tribute to 'the officers and men of the 2nd Worcesters . . . who gave their lives at Gheluvelt that civilisation might be saved'. This proud claim may seem hyperbole, but there is little doubt that the Worcesters, together with the South Wales Borderers, the Scots Guards and the gunners who supported them, saved Ypres on that day. They broke the spearhead of the enemy assault at the most vulnerable point along the Menin Road. Had the Germans been able to maintain the momentum of the offensive – as Haig feared when French visited him – it would have been hard to check a drive forward to Dunkirk and on to Calais.

During the afternoon General Bulfin ordered two battalions

from the 2nd Brigade I Corps – the 1st Northamptonshire and the 2nd Royal Sussex – to counter-attack southeast of Zillebeke, advancing with the bayonet through woods south of the village. Some half a mile was recovered; the battered remnants of Capper's 7th Division, to Bulfin's left, also rallied and regained lost ground. After dusk Bulfin recognized the need to adjust the line so as to accommodate 1st Division's needs west of Gheluvert. At last, at 7 p.m., Haig finally ordered the division to consolidate and hold their present positions. They were, however, to be ready to assist the French if Foch launched his proposed counter-attack next morning. Already General Dubois had sent a cavalry brigade and two infantry battalions to help the 1st Division, and another five French battalions strengthened the 7th Division in the Comines canal sector. At no other time on the Western Front was there such close Anglo-French collaboration, battalion to battalion, as during these early stages of First Ypres.[21]

Between the two world wars the Ypres League, an association of Salient veterans, chose to observe 31 October as 'Ypres Day', the turning point of the four-year campaign in Flanders. But on that night nothing marked off the sixth day of battle from the seventh: no Hallowe'en stillness shrouded the battlefield, no sound of Viennese waltzes drifted over the trenches as on the previous evening; there was only a short pause in the iteration of battle. During the small hours of the morning Fabeck, thwarted on the Menin Road, took advantage of the darkness to resume his assault on the weakest position along the allied line, the Wytschaete–Messines ridge, where the Germans had an advantage of almost 12 to one. Despite desperate resistance by the 6th Dragoon Guards and scattered companies of London Scottish survivors, Wytschaete fell shortly before 3 a.m. on 1 November although fighting continued along the ridge for another four or five hours. Later in the morning the 12th Lancers, supported by the 1st Northumberland Fusiliers and the 1st Lincolnshire Regiment, recovered ruined Wytschaete, though with the two infantry battalions suffering heavy casualties; the Lincolns alone lost over 300 officers and other ranks. French reinforcements from the 32nd Division tightened the allied hold but could not prevent the storming of the village by fresh troops from Pomerania, backed by Bavarian reserves, as dusk fell.

Possession of Wytschaete continued to be disputed during each of the battles along the Salient. The village was not finally cleared of the enemy until the last great offensive began six weeks before the Armistice.[22]

With Wytschaete in German hands there was no hope of holding on to Messines. The 1st Cavalry Division and the Oxford-shire Yeomanry withdrew about half a mile, down the steep, sloping edge of the narrow valley and over a small stream, the Steenbeek, to regroup on gently rising farmland to the west. As Bavarian troops took over the village, British guns were turned on Messines itself, a precursor of bombardments that devastated the area with thousands of shells over the next three and a half years. By nightfall on 2 November, Messines had become yet another burning village in this charred wasteland of war.[23]

The French counter-attacks, ordered by Foch for 1 November, ran into stubborn German resistance and failed to regain lost ground around Gheluvert. At one point confusion over French and British dispositions along the Menin Road gave the Germans the opportunity for another breakthrough, checked by the Black Watch and by the 2nd King's Royal Rifle Corps, but only after the regiment's first battalion had lost 446 officers and men, killed or taken prisoner. In the evening heavy shelling forced the 1st Irish Guards back to the edge of the woodland east of Zillebeke. A clutch of shells fell directly on one of the trenches in which the Irish had taken cover, killing 82 Guardsmen outright. Yet the survivors rallied and regrouped in time to repel the infantry assault that inevitably followed the bombardment. One in three of the bat-talion lay dead by nightfall, however.

Yet, despite the heavy casualties and the weariness of the opposing armies, the intensity of the fighting eased only slowly. On 6 November an attack by German reserve divisions (including the 6th Bavarian Reserve Division, in which Hitler was serving) dislodged French battalions covering the right flank of the British position at Klein Zillebeke. The German advance was checked by a charge of the Household Cavalry, though the horsemen suffered heavy losses, including the death of 11 officers who came from some of the best-known families in Edwardian society. Among them, serving in the Blues, were the first member of parliament to be killed in the war, Captain the Hon. Arthur O'Neill, the

Unionist member for Mid-Antrim, and Major the Hon. Hugh Dawnay, a close friend of Churchill and a veteran of Omdurman.[24] At the same time, isolated attacks were made on the French trenches at Broodseinde and the British at Ploegsteert, but they were not pressed home.

Kaiser Wilhelm recognized that the prospect of a triumphant entry into Ypres was fast receding. On Saturday, 31 October, he ventured to within 2 miles of the front line. Near Warneton he chatted amiably in English to wounded prisoners of war, much to the consternation of his attendant generals, who were dismayed by the likely response of their troops to such apparent fraternization. There was already unease among the Prussian professionals at Rupprecht's closeness to the Belgian royal family. Although now a widower, he had been married to Queen Elisabeth's favourite sister, who died in 1912. After the Warneton incident the kaiser was discreetly reminded that the troops expected their rulers to show that hatred of the enemy they were themselves encouraged to display.

Over the weekend Wilhelm lingered at Douai and Thielt, but by Monday evening he became restless and his staff began working out details of the return to Charleville. His 'military cabinet' – the senior army and naval officers whom he had selected to serve in his retinue – stressed to their master the need to strengthen the Eastern Front, where the Russians were amassing new armies after their initial defeats.[25] Although at times Falkenhayn railed at the influence of the kaiser's entourage, he respected the views of Colonel-General von Lyncker, the chief of the military cabinet, and he, too, looked to the East again. As early as 10 November, Falkenhayn accordingly broke up Army Group Fabeck, preparatory to sending the general himself and three army corps to serve under Hindenburg in central Poland.

But Falkenhayn still believed Dunkirk, Calais and Boulogne were within his reach, if only he could boost the power of his artillery with a concentration of infantry of the highest calibre. For the third time in three months he shuffled his pack of army corps. The trains that stood ready to take Fabeck's divisions back eastwards had reached Lille carrying men and equipment from the Prussian 4th Division and a Guards Division that had been fighting in Artois. It included two brigades of the Potsdam élite, the

Prussian Guard: surely troops of this calibre could cut their way through the battle weary defenders of the Menin Road before the full rigours of winter froze the battlefield?

'Horrible smell caused by dead men and horses which are lying everywhere. Ypres burning furiously,' noted Gunner Burrows in his diary for Saturday, 7 November. 'We expect a big attack soon,' he added. Heavy shelling continued on Sunday and Monday, but it quietened down before midnight on Tuesday, the twenty-fourth day of battle, by his reckoning. The stillness continued into the small hours of Wednesday, giving Burrows the opportunity to turn early to his diary: 'November 11th, 4.30 a.m. All quiet for once. Expect they are fed up attacking,' he jotted down optimistically.[26]

His hopes were soon dashed. At 6.30 a.m. the heaviest bombardment yet experienced struck the British and French positions along a 9-mile front, reaching a crescendo around nine o'clock in the morning. Twelve and a half German divisions were poised to go forward at carefully staggered intervals as the shelling abated. The first breach in the line was made on the western edge of Polygon Wood, close to the ground covered by the Worcesters on 31 October: a battalion of Zouaves – Algerian infantry in a regiment that had served France well for 73 years – cracked under the strain of more than two hours' shelling. The Prussian Grenadiers exploited the gap, enfilading the Royal Fusiliers on the other side of the Menin Road and, as Falkenhayn had anticipated, wreaking havoc among them: Haig says the regiment was reduced to two subalterns and about 100 men; Corporal Holbrook, who was in the thick of the fighting, reckoned that his battalion, 500 strong overnight, had no more than 34 fit men by 9 a.m.[27] The Royal Scots and the Royal Sussex were hurried forward from reserve to plug the gap before the Prussians could dig in.

Other alarms followed throughout the daylight hours. To the right of the Menin Road a fusilier battalion broke from the cover of Veldhoek Woods in the mist but were not supported. A Zouave detachment, entrenched before Veldhoek chateau, held them in check until the 1st Gloucesters and the 2nd Duke of Wellington's Regiment forced them back. To their right the Prussian 1st Guards Brigade, commanded by Prince Eitel Friedrich (the kaiser's second son), lost itself flushing out pockets of resistance in Polygon Wood instead of continuing a planned – and potentially threatening – drive on Veldhoek. Around Zillebeke, close to the scene of Friday's Household Cavalry charge, the German infantry did not attack until noon but, once again, a long and sustained bombardment forced a French battalion to leave its trenches.[28]

By now it was becoming hard to slow the impetus of the crack Prussian infantrymen; the 1st Black Watch were swept out of their advance trenches. But the character of the day's fighting was changed through the determination of some 140 men of the battalion manning barbed-wire 'fortifications' improvised on the southwestern fringe of Polygon Wood and around a neighbouring farm (its fields swept away by the A19 motorway).[29] The Prussians, frustrated by Scottish resistance, sought an alternative way forward through Nonneboschen (Nun's Wood), where chestnuts and oaks gave denser cover though the undergrowth was thick and cloying.

A fresh adversary pounced upon them. At Waterloo a battalion of the 52nd Light Infantry had broken the veterans of Napoleon's Middle Guard, until then thought invincible.[30] At Nonneboschen the second battalion of the 52nd, now known as the Oxfordshire and Buckinghamshire Light Infantry, surprised the Prussian Guard by a sudden attack before they could dig in. Some of the enemy turned and ran when the Ox and Bucks were still 30 or 40 yards away; others surrendered. The Ox and Bucks then began beating the woods, two by two with 12 yards or so between them, as if flushing out pheasants on a peacetime shoot. They reached the morning's lost front line but were forced to halt when, as darkness fell, 'friendly' French artillery began shelling the open ground ahead of them. Remarkably, no more than five of the Ox and Bucks were killed that afternoon and 22 wounded. The German casualty figure ran into several hundred.[31]

Brigadier-General Fitzclarence VC, who had brought the Worcesters into action 12 days previously, was now eager to send the regiment forward as vanguard of a night attack to recover trenches in his brigade's sector lost in earlier encounters. The 2nd Highland Light Infantry would support the Ox and Bucks (as they had in the afternoon), together with battalions from the Grenadiers and Irish Guards. As it was a wretched night, very wet and bitterly cold, the attack was put on hold until the small hours of 12 November, when it was thought the weather would improve. But the postponement posed a new question: had the Prussians found time to dig themselves in? When all was dark and still, the brigadier went forward on a personal reconnaissance. Tragically an unauthorized shot from an overwrought Irish guardsman alerted the Germans. At that moment the moon, breaking through quickly moving cloud, lit up the scene. A German sniper spotted a figure silhouetted against the trees, and Brigadier-General Fitzclarence fell dead in a burst of rifle fire.

His death came as a great blow to Haig and to French. Fitzclarence had emerged as the outstanding tactical commander in the BEF, responding swiftly to the dangers of 31 October and 11 November. On both occasions it was he who took the decisions that plugged the gaps on the Menin Road. With his death, the proposed counter-attack was abandoned. After 20 hours of intense fighting, Gheluvert and the old British positions remained in enemy hands. But the Germans were denied the victory that had seemed so close on the previous morning. Once again the BEF had thwarted Falkenhayn's determined drive to seize Ypres.[32]

Falkenhayn could delay the transference of regiments to Hindenburg no longer, for a Russian concentration in central Poland seemed to threaten the flanks of both the German and the Austro-Hungarian armies. To cover the gradual withdrawal, the battle continued south of the Menin Road, though as a series of isolated encounters lacking the habitual order and cohesion of Prussian planning. At Klein Zillebeke later that Thursday, Lieutenant Dimmer of the 2nd King's Royal Rifle Corps gained a Victoria Cross by breaking up another attack. Although wounded and the sole survivor of his machine-gun detachment, he turned his last gun on the advancing Prussians and fired off 900 rounds before falling unconscious. As the son of a south London railway worker who rose from the ranks into a fashionable corps, Jack Dimmer became a newspaper idol on his return home, only to be killed at St Quentin eight months before the war ended.[33]

By now the weather had broken across much of western Europe, after an exceptionally dry October. Some 30 years later people in Oxford were still recalling 'the first November of the war' as 'the wettest of all', although statistics local to Flanders show nothing unusual: Lille, barely 15 miles away, recorded no more than

1.5 inches over the whole of November. In the second week, however, the rain fell with torrential intensity on several nights, and there was an unseasonable localized thunderstorm.[34] Around Polygon Wood and across the Gheluvert plateau the soil was light and sandy, soon churned by rain and the passage of arms into glutinous slime. Many roads became impassable, their unpaved sides pitted with shell holes. West of Ypres horse-drawn wagons – still the main means of getting food and munitions to the Front – made use of the railway track, at least until the relentless bombardment tore away rails and sleepers. 'Mud, mud, mud up to the knees,' a sergeant in the Royal Horse Artillery recalled.[35]

Captain Sir Morgan Crofton of the 2nd Life Guards led his men into the trenches for the first time on 17 November and noted in his diary: 'We climb a Bank, and over into a muddy field, down a slope we go, the mud over our ankles, over a small muddy stream, at the top of which 200 yards away is our Line of Trenches.'[36] Mud became an abiding memory shared by all ranks in that November, three years before Passchendaele.

Across the Salient, south of Messines and down towards the French frontier, the soil was more akin to London clay, less slippery but heavy going after persistent rain. The infantry, British or German, could do little apart from sending out tentative patrols into what was now called, for the first time, 'no man's land'. Ditches and abandoned trenches, deeper in the heavier soil than to the north, became mantraps after dark. On 12 November, Lionel Tennyson, the cricketing subaltern grandson of Queen Victoria's poet laureate, fell into one of these trenches after dark while leading his platoon back from Ploegsteert Wood, a relatively quiet sector of the line that week. Last winter Lord Tennyson had played five Test Matches for England in South Africa: now, though soon rescued from the trench, his leg was so shattered that it seemed likely he would never bat again. Within a week he was back in London and in a West End hospital. So skilled were the surgeons that, by the summer of 1918, Major Tennyson was scoring runs for a star-studded XI in a charity match at Lords. In 1921 he led England in three Tests against Australia, and he captained Hampshire with legendary bravado for 15 of 21 inter-war seasons. But was it the Ypres experience that induced him to call his autobiography, *Sticky Wicket*?[37]

The rain clouds lifted on Friday night (13th), ushering in bright, crisp mornings instead of the bleak, autumnal days. Haig, a regular barometer-tapper, found the temperature creeping lower: light snow fell on 15 November, followed by a hard frost and heavy snow as early as 19 November. There was little prospect of mounting counter-attacks, nor any serious risk of the Germans renewing their offensive. By the weekend (13th–14th) Foch thought the main battle already over, although, on the Friday and Saturday, General Dubois's IX Corps was still heavily engaged checking Prussian assaults around the woods at Veldhoek, below Passchendaele Ridge. Sir John French was more cautious: he did not finally agree with Foch's assessment until Friday, 20 November, after intelligence reported a steady flow of troop trains heading east. Falkenhayn, aware of personal enemies in the kaiser's suite happy to see him discredited, delayed confirming the end of his offensive in the West until 17 November. Even then he took the decision only under pressure from Prince Rupprecht of Bavaria. It was another week before, on 25 November, Falkenhayn finally ordered the armies in the West to take up defensive positions and make secure their conquests down the whole length of the Western Front.[38]

The month-long battle did not die away like a passing storm. There had been no lessening of Ypres's ordeal. The shelling continued day and night. By the second weekend of November few civilians remained in the town, although some refugee families travelled no further out than Poperinghe, notably the indomitables who continued to make and sell lace in the hope of sales to soldiers returning to England on leave. Worse was to come. On Sunday, 22 November, the heavy guns that had shelled the town for more than three weeks targeted the Gothic heart of Ypres. They were supported by an armoured train firing from Houthem, 4 miles to the southeast, on the railway to Lille. The Cloth Hall had already been hit on four occasions: now the main objective was destruction of the city's towers. A post-war apologist for OLH alleged that they housed observers in touch with allied batteries and reporting the effectiveness and accuracy of any counter-bombardment: there is no evidence they were used in this way.[39]

The first shells burst in the Grand Place soon after six that Sunday morning. Once the morning mist dispersed observers from the slopes of the Passchendaele Ridge could focus their field glasses on the grey and black puffs rising from the town centre, and by nine o'clock the guns had found the range of the Cloth Hall. The first shell hit the top of the tower, making the upper pinnacle fall inwards. Within minutes the belfry clock, with its carved figures, was destroyed. Other shells wrecked the cathedral of St Martin, immediately north of the Hall. About eleven o'clock a Benedictine nun, Sister Marguerite-Marie, heard the carillon collapse.[40]

It must have been soon afterwards that the finest photographer of pre-war days, 'Antony of Ypres', set up his camera once more in the Grand Place to capture the last hours of the prized relict of medieval grandeur. A solitary figure stands sombrely upright in the square watching smoke billowing from the tower in a northwest wind. Two other civilians crouch closer to the burning building, keeping low, perhaps because 30 yards to their left a shell had brought down a section of ground-floor wall. A gap in the first-floor façade and tumbledown debris on the corner show where earlier bombardments made their mark. Otherwise the square is empty: the few townsfolk who remained in Ypres were sheltering in the casemates of the ramparts beside the Lille Gate. Later that day Maurice Antony brought his camera nearer the Cloth Hall; by then the wooden scaffolding left in place by Coomans's restorers was feeding the flames inside the building.[41] Out in the trenches, or by now from their billets around the town, survivors of the battle could see the fire well into the night. Through the smoke the flames of the skeletal belfry and cathedral spire stood out like candles burning at a Requiem for the Fallen.

8

DEADLOCK IN THE TRENCHES

First Ypres was over. To all four nations locked in battle in Flanders, its passing marked an end and a beginning. For Germany there would be no more variations on a Schlieffen theme, at least for a quarter of a century. The German army in Flanders was, in Falkenhayn's words, a 'broken instrument' needing careful repair. With nearly 500 miles of trenches running from the North Sea to the Swiss frontier, troops steeled to attack had to learn the disciplined restraints of siege warfare on a national scale. Deep fall-back positions, with bunkers and well-sited machine-guns, were required behind the forward trenches. German superiority in artillery was never in doubt; the need was for specialized storm detachments of infantry, led by junior officers of initiative able to open and exploit any gaps made by the bombardment. For the moment, however, Germany could mount no major offensive in the West. Despite his mistrust of the Hindenburg–Ludendorff partnership Falkenhayn was prepared, reluctantly, for OHL to support their proposals for a decisive blow to be struck against Russia in the East. By mid-January he was again contemplating probing assaults in Flanders, with limited objectives, but for the next two and a half years the line of battle across Belgium and France did not move as much as 10 miles in either direction.

Before the year 1914 ended the French made a final attempt to avoid stalemate: in mid-December, Joffre approved a thrust by Foch in Artois and a near simultaneous attack in Champagne. Both battles were thwarted by rain, sleet, mud and fog and together added more than 10,000 names to the casualty list. Only after this harsh lesson did Grand Quartier Général, like OHL, recognize the need to curb the offensive spirit. Over the last decade before the war, teaching at the École Supérieure de Guerre had boosted collective self-confidence. Now, with ten of the republic's 90 *départements* behind German lines, Foch's doctrine of *la guerre à outrance* – 'war up to the hilt' – became dependent on Joffre's propensity for *grignotage*, a 'nibbling away' at enemy defences by localized attacks. This strategy of attrition was wasteful and ultimately demoralizing; it imposed the burden of psychological endurance on an army in which 306,000 men had already died in five months of battle. At the turn of the year 'Papa Joffre', now at GQG in Chantilly, was still widely respected for having conjured up victory on the Marne, and no commander had as yet appeared who could challenge his rule over 430 miles of Front. But the length of the casualty lists made the more perceptive politicians uneasy. Amid Chantilly's reflective peace, Joffre was said to be perfecting plans for the coming year with all his habitual calmness, but for some in Paris there was a fear that his legendary imperturbability might be drifting comfortably into complacency.

Belgium, like France, had suffered grievously. More than nine-tenths of the kingdom was under enemy occupation, and the remaining un-invaded segment formed a war zone: 30,000 soldiers were dead, an even higher proportion of males of military age killed than in France or Germany. The fighting along the Yser showed the value of light field guns, infantry mobility and adapting tactics to the terrain, aspects of military science neglected under the stultifying legacy of Brialmont. The resilience of the Belgian army owed much to King Albert personally, and he was held in high esteem abroad, especially in Britain. At Christmas the *Daily Telegraph* published *King Albert's Book*, a collection of tributes that presented him as a chivalric figure, St George incarnate. In reality, the king was a shrewd, conscientious national commander-in-chief who lacked the resources to create a new model army without aid from his allies. Military dependence on France was fraught with dangers that they failed to comprehend. Although the king was at La Panne and the government operating from Normandy, political life continued within occupied Belgium through improvised institutions tolerated by the Germans. If the kingdom established in 1830 were to survive, it was essential for Albert to retain his prestige as a soldier–king to ensure that, once the war was over, Walloons and Flemings worked together as a united people. Already there

was a Young Flanders movement, based upon Ghent, that sought
German backing for the breakup of what they held to be a French-
dominated Belgian state. Small wonder if at times in the coming
year King Albert irritated Paris and London by asserting a haughty
independence. 'Brave little Belgium' was not a nation to be
patronized.

It was among the British, the people least materially harmed by
the fighting, that the concept of warfare changed most. The
experience of imperial adventures and colonial wars had served
the BEF well during the retreat to the Marne, the pursuit to the
Aisne and even the fluid early fighting outside Ypres. Although the
internal-combustion engine, powering both aeroplanes and armoured cars, soon took over the horse's deep reconnaissance role,
cavalry had still provided a protective screen for the rear of II Corps
on the exhausting march south and for a brigade of the 7th Division
harassed by Bavarian troops on 26 October, near Zandvoorde.
Moreover, both Mons and Langemarck confirmed the skills and
value of the '15-rounds-a-minute' riflemen. But the second phase
of First Ypres – the fighting along the Menin Road and across
Messines Ridge – showed the growing importance of good
entrenchment as a buffer against assault. The hastily dug shallow
ditches of early days had left troops almost as vulnerable to shrapnel
as in the open. Like Falkenhayn, the British commanders saw the
need for a systematic pattern of trenches in depth, well protected by
barbed wire and parapets, zigzagged to lessen the threat from blast
or flying shrapnel and served by sunken communication lines.
Static warfare of this character ran counter to traditions cherished
throughout the late Victorian and Edwardian era.

'More than once,' Grey recalls Kitchener as saying to him, ' "I
don't know what is to be done – this isn't *war*!" ' Yet the
commanders in the field were more conservative than the secretary
of state for war. Kitchener's mind was cautiously receptive to new
ideas in weaponry and strategy. Long ahead of French, Haig or
GQG he recognized that the German defences across Belgium and
France formed a fortress impervious to frontal assault and incapable
of complete investment. He accepted the primacy of the Western
Front in the grand strategy of the war in Europe, but he never
became a totally convinced continentalist.

'The defence of Ypres is the chief glory of our old army, which in its performance practically ceased to exist,' reflected the Oxford historian and Territorial veteran Cruttwell 20 years later.[1] Approximately a third of the original BEF were dead by December 1914. Some battalions were left with no more than one officer and 30 men from among those who crossed the Channel in August. Three brigadiers and 18 colonels were among the Ypres dead. In all, some 54,100 officers and men of the regular army fell during First Ypres. They were drawn from 88 infantry battalions, 22 cavalry regiments and 95 artillery batteries. The BEF's fully trained 'part-timers' – four regiments of yeomanry and seven Territorial battalions – suffered another 4,000 casualties. Hardest hit of all the divisions was the 7th, even though it did not sail from England until after the Marne and the Aisne and was withdrawn from the line before Falkenhayn's final push. Of 17,948 men in the division who landed at Zeebrugge on 6 October, 9237 were dead, missing or incapacitated by 5 November.[2]

When the year ended another 16 Territorial battalions were serving in or behind the Western Front, all integrated in existing divisions. In the months ahead more and more Territorials would come up to the Salient, but the first entirely Territorial division – the 46th North Midlands – did not cross the Channel until early spring. Other reinforcements were in camp on Salisbury Plain. The full might of the British Empire overseas was being marshalled to fight in Europe for the first time. Four infantry and two cavalry divisions of the Indian army were already in France. Now some 30,000 Canadian volunteers had reached England, having disembarked at Plymouth in the third week of October 1914. The vanguard, a battalion of Princess Patricia's Canadian Light Infantry, landed at Le Havre three days before Christmas and were attached to the 80th Brigade of the 27th Division. All were veterans of the Boer War, raised and commanded by Major Hamilton Gault, a wealthy businessman from Montreal. The remaining Canadians encamped on Salisbury Plain.

Also in England but retained for further training and fitting out were the four 'New Armies' of recruits who had responded to the call, 'Your Country Needs You'. But the great recruiting marshal at the War Office hesitated over their use. French and Haig hoped the New Army would swell the BEF by coming as battalions to be incorporated in existing corps instead of as divisions, each with a newly constituted staff. Kitchener, however, always kept his cards close to his chest. Rather than consign 24 embryonic divisions prematurely to the cauldron in Flanders and France, he saw them as a reserve, either to redress the balance in the West at a later date when his allies were exhausted or to strike decisively against German interests in a more distant theatre of war.[3] In early spring 1915 he reluctantly sent two of these New Army divisions to augment the BEF and two to Egypt, either to protect the Suez Canal or support the landings on the Gallipoli peninsula. There was as yet no shortage of men; the great concern was the dwindling supply of ammunition. The shell problem, in particular, was soon to intensify.

As late as 9 October, Colonel Weygand, Foch's chief of staff, had written in his diary, 'I think that we shall be home by Christmas.'[4] That lingering hope dissolved for French, British and Germans alike in the smoke and fury of the next three weeks. As the days shortened so the casualty lists lengthened. Berlin, Paris and the West End of London maintained a brittle gaiety, but away from the forced frivolity of the bigger cities it became a sombre winter, especially in England. Vera Brittain, returning home to Buxton in Derbyshire after her first term at Oxford, found Christmas 'strange and chilling . . . A good many people have decided they are too poor and too miserable to remember their friends,' she observed.

Punch sought to amuse its readers with 'news from behind the Front', light-hearted titbits served with a heavy hand. Black humour tinged the cartoons: over breakfast a well-scrubbed prep-school boy tells his mother, 'I hope I shan't die soon. It would be *too* awful to die a civilian.' But *Punch* could also be sombrely reflective. The Christmas number included a fine drawing by Sir Bernard Partridge. Under the caption 'The Children's Truce' the Angel of Peace peers down with compassion through a window at a children's party: 'I'm glad that they, at least, have their Christmas unspoiled,' the Angel says.[5]

As so often in his work Partridge reflected a sentiment common to all people: the grief of war forged social cohesion. Yet across Britain class barriers persisted. Officers' families would receive telegrams to inform them of loved ones killed in action, missing or gravely wounded. The families of other ranks were dependent on the postman: buff-coloured envelopes pushed through a letter-box might contain the gas bill, an income-tax demand – or grim news from Flanders. The daily papers gave prominence to names familiar in Society gossip columns before the war, particularly the scions of the great families: the sons of the Duke of Westminster and the Earl of Dudley, Hugh Grosvenor and Gerald Ward; Lord Bernard Gordon-Lennox and Lord Congleton of the Grenadier Guards, killed at Zillebeke, and Lord Charles Worsley who was a son of the Earl of Yarborough and had recently married Lady Haig's sister. Many, including Worsley, Grosvenor and Ward died at Zandvoorde on 30 October in the engagement in which Fabeck's infantry trapped two squadrons of Household Cavalry already dazed by a heavy bombardment.

Other names listed as dead or missing recalled news items from earlier years. 'Captain A. E. J. Collins' of the Royal Engineers, killed on 11 November, is still remembered as the 13-year-old cricketer who in 1899 scored an unmatched record innings of 628 not out in 6 hours and 50 minutes for his house at Clifton College, Haig's old school. 'Lieutenant G. Archer-Shee' was the naval cadet expelled from the Royal Naval College at Osborne for allegedly stealing a postal order but vindicated in a court case brought by his parents against the Admiralty. His parents' dogged fight to clear their son's name gripped the newspaper public for several months during 1910 and, long afterwards, it formed the basis of Terence Rattigan's play and film, *The Winslow Boy*. Young Archer-Shee, unable to return to the Royal Navy, was commissioned in the army on the outbreak of war and killed in October's fighting. His body was never found. Like Lord Grosvenor and the Hon. Gerald Ward, Archer-Shee's name is carved on the Menin Gate, in this instance among late additions on Panel 37, at the top of the main steps. Immediately above his name, the panel honours Captain J. F. Vallentin of the South Staffordshires. He was posthumously awarded the Victoria Cross for leading an attack that recovered a vital trench at Zillebeke on 7 November, one of the few days officially described as 'quiet' amid the turmoil.

As Christmas approached, there seemed a prospect of longer days of genuine 'quiet' ahead. The mirage of victory was fading, and war weariness spread among survivors of the battle and their families at home. In England the wish for an end to the fighting was reflected in the local press rather than in national newspapers, but the political leaders were well aware it existed.

As First Ypres began to lessen in intensity Churchill received a letter from a friend in the Oxfordshire Hussars. Captain Valentine Fleming MP wrote of 'an English line battalion marching back from the trenches . . . a limping column of bearded, muddy, torn figures slouching with fatigue . . . but able to stand the cold, the strain, the awful losses, the inevitable inability to reply to the shell fire, which is what other nations *can't* do'. Fleming concluded: 'On both sides every single man in [the war] wants it stopped *at once.*' Churchill forwarded this 'impressive letter' to his wife on 23 November with the reflection, 'What wd. happen I wonder if the armies suddenly and simultaneously went on strike and said some other method must be found of settling the dispute!'[6]

A dramatic down-tools strike was, as yet, unlikely, but a pause in the fighting had become a distinct possibility. Some form of Christmas truce was championed by neutrals in Catholic Spain and Protestant Holland and by an influential United States senator. On 7 December the newly elected Pope Benedict XV called for 'the clang of arms' to cease 'while Christendom celebrates the Feast of the World's Redemption'. Germany accepted the proposal, provided all the other belligerent governments agreed to observe a truce. They did not: a German ruse was suspected, a means of lulling the enemy into inactivity while secretly massing troops for the next offensive. Moreover, as a senior British staff officer wrote to his wife from Ypres, 'If accepted, I don't think hostilities will be resumed.'[7] There were many combatants who longed for an end to the fighting, as Captain Fleming's letter to Churchill had shown, but a *de facto* armistice after five months of war would have left a huge segment of France and most of Belgium under German administration. That was unacceptable to London and to Paris. 'Our Christmas initiative has not been crowned with success,' a saddened Pope Benedict admitted on 13 December.

The papal seeds did not, however, fall on stony ground. In the closing days of First Ypres a change had been made in the disposition of the BEF, partly to await the arrival of reinforcements from England but also to avoid the confusion that arose when French regiments were inserted at points in the British line. On 22 November the French added the defence of Ypres from the northeast to their existing responsibilities, allowing the BEF to regroup along a 21-mile sector from Wytschaete southwards across the border to Givenchy and including the Messines Ridge, Ploegsteert and Armentières. This realignment led, coincidentally, to a mainly Franco-Prussian confrontation in the north while the troops facing the British in the south came largely from Roman Catholic Bavaria and Baden or Württemberg (where there was a sizeable Catholic minority) or Saxony (Lutheran, though with a Catholic royal family). The pope's appeal for a truce had received much publicity across all of Germany, and it is hardly surprising that in the last days before Christmas, patrol activity, sniping and the customary intermittent shelling died down in the Messines–Ploegsteert southern sector of the line. The British were puzzled, but held their fire.

On Christmas Eve, Henry Williamson, an infantryman serving in a Territorial battalion of the London Regiment, looked across no man's land and 'saw dim figures on the enemy parapet'. He also saw 'with amazement . . . that a Christmas tree was being set there, and around it Germans were talking and laughing together'. Soon after midnight by German time 'a rich baritone voice began to sing . . . *Stille Nacht! Heilige Nacht*'. Soldiers manning opposing trenches only 40 or 60 yards apart began calling out Christmas greetings to each other and singing carols. On a 'white-rimed Christmas morning' they emerged from the trenches to talk together and exchange small gifts in no man's land. Williamson was astonished to find himself 'face to face with living Germans, some of them actually smiling as they talked in English'. By the afternoon impromptu football games were in progress, with at least one keen contest apparently won by Germany. In Williamson's sector the truce 'lasted for several days'; others have written of a pause in the fighting that continued into the New Year.[8]

News of these 'most extraordinary sights' soon reached homes in England by letters that, curiously, the censors seem to have ignored, provided no names of places or units were revealed. The provincial press printed extracts from letters supplied by proud parents or wives, but the London newspapers inflated the news, even *The Times* converted a football kick-about into an international. The truce was a localized affair, although there were instances of fraternization on the Eastern Front despite a difference of date for celebrating Christmas in the Orthodox churches. Effectively the truce was limited to one-third of the BEF's line, no more than 5 or 6 miles on either side of the Franco-Belgian border. The French and Belgians were reluctant to fraternize with the invader: one French infantry battalion did respond to an invitation from Badenese troops to visit their trenches on Christmas Day but shelled them on Boxing Day. The truce was ignored by Haig's I Corps and by 19 of the 24 infantry battalions in Smith-Dorrien's II Corps. But men and junior officers in two divisions of Pulteney's III Corps and two divisions of Rawlinson's IV Corps participated, some with the tacit approval of more senior officers. Many 'fraternizers' were recent arrivals, Henry Williamson among them.

Veteran officers waxed indignant. 'This is War, Bloody War, and not a mother's meeting,' 35-year-old Sir Morgan Crofton, a captain in the 2nd Life Guards, commented in his diary, 'Boshy papers of the halfpenny type slobber over this rubbish, but everyone out here condemns it. I am glad to say that General [sic] French fired in a snorter which should put a stop to these unsoldierly antics.' The 'snorter', sent from GHQ on New Year's Day, warned all officers against any repetition of 'unauthorized intercourse with the enemy'.[9]

Falkenhayn's reaction was similar to French's: further fraternizing would be treated as an act of treason, an Army Order of the Day sent out on 29 December declared. Corporal Hitler, who three weeks earlier had received the Iron Cross (Second Class) for bravery in the fighting on the Menin Road, strongly disapproved of the friendly exchanges and carol singing of his Bavarian comrades: 'There should be no question of something like that during war,' he told them.[10] Several letters home to England showed surprise at the easy amiability of these 'Bavarians', though the word may have been used generically for all southern Germans. The British seem to have found Saxon troops the friendliest of their enemies. Some Saxons hardly bothered to conceal their dislike of Prussia and contempt for Prussian values.

Not all Crofton's 'boshy halfpenny' dailies 'slobbered' with passing pacifism. One newspaper followed up tales of the truce with a diatribe against 'wild beasts fighting under the German flag'. On 9 January the *Daily Sketch* accompanied a French report of alleged atrocities in Belgium with a double page spread of 24 pictures of the evil-doers: many were portraits of princes and generals from Bavaria and Würrtemberg. For once the invective spared specifically Prussian militarism, the customary target of hate propaganda. No German could be trusted, the *Sketch* insisted: 'Incendiarism, murder and pillage form part of the German military equipment as definitely as do big guns.' A headline splashed across page two reminded readers of the right patriotic response: 'Can you still hang back? It may be your sister next.'[11]

The prime minister spent Christmas near Malmesbury but saw the New Year in at Walmer Castle, within sight of the leave boats crossing the Channel. Red boxes followed him constantly. Neither Colonel Maurice Hankey nor Churchill could give their minds a rest from the war: both sent Asquith long memoranda. So, more surprisingly, did his unmilitary chancellor of the exchequer, Lloyd George: he had visited the BEF sector on 19 October, where he met Foch though not French, who was preoccupied with the opening exchanges of First Ypres. All three memoranda – drawn up independently of each other – accepted that the Western Front was the decisive theatre of operations but argued that the war could not be won there by conventional frontal assaults without heavier and heavier casualties. Improved weapons and new devices, specifically designed for trench warfare must be found but, above all, 'outlets' in Europe or the Middle East were needed for surprise thrusts to take the enemy by surprise. 'Are there not other alternatives than sending our armies to chew barbed wire in Flanders?' Churchill demanded with characteristic vigour.[12]

His personal choice was for a landing on the island of Borkum or the Baltic coast, with entry into the Dardanelles as the surest means of striking effectively at Germany's Turkish ally. Hankey advocated co-operation with the Serbs in their resistance to Austria–Hungary or landings on Turkey's Asiatic shore; Lloyd George argued in favour of 'bringing Germany down by the process of knocking away the props under her' either by an amphibious operation in Dalmatia or a Balkan campaign with the Serbs and Greeks, including sending 'an advance force through Salonika to assist Serbia'. Asquith was critical of much contained in these memoranda, pointing out in particular the geographical obstacles facing any Balkan expedition, but he convened a series of 'War Council' meetings in the second week of January to examine the suggestions in detail. Also on the agenda was a plan that seems to have originated with the admirals at sea for a raid on Zeebrugge; after consultation with Sir John French, Churchill suggested developing it into a major joint operation to clear the enemy from the Belgian coast and advance from Dixmude to the Dutch frontier. The War Council blew hot and cold over the option, rejecting a land offensive on 7 January but having second thoughts when it seemed possible the 'coast game' (as Churchill unofficially dubbed the project) might tempt Holland to join the allies. On 13 January the War Council approved the Belgian option, at the same time proposing that the Admiralty should prepare for an expedition 'to bombard and take the Gallipoli peninsula' in February with 'Constantinople as its objective'.[13]

Independently, on Boxing Day, Sir John French had suggested to Kitchener a bombardment by 'big gun ships' to support an advance northwards from Nieuport, and he was attracted by the proposed 'coast game'. At Christmas he had secured reorganization of the BEF into two armies with Haig in command of the First Army (I Corps, IV Corps and the Indian Corps) and Smith-Dorrien the Second (II Corps, III Corps and the 27th Division). Both generals, and Allenby of the Cavalry Corps, were summoned to GHQ at St Omer on 4 January to discuss an advance in support of a landing near Ostend 'before March'. They welcomed the idea, but the project soon ran into difficulties. The Admiralty had second thoughts; any bombardment of Zeebrugge should be postponed until new shallow-draught monitors were completed. The Belgians were unenthusiastic, not least because further flooding of Flemish farmland was anticipated in order to create a new water barrier once the coast had been secured. There was a feeling (well justified) that the British were interested not so much in liberating Belgian towns and villages as in denying the German navy facilities for U-boats at Ostend, Bruges and Zeebrugge. King Albert bluntly told French that 'national unity would be imperilled' if the Belgian army were placed under foreign command for operations over which neither he nor his government were consulted. Finally, Joffre came down firmly against a coastal advance that would require French troops needed for attacks he was planning in Artois and Champagne. GQC remained suspicious of projects that could strengthen Britain's hold on the North Sea littoral: might 'perfidious Albion' seek the lease of a Belgian port or even Dunkirk in the eventual peace settlement? Away from the heat of battle, the Entente Cordiale looked at times extremely frail.

On 28 January the War Council in London shelved the Zeebrugge project. It reappeared in various forms over the next three years.[14] For six months strategic planning revolved around the Dardanelles and the tragic frustrations of the Gallipoli campaign. French, who visited Chantilly in late January, felt obliged to commit at least one corps to potential 'barbed wire chewing' in support of Joffre's planned attack in Artois. There had been intermittent fighting since October some 20 miles south of Ypres on the edge of the British sector, where ridges similar to the long hump of Wytschaete and Messines looked out across the industrialized plain beyond Lille. Shortly before Christmas the newly arrived 8th Division raided the German lines here, around the village of Neuve Chapelle, an operation in which Lieutenant Philip Neame of the Royal Engineers won a Victoria Cross for leading and rescuing a party of sappers caught in heavy crossfire.[15] This was the region Haig selected to mount the probing attack French envisaged, pressing ahead with the planning even after Joffre postponed his proposed March offensive in Artois.

For more than a month First Army's staff meticulously planned a set-piece battle aimed in the first instance at recovering Neuve Chapelle, by now in ruins. The main objective, however, was Aubers, on the crest of a ridge a mile to the north. With carefully contrived concealment, the reconstituted 7th Division and the Indian Corps's Meerut and Lahore divisions were brought south from the Salient to reinforce the 8th Division already holding the line. Pioneer aerial photography by the RFC provided clear intelligence over enemy positions. Officers were issued with large-scale trench maps. Some 500 guns, supplied with more shells than had been fired in three years of war in South Africa, were sited to bombard four and a half miles of German trenches. On 9 March, Haig's eve-of-battle Order of the Day rang with confidence.[16]

The Germans were taken completely by surprise. There was no preliminary bombardment, always a clear warning that an attack was pending. Instead, the guns thundered with unprecedented intensity for 35 minutes before the infantry went forward. They then shifted their target to the rear, in order to prevent the enemy from bringing up reinforcements. On paper every advantage lay with the 14 infantry battalions Haig initially committed to the attack: they outnumbered the enemy by more than four to one.[17]

By half-past eight in the morning of 10 March the infantry had cleared the first trenches and broken the enemy line for the first time on the Western Front. At this point, however, they were frustrated by the rigidity of Haig's orders. First Ypres had seen tactical decisions taken by commanders in the field, notably Fitzclarence in the fighting along the Menin Road: the attack at Neuve Chapelle had to conform to a strict timetable, each move forward determined by headquarters 5 miles behind the battle line. With telephone links destroyed by shelling, long periods of inactivity were inevitable. The Germans soon reorganized their defences. The British bombardment had failed to dislodge two nests of machine-guns northeast of the village, towards Aubers. The machine-guns mowed down several hundred men of the 2nd Middlesex and 2nd Scottish Rifles. West of Neuve Chapelle, some 9,000 Indians waited for orders to go forward for nine and a half hours. By half-past five, when the advance was at last resumed, darkness already enveloped fields where the shells had churned up the broken ground. No progress could be made. Despite the artillery preparation and the superiority in numbers, by nightfall the line had been pushed forward by a mere 1,200 yards along a front of less than 2 miles.

The battle continued for two more days. Falkenhayn sent down reinforcements from the approaches to Ypres, among them the 16th Bavarian Reserve Division (in which Corporal Hitler was a battalion runner). By the third morning 16,000 German troops blocked any advance towards Aubers Ridge. Both the British and the Germans attempted frontal assaults, with increasing loss of life. At last, long after nightfall on 12 March, Haig called a halt to the fighting. The British only held the village and the area taken in the first hours of the battle. Some 1,600 Germans were made prisoner, but casualties on both sides were heavy. Slightly over 11,600 British and Indian troops were killed, wounded or missing, 3,000 more than their enemy. Neuve Chapelle was an augury of what must come further north, around Ypres, unless new weapons, a speedier chain of command and inspirational tactics could break the dead-lock of the trenches and restore mobility to the armies.[18]

Neuve Chapelle had repercussions within the Salient. Soon after midday on 12 March an assault was made on German positions along the spur of Spanbroekmolen, a mile and a half east of Wytschaete. The Bavarians were known to have withdrawn troops from this sector to defend Aubers Ridge, and it was hoped to overrun their trenches at relatively light cost and capture a strategic rise of value in planning a later offensive. In reality the Bavarian regiment that moved southwards came, not from the front line but from the reserve, and the hill's defenders remained strong enough to offer spirited resistance, with one deep-cut trench in particular checking the advance. In desperation, Lieutenant Cyril Martin of the Royal Engineers led six sappers forward and cleared the trench with hand grenades. Although he was wounded, Martin then reversed the firing position and held the line until darkness fell and the attack was called off. For his valour and enterprise that afternoon, Martin received the Victoria Cross, but the crest of Spanbroekmolen remained in German hands. There were, how-ever, lessons learnt from this relatively small-scale probing raid, in particular the effectiveness in trench warfare of the newly invented time-fused hand grenade; like Neuve Chapelle, Spanbroekmolen revealed the mounting sophistication of the German trench sys-tem.[19]

Two days later came another innovation: the war underground erupted. Already, on 20 December, the Germans had exploded ten small land mines around Givenchy, killing and wounding many Indian troops, but what happened on 14 March was on an ominously bigger scale. The hamlet of St Eloi, little more than 3 miles south of Ypres's Lille Gate, had been the scene of intermittent fighting since the third week of October. By March it was in ruins, its inhabitants dead or fled, with a last echo of domesticity in the pathetic mewing of the few cats whose pro-verbial nine lives had carried them though shelling and bitter frosts. To the west of St Eloi was a disused brickworks, from which the spoil created a mound some 110 yards long and 30 feet high. This ugly hump provided the British with a good vantage point for a machine-gun section threatening the enemy lines out towards Hollebeke. For some weeks German sappers had been tunnelling under the mound, but their activity went undetected. Two large mines were exploded almost simultaneously at 5.30 p.m. on 14 March, destroying the machine-gun position and inflicting heavy casualties. Specially trained light-armed stormtroopers pressed forward across the newly made craters, using stick grenades to force back the dazed survivors, who came mainly from the 2nd King's Shropshire Light Infantry (KSLI) and the 4th Rifle Brigade. Before the light faded all the defensive positions in St Eloi were in German hands. Support troops, again carefully trained for their task, speedily threw up barbed-wire barricades among the ruined buildings in the hamlet and set up machine-gun posts commanding the road intersection. There was none of that hesitancy in following up initial gains that had proved so costly for Falkenhayn during First Ypres.

In the small hours of the morning three battalions of Irish infantry (1st Leinsters and 1st and 2nd Royal Irish Fusiliers) were brought up from reserve to support the KSLI and the Rifle Brigade. Bayonet attacks in the dark were grimly effective, but the defenders had the advantage of cover from the gaunt walls of the old cottages. The 200,000 shells that fed Neuve Chapelle's 500 guns had left the British short of artillery and munitions, and without field-gun support it was hard to break through the barricades. After more than 12 hours of confused fighting, the Irish cleared the Germans from the hamlet, but in a last assault to take the remaining improvised stronghold a Fusilier platoon was scythed down by machine-gun fire from a cellar aperture at ground level. Although the Germans fell back from St Eloi itself they could not be prised from what remained of the mound.[20]

The British and Irish sustained more than 800 casualties that day. Among the dead was Second Lieutenant George Llewelyn Davies of the 6th King's Royal Rifle Corps. He was the eldest of the five Kensington Gardens children befriended by J. M. Barrie, the Scottish dramatist: he became their legal guardian when they were orphaned in 1910. George completed his schooling at Eton and was in his second year at Cambridge when the war began. As Barrie acknowledged, George inspired his best-loved whimsically sentimental play. Now, like so many young subalterns, George fell victim to a German sharpshooter, a bullet penetrating the temple while being briefed by his colonel. For the tenth-anniversary production of *Peter Pan*, at Christmas 1914, Barrie had already cut the mournful line 'To die will be an awfully big adventure', and it was not restored until the bloodshed was over. By then the inspirer of Peter lay in a war grave at Voormezele cemetery, on the road to Mount Kemmel.[21]

At Second Army Headquarters in Hazebrouck, Smith-Dorrien's staff had been examining the feasibility of mine tunnelling for several weeks before the Germans seized the initiative at St Eloi. Mining was impossible during the winter months in the water-logged region east and northeast of Ypres, and tunnelling did not begin in the geologically more promising soil of the Messines Ridge until 1916. In February 1915, however, Second Army took over the Zillebeke sector from the French including Hill 60, the artificially created hillock beside the railway cutting to Comines and Courtrai (for the siting and creation of Hill 60, see chapter 2, p. 12). The British found preliminary work in progress on a small tunnel in which mines could be exploded to destroy the German observation post on the crest of the hillock. The Royal Engineers took over the dig, and as early as 17 February a small, experimental mine was blown without alerting the enemy.

In the first week of March the 173rd Tunnelling Company, Royal Engineers began cautiously digging here parallel tunnels. The main tunnel ran under the hill itself: two subsidiaries enabled mines to be planted under the approaches to adjoining trenches. Excavation proved both exhausting and harrowing. Near the surface the diggers unearthed the bones or putrefying remains of casualties from earlier fighting.

Beneath them the soil was in places little firmer than a child would find with bucket and spade on a beach, though there was also good solid earth thrown out by the navvies who built the railway. Tunnelling was dangerous on at least two counts: a tunnel could well collapse, burying the diggers; the Germans, alerted by subterranean sounds, might dig deeper and explode their own mine beneath the sappers. Once excavation was finished, 94 bags of gunpowder were hauled silently into position. In the main tunnel under the hill this necessitated a drag of 100 yards. On 15 April five

charges were set: a pair of mines together in the centre and opposite
the first German trench; a smaller mine outside the second line.
The sappers' activities remained a closely guarded secret within the
BEF. The German garrison on Hill 60 – the 65th Royal Saxon
Infantry Regiment – had no more inkling of what was happening
beneath them than the British on the St Eloi mound a month
previously.[22]

'Things are fairly quiescent here in this sector,' Sir Morton
Crofton of the 2nd Life Guards wrote in his diary for Tuesday, 13
April. In the previous week Bishop Winnington-Ingram of London celebrated Easter communion for 200 officers and men in a
barn behind the trenches and preached at a service where 'aeroplanes circled about overhead to guard the attractive target of 4,000
kneeling officers and men with a Bishop in their midst'. Crofton
reported signs of war weariness in Duke Albrecht of Württemberg's Fourth Army; on Easter Sunday notes were thrown into the
British trenches tied around stones: 'Let us have Peace on Earth
before the cherry blossom comes out, or do you want to go on for
ever sitting in these damned trenches?'[23]

But Peace on Earth was not in sight. Soon after seven o'clock on
17 April, a gloriously fine Saturday evening, the five mines at Hill
60 exploded at five-second intervals: 150 Germans were blown to
pieces or buried alive. Before the smoke had lifted the 1st West
Kent ('Buffs') and 2nd Scottish Borderers stormed the Hill and
secured it with, initially, light casualties. Their orders forbade them
going down into the craters for at least half an hour because of
poisonous fumes lingering from the compressed gun cotton used to
fire the charges. The central crater was 60 yards long and 30 feet
deep, about three times as big as the two outer craters.

The German response showed no trace of that lowering of
morale Crofton thought he had detected among the Württem-
bergers. After a short respite, their guns began a heavy bombardment that continued throughout the night. It was followed by a
counter-attack after dawn on Sunday and two hours of hand-to-
hand fighting, not only on the hill but also along the 'Caterpillar'
and the 'Hump', neighbouring earthworks thrown up by the
navvies who cut and laid the Courtrai railway. About 8.30 a.m.
the Duke of York's Regiment – Yorkshiremen from the West
Riding – brought relief to the Buffs and, three hours later, to the

Borderers, but they suffered heavy casualties. So too did six other battalions in the Infantry Brigade that reached the line during the next 24 hours: Queen Victoria's Rifles (QVR), Territorials in the London Regiment who had been serving in France or Flanders for five months; the 1st Bedfordshire, 1st Cheshire, 1st Devonshire, 1st East Surrey and 1st Norfolk regiments. On Monday, 19 April, the intensity of the fighting eased, only to be followed by two days and nights of grim encounters at close quarters, with the QVR Territorials and the East Surreys holding the craters despite hail-storms of grenades and shelling by field guns barely 300 yards away.[24]

Three Victoria Crosses were won by two officers and a private in the East Surreys for acts of valour at Hill 60 during 20–21 April: Second Lieutenant Benjamin Geary for improvising defences in an outer crater and holding it through heavy bombardment; Lieu-tenant George Roupell who 'though wounded in several places' kept his company together and beat off one of the strongest German attacks; 19-year-old Private Edward Dwyer who, after rescuing wounded comrades beyond the trench parapet, won what was virtually a hand-grenade duel with the attacking Saxons. In the QVR, Lieutenant Harold Woolley became the first Territorial to receive the Victoria Cross. For several hours on the Tuesday night he was the only officer on the hill, organizing resistance in two of the craters until he and the 14 QVR men still able to walk were relieved by a company of the Devonshires. Like Geary, Woolley became a priest in the Church of England after the war.[25]

Captain Andrew Johnston, the commanding officer of the signals company at 5th Division headquarters, commented in his diary entry for 22 April on a lull in the fighting around Hill 60. The previous night had been 'fairly quiet'; with the return of 'heavy guns' from Neuve Chapelle 'our position ought to be more secure'. A few German bombers on the broken ground north of the hill 'are rather a nuisance', he admitted, but in general he wrote as if Hill 60 were already won. It was not. Soon the fighting for the artificial knoll became absorbed in a greater clash of arms.[26]

By now there were signs that the Germans might be about to launch a spring offensive. On 19 April they sealed off the Dutch frontier in a bid to prevent knowledge of their activities reaching allied intelligence agents and foreign journalists in Amsterdam and

The Hague. Yet there were no reports of any concentration of troops. On cloud-free mornings – though there were few of them – the RFC and RNAS flew deeply into Belgium, as on the eve of First Ypres. But on this occasion their observers saw no signs of military build-up, and the aerial photographs revealed nothing unusual. Could it all be an elaborate feint to cover the movement of divisions away from the West, to serve under Hindenburg, Ludendorff or the highly gifted General von Mackensen in Galicia on the Eastern Front? Then, soon after midday on 22 April, Ypres suffered the heaviest bombardment since 11 November. The shelling reached a new intensity in the late afternoon, with the roads into town from the Belgian sector the main target. Sir Horace Smith-Dorrien, the commander of the Second Army, who had been visiting the 14th Infantry Brigade a mile beyond Ypres, was surprised by 'the terrific bombardment' as he walked back to his car in the town. It seemed unlikely the cautious Falkenhayn would open an offensive in the fading light of an April evening: would he launch one at dawn next morning? But even before Sir Horace's car left the town, Second Ypres had begun – and in a dramatic form.[27]

9

WEAPONS OF TERROR

'Cor, look at the lyddite shells bursting along Jerry's trench,' a look-out in the trenches east of St Julien called down from the parapet to his pals below on the afternoon of 22 April. Lyddite was a novelty, a British-patented high explosive based on picric acid that emitted puffs of yellow smoke on impact, and it was good to see 'our guns' pounding the enemy lines. But, as he watched, the look-out was puzzled: there was something strange about those puffs. A few seconds later he gave a louder yell: 'Blimey, it's not lyddite, it's gas!', he warned; the 2nd battalion, Lancashire Regiment, discovered they were facing a new and terrible weapon.[1] The Germans had released 168 tons of chlorine from batteries of 6,000 cylinders along more than 4 miles of front from the Yperlee canal at Steenstraat eastwards to the Ypres–St Julien–Poelcapelle road.

To those who lived through that first experience of gas warfare, the evening of 22 April was unforgettable. Lieutenant Louis Strange of No. 6 Squadron, RFC, had a unique view: 'I was cruising up and down over the Salient . . . watching out for gun flashes in the fading light when suddenly my attention was attracted by what appeared to be streams of yellowish-green smoke coming from the German front-line trenches. This was such a strange phenomenon that we dropped to 2,000 feet to have a good look at it. At first I was completely puzzled but finally my brain connected it with rumours about poison gas,' he wrote in his memoirs, adding: 'We raced back full throttle to Poperinghe.' From there he and his observer were taken straight to V Corps headquarters to make their report to General Plumer in person.

Down in the trenches south of Langemarck a Canadian officer watched with awed fascination as two 'greenish-yellow clouds' filled out and, carried westward by a light wind, became a 'bluish-white mist, such as seen over water-meadows on a frosty night'. Another Canadian, Private Underwood, was to recall how 'It was the first gas anyone had seen or heard of'; Sergeant Dorgan of the 7th Northumberland Fusiliers explained, 'We'd no training for gas prevention, never heard of the gas business.' Within minutes of the first alarm Lieutenant-Colonel Beckles Willson was appalled to see, sweeping down the road to Ypres, 'a panic stricken rabble of Turcos and Zouaves with grey faces and protruding eyeballs, clutching their throats and choking as they ran'. The gas had enveloped the French colonial troops' trenches, and all discipline was gone. Further west, a regiment of French Territorials was in little better shape, with those who had fled the toxic smoke staggering wearily on towards the Yserlee canal without guns or equipment.[2]

The terror weapon created a gap of some four and a half miles in the allied line, achieving in little more than five minutes the decisive breakthrough that had eluded Falkenhayn throughout First Ypres. It swept down not only on the French and the Canadians but also on the British 28th Division and on the Belgian Grenadiers and Carabiniers defending the line of the Yperlee around Boesinghe. Behind the gas cloud the 45th, 46th, 51st and 52nd Reserve Divisions of the Duke of Württemberg's Fourth Army advanced with impregnated gauze pads protecting their mouths and noses. The 45th Division soon took Steenstraat; the 40th crossed the canal at Het Sas; the 51st entered Langemarck and, half an hour after the gas's release, the 52nd were in Pilckem, only two and a half miles from Ypres's Menin Gate. Before nightfall these four advancing divisions – some 50,000 men – had captured 51 guns, mainly French 75-mms, and rounded up 2,000 dazed or wounded prisoners. Then to the relief of their adversaries the Germans began to dig in rather than continue to press forward on Ypres itself. Their orders stipulated that the immediate objective was the seizure of Pilckem Ridge, and this task was soon accomplished. The Duke of Württemberg was without reserves on hand to back up what Falkenhayn had regarded in the first place as essentially a strategic diversion embodying an experiment in weaponry.[3]

*   *   *

Although the allied troops in the trenches were taken by surprise, the possibility of resort to chemical warfare had long been recognized by governments and by humanitarians seeking to limit the horrors of war. The Hague Convention of 1907 condemned the development of weapons capable of spreading poison among combatants or civilians; Britain, France and Germany were among the signatories. Nevertheless individual scientists continued research into chemical warfare. Among them was the 12th Earl of Dundonald, a retired cavalry general and friend of Sir John French, who revised proposals put forward by his great-grandfather during the Crimean War for the emission of sulphurous fumes to prise the enemy out of prepared fortifications. In 1854 the great Michael Faraday authenticated the feasibility of the Dundonald project, though it was never tested. Sixty years later the revised version aroused little interest. At French's request, Haig received Dundonald on 12 March, at the height of the battle of Neuve Chapelle but was dismissive. 'I asked him how he arranged to have a favourable wind,' Haig commented contemptuously in his diary.[4]

The Germans treated science with respect and took inventors more seriously. Research scientists at the Kaiser Wilhelm Institute in Berlin worked closely with IG Farben's chemical experts, and the Prussian Ministry of War showed interest. Soon after the start of war, Pioneer Regiment No. 36 was established to develop weapons capable of discharging chlorine. Field howitzers fired shells containing lachrymatory gas against the Russians at Bolomow, near Warsaw, on 3 January 1915 but with no effect. As an alternative way of discharging gas, orders were given for the manufacture of cylindrical tubes, of small diameter and some 5 feet long. Training was then given to selected 'gas pioneers', serving soldiers who possessed some knowledge of science. The pioneers were to place the cylinders in position under cover of darkness, sited on their objective but concealed from prying eyes or cameras. Before the start of an infantry attack a pioneer wearing a primitive respirator would remove the cap on the cylinder, enabling the gas to be forced out of the tube by its own pressure and wafted into enemy lines by the prevailing wind. No explosive charge was required: all that was needed was a steady wind, fresh but not gusty and blowing from the right quarter.

Generals proud of the superior fire-power of Krupps big guns had no confidence in this bombardment by drain-pipe. Some 17 years later the Reichsarchiv history of the Ypres campaign recalled that officers and men 'almost without exception mistrusted the still untried weapon, if they were not totally against it'.[5]

But despite these doubts, the first cylinders arrived in Flanders in mid-March. Soon afterwards prisoners taken by the French blabbered carelessly about the new weapon, enabling General d'Urbal of France's Tenth Army to circulate an intelligence assessment on 30 March that described the cylinders with remarkable accuracy. By then, however, d'Urbal and his Tenth Army had left the Salient and were 100 miles away, fighting in Artois. General Smith-Dorrien does not appear to have heard of the Tenth Army's discovery until the second week of April, the news being followed by reports of a German captured in the Yserlee canal sector of the Salient who was carrying a protective gas pad. No. 6 Squadron, RFC, was ordered to search from the skies, but the gas-release batteries were so effectively concealed that neither pilots nor observers saw any signs of the cylinders. On 15 April, Smith-Dorrien noted in his diary that he had received information about 'enormous tubes of asphyxiating gas', adding the comment: 'In case there is any truth in it, I have let all commentators know.' General Plumer passed the report on to his divisional commanders 'for what it is worth', and Sir John French, who had also heard tales of a gas weapon, was no less scornful. When rumours of a German attack for the night of 15–16 April proved unfounded, this widespread scepticism seemed justified. Through the following week the fate of Hill 60 held the generals' attention.[6]

Falkenhayn originally contemplated no more than a limited offensive along the Menin Road, where he had been thwarted five months earlier, and the gas cylinders were stored near Gheluvelt. It was not a good site: Passchendaele Ridge acted as a wind shield, and promising north-easterlies – rare anyhow in western Belgium – tended to veer round unpredictably, threatening to blow back a gas cloud towards the attackers. In mid-April the cylinders were moved to the northeast sector, where the ridges were lower and ran for the most part parallel to the line of attack.

Poelcapelle, the pivotal village for the German assault, faced what was at that moment the most vulnerable defensive position in the Salient, for the Poelcapelle–St Julien road marked the northern boundary of the British Second Army's sector. West of the road the line was held by the 87th French Territorial Division and the 45th Algerian Division, both under the command of General Putz. They had only recently moved up to the Front and were assigned some four and a half miles of trenches, reaching out to the Belgian Army's southern posts along the Yserlee canal, slightly north of Steenstraat. The Territorials included elderly Breton reservists, *les pépères* ('grandads'), while the 45th Division comprised Zouaves and a far from reliable 'white' punishment battalion as well as the so-called 'Turcos', native Algerian riflemen.

To the east and south of the road was the 1st Canadian Division, who had already seen action at Neuve Chapelle. Like Putz's motley force, the Canadians were newcomers to the Salient, though they were troops of very different mettle. Their three infantry brigades formed part of General Plumer's V Corps together with (from north to south) the 28th, 27th and 5th British divisions. The most experienced Canadian regiment, Princess Patricia's Canadian Light Infantry – the veterans who had landed in France shortly before Christmas – remained attached to the 27th Division until November 1915, and on 22 April they were too far south to be caught under the asphyxiating yellow cloud. But within a fortnight 'Princess Pat's', too, were to be caught up in Second Ypres, fighting desperately around Frezenberg and Wieltje as the battle moved into its final phase.

The initial success of the German attack carried them forward almost 3 miles in less than five hours. Fortunately the Canadians, on the left of the allied centre, held firm throughout the night of 22–23 April. Smith-Dorrien realized that the Front could only be stabilized if the French found substitutes for the two divisions that had fled in panic. But Foch was slow to respond: GQG was engrossed with preparations for their own offensive in Artois, and Joffre could not spare more troops for Flanders. The best Foch could offer was General Putz's reorganized Territorials, augmented by some 'loose' battalions from his 10th Division. There was, however, no prospect of effective French aid plugging the gap earlier than the evening of 23 April, and it was left to Plumer and to Brigadier-General Turner VC of the 3rd Canadian Brigade to douse the German dragon's fire and fury throughout St George's Day.

Plumer ordered the consolidation of a line already improvised south of the Bois de Cuisiniers, an extensive copse off the Menin Road near Hooge, soon anglicized as Kitchener's Wood (but no longer extant). At a quarter past four in the afternoon the 6th Duke of Cornwall's Light Infantry and the East Yorkshires pressed a counter-attack forward towards Pilckem. The Germans, however, had placed machine-gun nests on the slopes of the ridge, with tragic consequences. As soon as the attackers broke cover, they were mown down by machine-guns and suffered appalling losses. After three hours of heavy fighting the East Yorkshires, who had a nominal strength of 2,000 men at the start of the day, were left with only seven officers and 280 men alive and unwounded. Everywhere around the edge of the ground lost on the previous day Württemberg's artillery rained down what was in effect a protective screen.

Next morning (Saturday, 24 April) the Germans turned their attention to the exposed apex of the Canadian trenches, releasing gas cylinders well before dawn. The artificial cloud on this occasion was some 15 feet deep and, caught by a strong wind, soon swept down on the Canadians. They had no respirators, but they gained some protection by taking advantage of the soluble character of chlorine and covering their mouths and noses with wet towels or handkerchiefs, sometimes kept damp with urine. Remarkably three-quarters of the defenders were fit enough to continue the fight after the gas dispersed, and the Canadian field guns gave the infantry steady support.

By nine o'clock the battle had become an artillery duel, in which the Germans possessed heavier howitzers, capable of shelling support roads and destroying signal wires. It was hard for Smith-Dorrien, and even Plumer, who was much nearer the fighting, to keep in touch with the balance of a battle that was constantly changing: it was harder still for Sir John French, studying the map out at headquarters in Hazebrouck, to appreciate the problems in the forward trenches. Yet, despite the difficulties of communication, GHQ accepted that a general directive was needed for commanders in the field. It came soon after four o'clock on that Saturday afternoon: Plumer received from French the laconic order, 'Every effort must be made at once to restore and hold the line at St Julien.'

But St Julien was not, like Gheluvert and St Eloi, a village at a strategic crossroads. It was little more than a hamlet, 2 miles south of Langemarck and straggling along a road beside the Hannebeek, one of several small streams coming down from Passchendaele Ridge. A single day's fighting had already reduced the line of cottages to ruin. When the 10th Brigade sought to fulfil French's orders, in heavy rain early next morning, the 2nd Seaforth Highlanders and 1st Warwickshires were exposed to enfilade fire across the fields and shelling from the adjoining slopes, while also checked by machine-gun nests set among the rubble. Almost 2,500 of the brigade's 4,000 officers and men were lost during the attack and to little purpose. The Germans remained firmly in control of the charred stones that had been St Julien, though the 10th Brigade succeeded in blunting the impetus of their assault. Later on that Sunday and 2 miles further east, a composite Landwehr division struck at the flank of the battle-weary Canadians and captured the village of Gravenstafel.

In the early evening most units of the 1st Canadian Division were pulled back from the forward trenches into reserve. The division, numbering some 10,000 men at the start of the battle, had lost 1,700 killed in the 72 hours that followed the first release of gas, with more than 2,500 wounded. But the Canadian casualties were not limited to the 1st Division. Today, Chapman Clemesha's magnificent 35-foot high *Brooding Soldier* statue stands at Vancouver Corner, where the N313 to Poelcapelle meets the Zonnebeke–Langemarck road. The statue carries an awesome tribute as unadorned in its proud simplicity as the monument itself: 'This column marks the battlefield where 18,000 Canadians on the British left withstood the first German gas attacks, the 22–24 April 1915; 2,000 fell and lie buried nearby.'[7]

Individual acts of valour during the ordeal of the Canadians were subsequently recognized by the award of two Victoria Crosses, both posthumously. Lance-Corporal Frederick Fisher braved heavy artillery fire to cover troops in a support trench with his machine-gun; Sergeant-Major William Hall twice left his trench to bring back wounded men under heavy fire. The shelling persisted even as the division pulled back, adding more names to the long casualty list. On 25 April, Captain Francis Scimager, a doctor serving at an advanced dressing station in a farm, won a third Canadian VC for saving his wounded patients when the farm buildings became a target for the German guns.

A week later, in a neighbouring dressing station, the death of a Canadian officer inspired an enduring tribute to those who took 'up our quarrel with the foe'. At Essex Farm, Colonel John McCrae was saddened by the fate of his friend, Lieutenant Helmer, who was receiving treatment when he was hit by a German shell. After the fighting died away McCrae mourned Helmer in an elegy for the thousands killed in the springtime of their lives and buried close to where they fell. *Punch* published 'In Flanders Fields' on 8 December 1915, to rekindle emotions aroused earlier in the year by the war sonnets of Rupert Brooke. McCrae immortalized the image of the blood-red poppies that 'blow between the crosses row by row'. His deeply moving sincerity has survived changes of attitude towards war through four generations.

After less than three days of battle it seemed as if Württemberg's troops had secured a potential victory of far greater value than Falkenhayn ever anticipated. They were across the Yserlee canal at Lizerne, though the Belgian Carabiniers continued to offer stiff resistance. Their field artillery maintained a steady bombardment of forward positions from three sides, and their heavy guns pounded the congested roads along which relief columns were making their way to the Front. There was, it appeared, no answer to the improved Maxim machine-guns, and the constant fighting exacted a heavy toll of the best troops. It was a harsh week for George V's armies. Across Europe, the first landings had been made at Gallipoli on 25 April; the British at Cape Helles suffered 1,700 casualties on that morning, and further up the peninsula 1,252 Australians and New Zealanders (Anzacs) were killed over the next six days, one-in-four of those who landed.

Yet although the Germans in Flanders had prised the latch off the gate barring access to the Channel ports, they failed to press forward into the open country beyond. The unexpected always caught Falkenhayn off balance: he hesitated, and time overtook him. The French recovered Lizerne on 27 April and supported the Belgians in clearing the western bank of the canal by mid-May; though the British continued to suffer heavy losses in counter-attacks, their line was never broken.

On 1 May the 15th Brigade of the 5th Division thwarted a gas attack for the first time, made on Hill 60. The 1st battalion Dorset Regiment were among forward troops issued with gauze and flannel pads to be hung around the neck, ready to be wetted by means unspecified when a gas alarm sounded. The attack, launched at 7.15 in the evening, took the Dorsets by surprise, but a young subaltern, Second Lieutenant Kestell-Cornish had the enterprise to seize a rifle and, with the only four men in his platoon still able to stand, fired rapidly into the yellow cloud from the trench parapet checking the advancing Germans, who could reasonably assume a machine-gun post had remained unaffected by the gas. Reserves from the 1st Devons and 1st Bedfords brought support to the Dorsets, but for three hours there was close fighting in the trenches at the foot of the hill. Ninety men were fatally gassed in the trenches that evening. Of 207 wounded brought back to the dressing station, '46 died almost immediately and 12 after long suffering'. Kestell-Cornish spent two days in hospital, recovering from the effects of the gas, but he was back in the trenches within a week.[8]

Sadly the Dorsets' resolute defence was to no avail; a second German attack four days later could not be repulsed. The 1st Cheshires were brought up hurriedly from their billets in Ypres to bolster the Dorsets, 1st Norfolk and 2nd Duke of Wellingtons after the Germans discharged thicker gas from flank positions that ran the length of their trenches, causing heavy casualties. At one point the Cheshires were engaged for half an hour in a deadly exchange of hand grenades, their 'jam tin variety' bombs less effective than 'those horrid little black grenades that the Germans fling so accurately', complained Second Lieutenant Arthur Greg, a Rugbeian who cut short his studies at New College, Oxford, to enlist in the previous September. 'An officer of the Dorsetshire Regiment had his head blown off just as he was handing me a new box of grenades,' Greg wrote. 'I felt very upset.'[9] For 48 hours the British tried to hold the hill or recover it by counter–attacks, but they could not dislodge their enemy. Hill 60 remained in German hands for the next two years.

By 27 April, Smith-Dorrien had become seriously alarmed at the exposed position of V Corps and angered by the commander-in-chief's insistence on pressing ahead with inter-allied

counter-attacks. It seemed evident that GHQ at distant Hazebrouck did not realize the Second Army was short of troops and
that French support had proved limited in numbers and reluctantly
given. Without consulting Sir John, Smith-Dorrien ordered all
offensive operations to cease 'forthwith', and he sent an urgent
900-word letter to General Robertson, who had become the chief
of French's general staff in January. Smith-Dorrien respected
Robertson, known as Wully, the Lincolnshire lad who 38 years
back in time ran away from home to enlist as a private and rose to
high command through natural intelligence. Over strategic issues
Wully seemed a sensible realist, and the letter put forward a sound
case for pulling back to the so-called 'GHQ line', a defensive
semicircle 2 miles east of Ypres prepared by the French in
January.[10] But Robertson's realism was compounded of ruthlessness and ambition; he expressed neither agreement nor doubt. In
the early afternoon he telephoned Smith-Dorrien to say that 'the
Chief does not regard situation nearly so unfavourable as your
letter represents'. Smith-Dorrien was told to co-operate with the
French in a simultaneous combined attack with 'due regard to
previous instructions'. A letter would 'follow', brought by a staff
officer.

No letter came. Instead, Smith-Dorrien received that evening a
telegram sent *en clair* by a staff major ordering him to hand over to
General Plumer 'the command of all troops engaged in present
operations about Ypres'. Smith-Dorrien remained in the Salient
another ten days, still technically responsible for II Corps, out on
Messines Ridge. On 6 May, Smith-Dorrien received by telephone
the news he had anticipated: "Orace, you're for 'ome,' Robertson
allegedly told him. On this occasion formal, written instructions
did 'follow' the call: he was to return to England; Plumer would
succeed him in command of the Second Army. Thus was the most
senior general serving in the British army dismissed at the height of
a critical battle; no explanation was given.[11] Ironically, Plumer had
by then already retreated to the GHQ line or, more precisely, to
forward trenches hurriedly dug ahead of it. Sir John French would
accept proposals from the tactful Plumer that from his predecessor
would have been anathema. A feud between choleric generals
fighting the same battle was potentially disastrous, as the Russians
had found at Tannenberg in August 1914.

The slaughter of Second Ypres dragged on into May, irrespective of the retirement to the GHQ line. During the second week of the month the German 53rd Reserve Division attacked the 27th and 28th Divisions in great strength along a ridge that runs west of Frezenberg southwards from Wieltje to merge imperceptibly into a higher ridge, covering the woods and lake at Bellewaarde, to the east of Hooge chateau on the Menin Road. Heavy bombardment and persistent infantry assaults killed nine officers and 382 men in Princess Patricia's Canadian Light Infantry on 8 May, leaving the regiment only 154 survivors. At nightfall the 12th London Regiment, nominally 1,000-men strong, could muster a mere 53 other ranks and no officers. The German bombardment was so deep that one company (250 men), marching through darkened streets on the eve of the battle, suffered 80 casualties from falling masonry. Several eye-witnesses comment on the agonies of horses hit by shell splinters or by breaking their legs in potholes. A pitiful neighing backed the stench of rotting carcasses along the roads.

Four days later (12 May) the 'Cavalry Force', fighting as dismounted infantry, relieved the 27th Division. They had hardly reached the lines facing Frezenberg on that Thursday when the full fury of bombardment fell on them. The shellfire continued for eleven and a half hours, inflicting heavy casualties, particularly on the 1st Life Guards, whose trenches were destroyed. The Leicestershire Yeomanry lost 96 of the 282 men who set out from their billets on the previous day; of those killed, 83 had no known grave; their names are inscribed on the Menin Gate. Yet somehow the North Somerset Yeomanry's trenches continued to offer some cover despite the bombardment, enabling a counter-attack with bayonets to be made later in the day. Renewed shellfire checked two other counter-attacks by the regrouped cavalry during the afternoon.[12]

Personal tragedies abounded on that ghastly Thursday: one robbed England of yet another poet of budding talent. Julian Grenfell, a captain in the 1st Royal Dragoons, was gravely wounded in the trenches on the edge of the wood north of Hooge by a shell splinter that penetrated his skull. His 'Into Battle', completed a fortnight earlier, conveys the alternating emotions of fear and elation he had experienced five months previously during First Ypres, the contrast between the soldier's 'dreary,

doubtful, waiting hours, before the brazen frenzy starts' and that
'burning moment' when 'only joy of battle takes him by the throat,
and makes him blind' to all things else. Premonition darkens his
later stanzas: 'In the air death moans and sings'; calmly the poet–
soldier resigns himself to 'Destined Will'. The wound proved fatal;
Grenfell was taken fully conscious to a military hospital in Boulogne. There he lingered for 12 days until night could finally 'fold
him in soft wings'.[13]

Officially Second Ypres ended on 24 May, when four German
divisions made a final attempt to push forward from a line north of
Bellewaarde Ridge along the Menin Road. More gas was released
than in any earlier attack, but counter-measures were improving
day by day; East Enders working overtime at Allen and Hanbury's,
the pharmaceutists of Bethnal Green, enabled primitive respirators
fitted with eye-shields to be rushed out from London. But only
strong shields for the body could have given protection from the
thrust and counter-thrust with bayonet that followed when the
infantry clashed once the gas cloud lifted. The fighting continued
all day, until around eight o'clock in the evening the British 4th
Division pulled back from Wieltje to newly dug trenches extending GHQ line to the northwest.

After 34 days of battle the Germans had trimmed the Salient
drastically, though most of the territory was gained in the first two
days. The British suffered almost 60,000 casualties, the French
about 10,000 and the Belgians slightly more than 1500, a total of
71,500 allied dead, missing or seriously wounded. By contrast the
Germans sustained 35,000 casualties, less than half their enemy's
number. On war maps printed in the newspapers the ground won
seemed of little importance. Although Falkenhayn's troops were in
some places only 2 miles from the Grand Place, they had made little
progress towards those elusive Channel ports: Dunkirk was still 30
miles ahead of them, Calais some 50. But the crests of the arc of
ridges around Ypres were in enemy hands. From Bellewaarde and
from Hill 60 the Germans enjoyed clear views extending well
behind the British trenches. The roads to the French border had
long come under haphazard shellfire. Now observers could sight
the artillery on targets out at Poperinghe, Dickebusch and Vlamertinghe with ominous accuracy.

*   *   *

Sir John French admitted to Haig that he had spent 'several bad nights as the result of anxiety' over Ypres, but increasingly he was looking beyond the old frontier, tempted by the prospect of a battle for Lille.[14] By 6 May, Haig completed plans for supporting Joffre's spring offensive. In what might be regarded as Neuve Chapelle Mark 2, the First Army would make a second attempt to reach the high ground southwest of Lille, this time by securing Aubers Ridge, the objective that proved too distant two months earlier. The following day – while the Germans were massing their artillery in the Salient around Frezenberg – French summoned First Army's commanding generals to GHQ in Hazebrouck for a confident briefing on the favourable position of the allies across Europe and his hopes for Aubers Ridge and the simultaneous French assault on Vimy Ridge.

His optimism was misplaced. On the Eastern Front the Russians were forced back from the foothills of the Carpathians into Galicia; from Gallipoli the news grew gloomier by the day; in Artois the French advanced 3 miles and briefly held the crest of Vimy Ridge, only to be overwhelmed by counter-attacks, and on the same day – Sunday, 9 May – Aubers Ridge proved a costly disaster. The First Army and the Indian Corps incurred 11,500 casualties in 12 hours of battle. Haig lacked guns of heavy calibre, and the artillery was woefully short of high explosive. Shrapnel shells failed to cut through the barbed wire, exposing the infantry to merciless machine-gun fire. Haig wished to resume the offensive on the Monday, but each of his three corps commanders reported they did not have enough shells to support further attacks.[15] A second battle was fought around Festubert (15–25 May), when once again initial success was thwarted by lack of high-explosive shells.

On 14 May, the eve of Festubert, *The Times* caused a sensation in London with an article under the triple headline, 'Need for shells. British attacks checked. Limited supply the cause'.[16] Colonel Repington, the paper's military correspondent, based his article on figures fed to him secretly by Sir John French, who also sent his military secretary and an aide-de-camp to London to contact Lloyd George, knowing that the chancellor of the exchequer had for the past month been chairing a cabinet committee on munitions, from which Kitchener was pointedly excluded. On 21 May the *Daily Mail* – the paper with the largest circulation and, like *The Times,* owned by Lord Northcliffe – blamed the war secretary for the 'shell scandal'. To French's disappointment, however, Kitchener was not swept from office. Asquith had already resolved to strengthen the government's authority by bringing the Conservative Unionists into a coalition. Bonar Law, their leader, insisted on keeping Kitchener at the War Office: the head he demanded was that of Churchill, the initiator of Gallipoli.

On 27 May, when the Liberal–Unionist coalition took office, Churchill was removed from the Admiralty, while Lloyd George left the Exchequer to become minister of munitions. Sound administration, together with unprecedented powers of requisitioning, ensured that the manufacture of weapons and output of shells and ammunition were speeded up. Within a month shell production had risen to 4,000 a day and by the autumn it reached 10,000, but for Haig the improved figure was far from satisfactory: in battles on the Western Front the British guns could get through 40,000 shells in a single day. Lloyd George was convinced that in the spring of 1916 the BEF would have all the guns and explosives needed for a sustained offensive – but not sooner. And still lacking was any means by which infantry could penetrate sophisticated field defences, where concrete pillboxes and deep dug-outs seemed impervious to artillery.

The summer of 1915 became a season of ripe politicking. There were jointly productive Anglo-French talks over munitions problems at Boulogne; discussions over the extent of the British commitment in France at Calais on 6 July, with subsequent Joffre–Kitchener talks later in the month, and the first inter-allied conference over grand strategy, at Chantilly, on 7 July. Ever present in the background was the British fear that if the BEF failed to back Joffre's planned offensives to the hilt an exhausted France would seek a separate peace. To guard against this contingency Kitchener, while opposing 'a too vigorous offensive', pressed Sir John French to pledge his support for GQG even if the BEF suffered 'very heavy casualties'. The war minister left Sir John to face harsh decisions in the months ahead, sometimes taken against his own strategic instincts.

Meanwhile, as May came to an end, Plumer was made sharply aware of business left unfinished from Second Ypres. Hooge

The 2nd battalion, Scots Guards of the 7th Division nearing Ypres after marching along the road from Roulers, 14 October 1914

Weary survivors of the London Scottish after the Battle of Messines, 31 October 1914

The 2nd battalion of the Royal Warwickshire Regiment aboard buses as they pass through Dickebusch at the height of First Ypres, 6 November 1914

German soldiers of the 134th Saxon Regiment welcome a British party in no man's land, Boxing Day 1914. Brigadier-General Drummond took the photograph as he approached them

Officers of the 27th Magdeburg Regiment in a front-line dug-out, April 1915

Soldiers from the East Surrey Regiment in the trenches, Ploegsteert Wood, 11 June 1917

A stretcher party carries a casualty through the mud on the second day of Passchendaele, August 1917

Kaiser Wilhelm (*front row, second from right*) with Crown Prince Rupprecht of Bavaria (*on his right*) and the chief of his military cabinet, Colonel-General von Lyncker (*behind, centre*), June 1918. Kaiser Wilhelm appears to be talking to his naval brother, Prince Heinrich (*front row, far right*) who, as a courtesy general, is dressed in army uniform

Australian infantry pass the ruins of the Cloth Hall in Ypres on their way up the Menin Road, 25 October 1917

A howitzer battery precariously close to a swollen rivulet in the mud of Passchendaele, 31 October 1917

Field Marshal Haig (*right*) with General Plumer of the Second Army (*far left*) and General Horne of the First Army (*standing behind*), 1918

The *Grieving Parents* by Käthe Kollwitz, Vladslo Cemetery. (*See p. 3 and pp. 207-8*)

chateau remained a British outpost defying German mastery of Bellewaarde Ridge, and work began on a redoubt to strengthen an almost untenable position. On 2 June a heavy bombardment of the chateau grounds was followed by an infantry assault that forced the British to pull back before the redoubt was completed. Next day an attempt was made to recover the chateau, the 1st Lincolns pushing ahead to the ruined stables, but they made too good a target to consolidate their position. Careful planning was needed to loosen the German hold on either the chateau or Bellewaarde behind it. Much of the summer's deadliest fighting was a quest for the ridge with a view.

Over the next ten days the staff of V Corps – under Allenby's command since Plumer's promotion – meticulously planned an operation on 16 June committing the 3rd Division to recovering Bellewaarde Ridge. The attack followed two days of aerial reconnaissance, and Allenby's staff even provided the forward troops with carrier pigeons to let headquarters know of progress or setbacks should shelling cut telegraph links. The attack was preceded by a two-hour bombardment of the German lines, a barrage that dug deeply into the limited stock of shells.

At dawn the 9th Infantry Brigade went over the top, met surprisingly little resistance and headed north-eastwards beyond Railway Wood to the embankment carrying the line to Roulers. A second wave from the 7th Infantry Brigade – the 1st infantry battalion of the Honourable Artillery Company (1/1 HAC), the Liverpool Scottish, the 1st Lincolns, the 2nd Royal Irish Rifles – also went forward towards the embankment, advancing so rapidly that they came under shellfire from the British guns and, at the same time, from German positions along the embankment and on their flank. Casualties were heavy, and a German counter-attack drove them back to the trenches taken in the first attack. Out of 540 officers and other ranks in the Liverpool Scottish who fought on that day, 180 were killed and 218 wounded.

The dazed survivors of the brigade, now supported by the 3rd Worcesters, rallied and in the late afternoon attempted to resume their advance. 'There was great confusion,' Sergeant John Lucy of the Irish Rifles later wrote. 'The German front line occupied by us was filled with the dead and wounded of about eight regiments, and our men . . . had to go forward without direct artillery support, over muddy ground spurting shell explosions every few yards and raked by enemy machine-guns from an unprotected left flank.'[17] By the end of the day the British had to be content with taking more than 150 prisoners, capturing two machine-guns and a half-mile line of better-built trenches 250 yards ahead of the ones they held when the attack began. To achieve these gains the 3rd Division lost 140 officers and 3,391 other ranks in 14 hours of battle. Among the 9th Brigade's wounded was their brigade major, Archibald Wavell, who had been married in London on the day Second Ypres began. A shell splinter hit him on the forehead, blinding his left eye and threatening the sight of his right.[18] He recovered in hospital in London. Colonel Wavell was beside Allenby when the victorious general in Palestine made his formal entry into Jerusalem in December 1917, and he went on to command in the Middle East in 1940–41. Two years later he became the only field marshal appointed viceroy of India.

Most of the fighting in the Salient during the summer of 1915 took place around Hooge, the apex of the British defensive line east of Ypres. It was even the scene of the first spectacular duel in the skies. In the evening of 25 July, Captain Hawker, flying a single-seat Bristol Scout from Abeele aerodrome, completed the pursuit of three German two-seaters that had begun above Passchendaele by swooping down sun from 11,000 feet to within a hundred yards of the rear aircraft and sending it crashing in flames by a burst of Lewis gun-fire over Hooge; Hawker was awarded the Victoria Cross 'for most conspicuous bravery and very great ability'.[19]

A map recovered from the crashed aircraft identified the position of German batteries in the neighbourhood. It did not, however, give warning of the attack that would come five days later, when liquid flame projected from a steel cylinder Flammenwerfer added a second terror weapon to the horrors of the Salient. The German assault was triggered by the British explosion of a mine, which had destroyed a fortified post behind the ruins of Hooge village on the evening of 20 July, enabling the 4th battalion the Middlesex Regiment and the 2nd Gordon Highlanders to rush forward into and around the crater, occupying good trenches, dug recently. The Germans made every effort to prevent the British consolidating their gains but failed to dislodge them. Like Allenby in the previous month, the Duke of Württemberg ordered careful planning for a sustained attack.

It came soon after three o'clock in the morning of 30 July. 'There was a sudden hissing sound and a bright crimson glare over the crater turned the whole scene red', Lieutenant Carey of the 8th Rifle Brigade recalled. 'As I looked I saw three or four distinct sheets of flame – like a line of powerful fire-hoses spraying fire instead of water – shoot across my fire-trench.' Carey was the only officer of his company to survive the day; a neighbouring company 'seemed to have been almost completely obliterated'.[20] Flame-throwers were also employed in a simultaneous attack south of the Menin Road at the northern fringe of Sanctuary Wood. Inevitably the surprised defenders – mostly from the King's Royal Rifle Corps (KRRC) – fell back across the fields towards Ypres. Once again 'resting' battalions were ordered from their billets and hurried eastwards up the Menin Road, under renewed shelling. By the afternoon the 1st Sherwood Foresters – technically the Nottinghamshire and Derbyshire Regiment – and the 6th Duke of Cornwall's Light Infantry (DCLI) had joined the KRRC in blunting the impetus of the enemy assault, but nothing could shift the Germans from the crater and the chateau stables.

'I simply looked upon the coming adventure in much the same way that I looked forward to an exciting game of Rugger,' Private Pollard of the HAC wrote years later, as he recalled his feelings on the eve of the first attack on Bellewaarde.[21] At times it seems as if this terrible war, ever spawning agonizing ways to kill, had become trivialized into a deadly contest for possession of the ball among rival teams competing for a local trophy. No sooner had the British lost shell-pocked Hooge than they began for a third time to devise means to recover it and Bellewaarde Ridge, too. On this occasion resort was made to subterfuge: German airmen were able to see British and French troops assembling to the north, as if to bring the fighting back to Pilckem and Langemarck; observers at Messines could direct artillery on newly dug trenches that attracted attention, and there was constant movement out towards Zillebeke and Hill 60.

But at 2.45 in the morning of 9 August a half-hour bombardment of the Hooge crater area left no doubt of the objective. The 2nd Durham Light Infantry formed the vanguard of the 6th

Division's attack, together with the Sherwood Foresters. The day's heavy fighting, much of it with bayonet, brought some success. The line was pushed back east of Hooge hamlet and to the south of the Menin Road, but ferocious German shelling made it impossible to retain the furthest gains. In the end, the 6th Division had advanced the British position some 250 yards. Sensibly the Germans did not attempt to come forward again. The two armies were separated by a wide no man's land of broken tree stumps, shell holes filling readily with water and churned-up clay that a rain shower would turn into glutinous mud, even under the August sun. That night, as their colonel reported, the 2nd Durhams 'marched to billets at Ypres – strength 4 officers and 166 men . . . For our time in the trenches', they had lost 6 officers and 92 men killed, 6 officers and 262 men wounded, while another 100 were ominously listed as 'missing'.[22]

A billet in Ypres was hardly recuperative. 'The town is a mere heap of rubble, cinders and rubbish', the Life Guards captain, Sir Morgan Crofton, wrote in his diary a few weeks earlier. 'Not a cat lives there now, it is the abomination of desolation.'[23] It was also at times a death-trap, liable to attract attention from the German heavy guns whenever intelligence believed troops were massed inside the city. On 12 August a company from the 6th DCLI was caught by a bombardment of the Grand Place. Some sought refuge under the twelfth-century cloisters of the cathedral. There they were trapped when another round of shells struck St Martin's. Efforts to rescue them were frustrated by more shelling, in which their commanding officer was killed. After the war ended 40 bodies were discovered, entombed by fallen masonry.

'The Salient at Ypres is simply an inferno,' Crofton had added in his diary entry. 'It is not war, but murder pure and simple . . . As a strategic or tactical point Ypres is worthless. Why we don't give it up now, God alone knows.' It was, he assumed, a question of pride and prestige. Crofton was jotting down private opinions at the close of a hot and humid day, and perhaps his comments should not be taken too seriously, but he was an intelligent officer from a military family, and he may well have been right. Ypres was already symbolic, a name in the headlines for the last eight months, the town where in November the 'Old Contemptibles' denied the kaiser the triumphant entry he daily anticipated. Crofton thought 'this muck heap' should be evacuated, with the Germans denied possession by using 'our guns' to make the place 'untenable', though at the same time he deplored the shortage of guns and ammunition: 'If only we had shells, we would push through to the Rhine,' he wrote confidently. Other field officers, including on occasions Haig himself, considered straightening the Salient by withdrawing from the forward trenches and falling back on the canal and the remains of Vauban's ramparts. But Krupps and Skoda fire-power had already destroyed with ease Brialmont's fortresses: it is doubtful if improvised defences amid the rubble of Ypres could have long delayed a German advance to the Channel ports.

After the failure of Aubers Ridge and Festubert, the 'sleek deadheads of the Headquarters Staff'— as Crofton contemptuously called French's team[24] – turned again to plans for backing GQG's grand offensive. Joffre intended to strike at the German right flank at Vimy, and he suggested the BEF might find the Loos area 'particularly favourable ground' for an attack: Loos, 5 miles south-west of Lille, was an unattractive mining town in which a historic Cistercian abbey now served as a prison. Haig disliked the project from the first, insisting that First Army still lacked shells and artillery. French vacillated. He rode forward to a distant ridge on 12 July, peered down on the industrial murk of the Loos valley, where the slag-heaps, canals and miners' cottages revived memories of the difficulties of fighting in Mons, and he shared Haig's doubts. But assurances that he could now employ chlorine gas and would receive two divisions of Kitchener's New Army as reinforcements induced him to change his mind.

Haig's First Army launched the attack on Loos at 5.15 in the morning of 25 September, after four days of preliminary bombardment (in which 250,000 shells were fired). The town was taken, without the costly struggle French had feared, by the 1st (Scottish) Division – to Germans 'the devils in skirts'. The chlorine gas threw the defenders of the formidable Hohenzollern redoubt into such panic that it fell within the first hour of battle. But by half-past seven the gas cloud had drifted northwards; the British encountered the solid line of the German second position and could make no dent in it. The Germans summoned up reserves, including a guards division. But when Haig, in turn, called for reserves, they were held back on French's orders, for he feared Haig would commit them too early. By the time 12 battalions of Kitchener's New Army – 10,000 initiates – went into action on the second morning, the Germans had strengthened their positions, and artillery stocks were running low. In four hours the 12 battalions suffered 8,000 casualties. Like the battles in the Ypres Salient, the carnage continued long after the first two decisive days; officially the battle of Loos ended on 4 November. By then, 16,000 British soldiers were dead and more than 25,000 wounded: 2 miles of French soil was freed from the enemy.[25]

As a feint, intended to prevent German reinforcements from being drawn southwards to Lille, Plumer was ordered to mount a diversionary attack on 25 September along the Menin Road. At precisely the same hour that the chlorine gas enveloped Loos, the Second Army's 3rd division went forward on a mile-long front straddling the road between the lake at the foot of Bellewaarde Ridge and the northern edge of Sanctuary Wood. The brunt of the fighting was left to the veterans of the 1st infantry battalion of the HAC and the 2nd battalion Royal Irish Rifles (RIR). There was a shortage not only of shells for the gunners but of grenades and wire-cutters for the infantry as well. The RIR fought with particular tenacity, amid craters and shell holes familiar to them from the attack three months earlier. On this occasion the holes held more water and the churned-up clay made for slow progress. Little could be achieved; another 4,000 names were added to the lengthening casualty list of dead and wounded.

For the remaining weeks of the year the Salient was, officially, 'quiet'. In reality, there was constant activity and the imminence of a mortal wound never receded. Around Zillebeke opposing trenches were no more than 25 yards apart. For a tall man to raise his head above the fire parapet was to court a sniper's bullet. Any suspicious move sighted in a communications trench would bring a 'whiz–bang' crunching down, to be followed by an artillery duel that might drag on for more than an hour. The bitter cold, constant rain and need to wade through flooded communication trenches made life intolerable even without the proximity of the enemy, and spells of duty in the trenches rarely lasted longer than four days at a time, although the processes of being relieved and marching back again a few nights later were no less dangerous. The vibration of a bombardment would loosen the wet earth of dug-outs, which would then collapse and trap any troops taking cover within them. Shells exploding short of the trenches would leave gaps in the barbed wire.

On the night of 22 December, in bright moonlight, Second Lieutenant Roland Leighton of the 7th Worcesters was ordered to take his platoon forward to repair just such a gap in the wire. As he was supervising their work, a machine-gun already trained on the gap opened up, and he was hit by a bullet that penetrated his stomach. An ambulance took him, mortally wounded, to a clearing station 10 miles behind the lines, where he died the following night. He had been granted Christmas leave in England and his fiancée, Vera Brittain, by now a nurse with the Voluntary Aid Detachment, awaited him jubilantly at the Grand Hotel, Brighton. There on Christmas Day a telephone call from his sister told her Roland had been killed.[26]

Similar tragedies rent other grieving families across Britain and Canada, France, Belgium and Germany in that traditionally festive season. On Christmas morning a Bavarian gesture of fraternization tempted some Coldstream Guards, but it was sternly rebuffed on orders from their Corps commander. 'Our Artillery fired throughout the day as ordered,' Major-General Cavan assured Haig. There would be no Flanders truce over this second Christmas at war.[27]

10

'ORGY OF SLAUGHTER'

'Sir John French is played out. The show is too big for him and he is despondent,' wrote Major Charteris, one of Haig's most trusted staff officers in the aftermath of Loos.[1] The field marshal's health had been poor, even before the battle: he was confined to bed with influenza during early September but well enough to ride through villages close to the front line on the eve of Loos and spend two hours on the second morning visiting the wounded at a casualty clearing station: 'Poor dear fellows they bear their pain gloriously,' he wrote to his mistress, Winifred Bennett, a few days later.[2] Loos, however, finally discredited French: he was blamed for holding back three divisions of reserves when Haig urgently needed them on the first morning and ridiculed for not insisting on a direct telephone link from his battle-command post outside Lilliers to Haig's First Army headquarters at Hinges, 19 miles away. His subsequent doctoring of a dispatch to justify his conduct of operations and place the blame on Haig confirmed the doubts of those reluctant to shed their loyalty to a commander who remained popular with the old, long-serving soldiery.[3]

Only a decisive victory at Loos could have saved French from recall. Age intensified the unpredictability of a mercurial temperament and hardened his obstinacy: the fourth day of Loos was his sixty-third birthday. Too many in high places had become personal enemies, including Kitchener, and he placed too much trust in generals who were personally ambitious and more skilled than he in manipulating politicians, not least among them Haig and Robertson. King George V told Haig as early as 14 July that he had lost confidence in the field marshal, and he assured Kitchener he could rely on royal 'support in whatever action

he took in the matter of dealing with French'. In the third week of
October the king visited the BEF in France and Flanders and was
thrown from his horse and injured while inspecting the First
Army. Before the accident he had a further conversation with the
army's commander. 'French's handling of the reserves in the last
battle, his obstinacy and conceit showed his incapacity,' Haig told
the king, and he added, pointedly: 'For the sake of the Empire
French ought to be removed. I personally was ready to do my
duty in any capacity.' The king agreed with Haig having, he said,
heard criticism from other generals in the field, including Robertson. After his accident George V urged Asquith 'from his sick
bed' to get rid of French.[4]

The field marshal was reluctant to go. He was still responsible for
the BEF on 6 December 1915 when he attended inter-allied talks
at Chantilly. The conference accepted in principle Joffre's grand
design for 1916, a series of almost simultaneous offensives against
Germany and Austria–Hungary on every allied front across the
continent. But Sir John was by now a lame-duck commander-in-
chief. On that same morning Asquith received his resignation,
dispatched at last from St Omer on the eve of his departure for
Chantilly. In his letter French recommended Robertson as a
successor; Asquith appointed Haig, though Robertson would
become CIGS, the chief of the imperial general staff. When French
sailed for home the 19th Hussars, the regiment in which he was
commissioned a third of a century before, lined the quayside at
Boulogne and cheered him aboard the destroyer for Dover. Ahead
lay command of Home Defence and a peerage. It was as Viscount
French of Ypres that he took his seat in the Lords.

Haig assumed formal command of the BEF on 19 December
1915 at noon. He had no immediate plans to go over to the
offensive in Flanders. Nor, indeed, had the Germans. In a long
memorandum to the kaiser, drafted in the same week that French
resigned, Falkenhayn reviewed the possible battle fronts in search
of one that could bring Germany decisive victory. Flanders was
swiftly passed over: interestingly, he reckoned 'the state of the
ground' would make the exploitation of early successes difficult.
After considering all options, he recommended the seizure of
Verdun, the fortress whose fall in September 1792 had prompted
panic massacres in Paris. To save Verdun, Falkenhayn argued, Joffre

would throw in so many troops that the German army would be able 'to bleed France white'.[5]

Joffre, too, preferred France rather than Belgium as a chosen battleground for the year 1916. When Haig met Joffre at Chantilly on 29 December the French supreme commander developed further his grand design, outlining plans for a combined offensive in Artois and Champagne. On Boxing Day, however, Haig had entertained to lunch Admiral Bacon, commander of the Dover Patrol, who emphasized the need to deprive the German navy of the use of Ostend and Zeebrugge, thus reviving the idea of an amphibious landing and an advance northwards from the Yser.[6] At his meeting in Chantilly, Haig raised the possibility of undertaking such a drive and going forward to the Dutch frontier, but Joffre showed little interest. GQG wanted the 'new armies' of the BEF deployed further south, taking over more sectors from the French. Joffre therefore made two recommendations. The British would extend their line southwards and eventually hold some 110 miles of the 590-mile long Western Front; the spring offensive would be a massive joint operation aimed at clearing the centre of the Front and providing a Franco-British axis for a later advance into Germany.

With some reluctance, Haig accepted the obligation to extend the British commitment and to concentrate on preparing the newly arrived 'Kitchener battalions' for what was to become the battle of the Somme. By the spring the British would have a million men serving in France and Flanders. On 22 February the War Committee – Asquith's inner council of five ministers and four serving officers – received a letter to study from Haig proposing a British attack along 14 miles of the Front on the Somme in May or June. Also for the committee's reading that Tuesday morning came reports in *The Times* that the Germans had shelled Verdun on Monday to open what was clearly intended to become a major offensive.[7] For the next eight months the two terrible battlefields 150 miles apart polarized strategic thinking in London and Paris.

The first casualty of forward planning was Bacon's proposed amphibious landing and advance from the Yser to Ostend and Zeebrugge. Haig crossed to Dover on 25 February and told the admiral and his military co-ordinator, General Hunter-Weston, that, while 'the scheme should be worked out in the most complete detail' its execution would 'depend on the military situation'. Haig

then continued his journey to London for a discussion with
Kitchener, proposing that should the French find themselves
unable to counter-attack at Verdun the BEF would go forward
independently from an Ypres–Armentières line 'in the direction of
the Dutch frontier'. The two men agreed, however, that, as Haig
noted in his diary, provided all went well at Verdun the BEF must
attack alongside the French 'astride the Somme (as already proposed by Joffre)'.[8]

Throughout 1916 there were no major operations around Ypres. It
was not, however, a quiet sector of the Front, like the most
southerly points of the French line in the Vosges. There were
constant raids, notably by the Canadians at Spanbroekmolen in
front of Wytschaete early in the new year and again in February. In
late March and early April the fighting flared up around St Eloi
when the British sought to dislodge the enemy from the Mound,
the artificial hill captured by the Germans after mining operations
12 months previously. On 27 March 1916 no less than six British
mines were blown there. The 1st Northumberland Fusiliers and
4th Royal Fusiliers then launched an attack that destroyed the key
German observation post. The victors were relieved by troops from
the 2nd Canadian Division a few days later, but the newcomers had
hardly taken stock of their surroundings when a determined
German counter-attack on 6 April forced them gradually back
from the mine craters to the original British line. Such actions,
costly and ultimately futile, occurred all too frequently during these
months of apparent stalemate.

There were, too, occasions when a German initiative put
Plumer's Second Army briefly on general alert. In the small hours
of 30 April, two German regiments advanced behind a gas cloud on
to trenches held by the 10th Royal Welch Fusiliers at Spanbroekmolen, below Messines Ridge. The wind carried the gas down to
the 24th Division's trenches around Wulverghem before veering
and blowing back on the attackers, whose respirators offered some
protection from its effects. Only a few lines of trench changed
hands. The whole action lasted less than four hours, but the gas,
coming suddenly in the middle of the night, caused more than 500
British casualties, either in men killed or incapacitated by the
choking poison of chlorine or phosgene.[9]

The severest fighting in the Salient during the year came at the start of a very wet June. Although Falkenhayn's attention was concentrated on Verdun, where the Germans nearly broke the French line in the third week of the month, he also had to watch the new deployment of the BEF in the area northwest of the Somme. Crown Prince Rupprecht was ordered to launch a major diversionary attack on the one remaining section of rising ground east of Ypres in British hands. This slight incline was known as Observatory Ridge and ran eastwards from Zillebeke to the bare tree stumps that so recently had been Sanctuary Wood. The ridge culminated in the slopes of Hill 62 – 'Tor Top' – and neighbouring Mount Sorrel. As well as hampering the movement of the BEF southwards, the Bavarians would test the power of the Second Army, in the hope that defences weakened by loss of regiments to augment the Fourth Army on the Somme might crack and open up a new route into Ypres. At the same time the attack would strengthen the German position at Hooge, astride the Menin Road.

Facing the Germans was the Canadian Corps, deployed to defend Mount Sorrel under a British veteran corps commander, General Sir Julian Byng. He was only appointed on 29 May, four days before the German attack began and had not yet had an opportunity to see for himself the trenches as far south as Mount Sorrel.[10] Like so much fighting in 1916–17 the German assault was preceded by the customary bombardment as well as by tunnelling underground and the planting of mines. About one o'clock in the afternoon of 2 June the first mines exploded at Mount Sorrel. The Bavarian infantry broke through and within six hours captured three fortified positions in the British trench system. Canadian casualties were heavy: the 4th Canadian Mounted Rifles, holding the most southern line of trenches (covered by the guns of German-held Hill 60), lost 637 killed, missing or gravely wounded and ended the day with less than 50 fighting men.

Torrential rain ruled out an immediate counter-attack, but the appalling weather had the double advantage of leaving the Germans groping with mud while enabling Byng to prepare his response with more foresight than would have been possible in any hastily contrived speedy reaction. By now Lloyd George's drive to increase the turn-out of shells and weapons was paying dividends. Despite the artillery assigned to Fourth Army for the approaching battle on the Somme, Byng was able to call on more than 200 guns. They concentrated their fire on a sector of the line little more than a mile in length. With this support the Canadians were at last able to go forward on the night of 12–13 June and recovered the lost trenches south of the Menin Road in the first of the Dominion's epic triumphs on the Western Front.[11]

Beyond the Menin Road, however, the fortnight's fighting left the German hold on Hooge strengthened, with the British forward positions pushed back more than half a mile towards Hell Fire Corner and the Menin Gate. The new defensive line, unchanged over the coming 12 months, ran southwards into the remains of Sanctuary Wood. At some points, especially in the north, no man's land became, unusually, as much as 300 yards wide.

For the first five months of the year 1916 the former first lord of the Admiralty was serving in the trenches. A sense of humiliating frustration at his exclusion from any active role in the conduct of the war induced Churchill to seek a command in France in the late summer of 1915 with the backing of Sir John French, who would have been prepared to see him promoted from a major on the reserve to brigadier-general. Haig, however, was not so accommodating. After a month with the 2nd battalion Grenadier Guards at Neuve Chapelle, on New Year's Day he was appointed to command the 6th Royal Scots Fusiliers, 30 officers and 700 men in the 9th (Scottish) Division, recovering from heavy losses at Loos.

On 24 January the battalion went into the line at Ploegsteert ('Plug Street' in Tommy parlance), a village south of Messines and almost on the French frontier; Lille was only 11 miles to the southeast.[12] They would spend six days in the trenches, followed by six days back in reserve. Not once during Churchill's hundred days at the Front were the Royal Scots ordered over the top to attack the enemy facing them, although patrols went regularly into no man's land. The battalion was shelled day after day, and their commanding officer had more than one narrow escape. Churchill experienced many of the privations of trench life in winter, although no other officer arrived to take up his duties with, behind him, a limber containing a long bath and a boiler to heat the bath water. The weather was not so harsh as in the previous year, and supplies of brandy and port from London kept him internally well insulated when, at the start of February, the fields became covered with snow. To the surprise of his brother officers, on fine days their CO would set up his easel in the yard of the farm that served as headquarters and paint the scene, on one occasion remaining in a bad temper for several days 'because I couldn't get the shell hole right in the painting'. Some months earlier beyond Messines, a few miles from Ploegsteert, a Bavarian corporal had his brushes out, painting a sunken road at Croonaert, a hamlet near Wytschaete. But by the time Colonel Churchill was searching for the right shade of white to depict his shell hole, Corporal Hitler and the 16th Bavarian Reserve Infantry Regiment had left his sunken road for Fromelles, 10 miles across the French border.[13] Churchill, who spoke in the Commons while on leave in March, finally left the trenches in early May and resumed his political activities at Westminster as a critic of the government. His battalion disappeared, absorbed in a new formation ahead of the Big Push soon to be launched by General Rawlinson's Fourth Army on the Somme, 16 miles east of Amiens.

Hours of boredom interspersed with moments of terror were common to all who fought in the trenches, irrespective of their national allegiance. The Germans had a rest-house for their troops along the Yser in the woods of Praetbos, near Esen and Vladslo. It was a quiet spot that could never have attained the fame of the BEF's bustling Poperinghe. To raise spirits during spells of leave, football matches were organized for the Germans as also for the British, and there were cinema shows – Charlie Chaplin humour appealed to all nationalities. The BEF could enjoy athletic sports at times and, in the summer, opportunities to play cricket. Singsongs were popular, held sometimes in big barns and occasionally under canvas. Each of the British army divisions had a concert party. Much acting was in drag but The Fancies, a concert troupe from the 6th Division, included two camp-followers from Poperinghe nicknamed Glycerine and Vaseline: one had slipped out of Lille and counted as a refugee; the other, an innkeeper's daughter, may well have been the original 'Mademoiselle from Armentières', whose attractions were celebrated in a song popular with the Tommies. Nobody cared that neither Glycerine nor Vaseline could sing in tune, act or speak English; as one veteran recalled years later, it was enough in such a place at such a time that 'they were two buxom, bonny girls'.[14] Most of The Fancies' shows were staged in a converted hop-store at Poperinghe. Under their auspices, on Christmas Eve 1915, the Veterinary Corps presented W.S. Gilbert's *Box and Cox* there.

There are several references to The Fancies in the early numbers of *The Wipers Times*, for February and March 1916.[15] This 24th Division trench newspaper – subtitled 'Salient News' – was the inspiration of two officers of the 12th Battalion, Sherwood Foresters, Captain F. J. Roberts and Lieutenant J. H. Pearson, both of whom survived the war. Remarkably, it was first printed on a press found in ruined Ypres and restored in a casemate within Vauban's ramparts, down by the Lille Gate. The wry humour, realistic cheerfulness and gentle deflation of anything pretentious made *The Wipers Times* an instant success. Parody, of prose or verses, was a favourite vehicle of expression. Despite the shelling, the first four numbers were turned out by the improvised press regularly at fortnightly intervals. When, in April, the Sherwood Foresters moved down to Neuve Eglise, the title changed felicitously to *New Church Times*, but the character remained the same: even the gas attack at Wulverghem could be shrugged aside next day with a stoic resignation that echoes Kipling's *Barrack Room Ballads*. *The Wipers Times* rose above the hate propaganda of London dailies: the music-hall act featuring 'William O. Enzollern' and his son 'the celebrated male impersonator Little Willie' was ridiculed, not reviled. But, like *Punch, The Wipers Times* could turn from light-heartedness to moving sentimentality at the twitch of a handkerchief. On 12 February 1916 the first number records how a 'little maid of Flanders' was 'found playing' amid the ruins of the shell-shaken city 'not many days ago': the anonymous writer reflects on this, 'An omen . . . Ypres has died, but shall live again.'[16]

By then Poperinghe was already living again. The linen town that in the fourteenth century gave its name to 'poplin' was home to 11,000 people before the war. A brief incursion by Uhlans in October 1914 prompted rapid evacuation: fewer than 50 families were prepared to stay on and battle it out. The town was in effect a corridor, with the enemy less than 10 miles away on three sides. It fell within range of German artillery in the spring of 1915, and the area around the railway station suffered. The road out through

Vlamertinghe to Ypres, 7 miles to the east, gained a reputation for shelling second only to the Menin Road, but comparatively few shells hit the town centre. By late 1915 an influx of refugees from Ypres, combined with the presence of troops and all the services needed to support a modern army, lifted the population to over 200,000.

'Pop' soon became the BEF's principal rest centre in the Salient. Shops reopened and expanded; halls became 'picture palaces'; barbers were never without customers. Inevitably, Poperinghe had its brothels, like any garrison town, but they were carefully scrutinized by military police 'redcaps'. Some cafés along the main street that became Gasthuisstraat were temporarily famous: British officers raised the pre-war Hop Market Café in status to Skindles, named to recall the fashionable riverside hotel at Maidenhead. In quality of food and abundance of good champagne Skindles competed with A la Poupée, in the main square. This restaurant was generally known as Gingers, after Madame's daughter, Eliane Cossey, the very popular red-headed teenage waitress who told Edmund Blunden she was 'daily attending school at Hazebrouck': as Blunden rightly comments, 'A courageous feat'.[17] But even to live and continue working in Poperinghe needed a fatalistic iron will. Later in the war an officers-only club further up the road received a direct hit, killing the refugee family from Ypres who had opened it. The power of the blast threw the owner's decapitated body across the street.

Best respected of Poperinghe's amenities was Every-Man's Club, Talbot House, the creation of the Queensland-born Reverend, Philip Clayton. Talbot House – 'Toc H' in army signalese – was dedicated to the Bishop of Winchester's son, Lieutenant Gilbert Talbot of the Rifle Brigade, killed south of Hooge in 1915 on the day of the first flame-thrower attack. Clayton was a curate in a slum parish of Portsmouth when war broke out, but by the late autumn of 1915 he was serving as chaplain to the Buffs and the Bedfordshires of the 16th Infantry Brigade. His upbringing had allowed him to graft scholarly classicism on to egalitarian Australian common sense. His uncle Canon Horace Clayton – vicar of St Mary Magdalen, Oxford, for 40 years – possessed a formidable presence, tipping the scales at 20 stone and known from his undergraduate days as 'Tubby Clayton'. Although Philip's figure was less portly and more compact, he inherited the canon's nickname and much else, too, from Edwardian Oxford. His ideal, so he wrote on 30 November 1915, was to convert a 'jolly house' he was taking over 'to be the Pusey House of Poperinghe'.[18] Twelve days later, on the eve of his thirtieth birthday, Talbot House opened and, over Christmas, 500 men from the Rifle Brigade and 200 of the Queen's Westminster Rifles attended a celebration of the Eucharist in an improvised chapel on the first floor. In late January the attic 'Upper Room' was fitted out as a permanent chapel. Over the following two and a half years more than 25,000 soldiers made their communion at the altar.[19]

For many visitors the great attraction of Talbot House was the absence of the rigid officer/other ranks distinction of army convention. 'All Rank Abandon Ye Who Enter Here' ran a notice above the portal of the chaplain's room. Despite shells that severely damaged the building, the House survived as an oasis of peace, fostering communal bonds of faith and fellowship that the Toc-H brotherhood spread around the world between the wars.

War, however, is full of cruel ironies. Not least among them, in 1916–18, was the proximity of Talbot House to Poperinghe's Hotel de Ville, where 14 British 'Other Ranks' and one officer were shot at dawn strapped to the execution post in the town hall courtyard, barely 200 yards away.[20] The building had been requisitioned as headquarters for successive divisions serving in this sector of the line. All the condemned men were found guilty by Field General Courts Martial of desertion or alleged cowardice. Haig, as commander-in-chief confirmed their sentences. As well as the British soldiers executed, Coolie Wang Ch'un Chi'h of the 107th Chinese Labour Company was shot in the courtyard as late as May 1919, condemned for murder. Nine in ten of the death sentences imposed by courts martial and sent to Haig for confirmation were commuted to terms of penal servitude. Nevertheless, the way courts martial were conducted and uncertainty over standards applied in deciding for or against commuting the sentence led to disquiet in parliament at the time and to campaigns for posthumous justice that continued through three generations. Eventually in August 2006 the Ministry of Defence promised legislation to grant a general pardon for all who were shot at dawn, whatever the offence and irrespective of where it was committed. By then the execution post at Poperinghe had served as a macabre tourist attraction *in situ* for many years.

Belgian troops, too, found some rest in Poperinghe, though there were no specific facilities set aside for their entertainment. Most were stationed on the road to Elverdinghe, a large village in the rear of their lines along the Ypres canal. Life was extremely hard for the rank and file of the Belgians, the least publicized of any army on the Western Front. They held on desperately to the 'Trenches of Death' south of Dixmude or looked out from their positions around Pervyse and Ramscapelle across a lagoon of flooded fields, cut off from contact with their families under German occupation. By the spring of 1916 three in every four Belgian soldiers were Dutch-speaking Flemings. If Flemish by birth, they were denied all prospect of promotion unless they had mastered the French language. It is hardly surprising that their specifically Flemish local patriotism intensified, at the expense of commitment to the unitary kingdom.

In occupied Ghent, a Dutch pastor had founded a Young Flanders group as early as October 1914. Its members were ardently pro-German and published a daily newspaper, financed by the occupying authorities. Some copies of the newspaper reached unoccupied Belgium and circulated in the base camps. In February 1917 the Germans permitted the establishment of a separatist council of Flanders. The Young Flemings were too extreme in their views to appeal to the men in the trenches, but study groups of serious-minded and reasonably well-educated young men came into being, sometimes under the auspices of Catholic padres. When the war dragged on into 1917 and beyond, the Belgian military authorities came to mistrust this Flemish Front movement; as so often, political repression won over sympathizers, ultimately achieving more for Flemish particularism than any German-sponsored organization.[21]

There was no organized Resistance movement in the Belgian provinces under German occupation, as across Nazi Europe 25 years later. Some 30,000 young men succeeded in evading the guards and made their way to England for eventual enlistment in their national army. In Brussels, Belgian bankers established a National Committee for Help and Relief that, with American support, eased the burdens imposed by the British blockade. With the knowledge of the occupying authorities, loose links were maintained with the government in exile, who authorized the civil servants to fulfil their customary duties. Interference by the Germans with the traditional Belgian way of life was greeted with sullen, passive non-compliance. Burgomaster Max in Brussels and Cardinal Mercier, Archbishop of Malines, encouraged disciplined protest, notably on 21 July 1916 over attempts to ban the celebration of the National Day and in the subsequent successful campaign to halt deportation of workers to German factories and mines. Newspaper editors chose voluntary closure rather than accept supervision by the authorities. For four years a mood of resigned endurance prevailed throughout the occupied provinces.[22]

King Albert remained fully aware of his sovereign responsibility towards all his subjects, on either side of the lines of battle. In conversation with his allies, he repeatedly opposed any step-by-step invasion of Belgium. To attempt to roll back the Germans from the coast to the Rhine would, he argued, devastate his kingdom. As a soldier, he thought that the enemy would have little difficulty in checking an advance of this character. Visits in early 1916 by Joffre (who was accompanied by his chief of operations, Colonel Gamelin) and by Haig and Lord Curzon failed to make Albert change his mind. The right place to mount an attack was up the Meuse valley, nearer the German homeland, not across the Yser and through the forest of Houthulst, he told his two British visitors. And in the closing weeks of the year he was still pressing Colonel Maglinse, Gamelin's successor, that GQG must concentrate further to the east in order 'to carry the war into enemy territory'.[23]

The British government treated Albert with great respect, particularly Curzon, who was lord privy seal in the Asquith coalition. He appreciated the king's statesmanship and in particular the skill with which he held in check the annexationist ambitions of his ministers at Sainte-Adresse, the *plage* beneath the cliffs of Le Havre where the government survived the war in comfortable exile.[24] The Germans used Count Toerring-Jettenbach, husband of Queen Elisabeth's favourite sister, Sophie, to establish contact with Albert in the hope of inducing the Belgians to conclude a separate peace. In November 1915 and January and February 1916 there were several meetings in Zürich between Toerring and Emile

Waxweiler, an eminent sociologist who was a close confidant of the king. It is not clear how much Curzon knew of these meetings when he met Albert at La Panne in February but, with character-istic diplomatic finesse, he gave an oblique warning against uni-lateral action while emphasizing that the king 'enjoyed the total confidence' of the British government. 'If you have an idea, an opinion to give we would be very happy to hear it,' Curzon told Albert.[25] Nothing came of the Toerring–Waxweiller talks. The German proposals were inept: a suggestion by the king's brother-in-law that Albert might voluntarily surrender his sword and agree to be treated as a prisoner-of-war caused indignant amusement at La Panne; even the solemn sociologist was seen to smile. But with tacit approval from London, the tenuous link with non-Hohen-zollern Germany was not irremediably cut. Albert never ruled out the possibility of having to seek a negotiated peace.

Franco-Belgian relations were frequently strained, and a short visit to La Panne made by an ill-tempered President Poincaré and his querulous wife soon after Curzon did not ease old tensions. The French continued to resent the Belgian king's insistence on independence of command and were suspicious of the royal connections both with England and with the lesser German dynasties. While Albert found it easier to work with Haig than with his predecessor, he grew impatient with Joffre, angered by the Frenchman's feigned optimism, the easy assump-tion that, despite heavy losses at Verdun, the coming offensive would bring victory by October. Foch seemed to talk more sense in a visit to La Panne on 11 May: he thought an end to the war possible in the autumn of 1917. Albert questioned the readiness of the allied armies to launch the offensive in the coming four weeks, as Joffre proposed. Ominously, Foch shrugged his shoulders.[26]

As British regiments moved down from Flanders for the Big Push on the Somme other senior figures in Paris and London were beginning to doubt the wisdom of Joffre's plans. Georges Clem-enceau, chairman of the Senate Military Committee, visited Haig on 4 May to ask him to 'exercise a restraining hand' on Joffre after the terrible casualties suffered at Verdun: a second failure might pave the way for a government in Paris that favoured peace at any

price. A fortnight later Kitchener warned Asquith's War Committee that the Germans were close to breaking the French line at
Verdun and heading straight 'on to Paris'. In the Commons,
Churchill reminded the House that every 24 hours 'nearly a
thousand men – Englishmen, Britishers, men of our race – are
knocked into bundles of bloody rags', committed to 'futile offensives'. Maurice Hankey, writing in his diary two days before
Clemenceau's visit to Haig, noted that 'the Army want a regular
orgy of slaughter this summer and . . . plan . . . a great offensive . . .
which no member of the Cabinet and none of the regimental
soldiers who will have to carry it out believe in.' Trench storming,
whether in Flanders or Picardy, could never bring decisive victory.
It would be better, Hankey believed, to wait until the new secret
weapon, the 'caterpillar' or 'tank', was available, ready to break
through the barbed wire and restore mobility to the Western
Front.[27]

Haig wavered: he too wanted to see the caterpillars in action. He
met Joffre again on 26 May, urging postponement of the Big Push
until the middle of August. In his diary he wrote, 'The moment I
mentioned 15 August Joffre at once got very excited and shouted
that, "the French army would cease to exist if we did nothing till
then".' To calm down 'the old man', Haig settled for 1 July 'or
thereabouts'.[28]

The War Committee had still not given its final backing to the
offensive when on 5 June the secretary of state for war was
drowned: the cruiser HMS *Hampshire* struck a mine off the
Orkneys as she bore him on a mission to Russia. The news of
Kitchener's death, broken only five days after the first disturbing
reports of the naval battle of Jutland, caused dismay across Britain.
In London, 'groups formed round each purchaser of a paper, and
as the news sank in faces visibly paled and voices sank to a pained
hush'. Within the government, Kitchener's standing had dimin-
ished but, though he never expressed himself with clarity, no
other cabinet minister possessed such insight into the French
military mind. Asquith himself discharged Kitchener's duties as
secretary of state until the appointment of Lloyd George on 6 July.
But the greatest offensive as yet undertaken by any British army
was about to be launched at a time when there was no war
minister in office.[29]

Along 24 miles of Front – 16 miles held by British troops, 8 miles by French – the allies were ready to strike at dawn on 1 July. Confusion over objectives before 'Z-Day' for Third Ypres continued after the battle began.[30] Haig, as commander-in-chief, wanted Rawlinson's Fourth Army to break through the centre; Gough's Fifth Army would then come forward from reserve, with cavalry, and roll over shattered German defences to take the town of Bapaume, as the preliminary to a major drive north-eastwards. Rawlinson was more cautious, he favoured a methodical trench-by-trench advance, one bite at a time. It was agreed that General Allenby's Third Army was to mount a feint attack to the north of Fourth Army, but there would be no long bombardment in this northern sector, as it was hoped the diversion would take the Germans by surprise, forcing them to divert troops away from the principal line of attack. In the event, Allenby's 46th and 56th Divisions suffered heavy casualties, many caused by German booby traps left in apparently empty trenches.

There was certainly no element of surprise in the main attack: over the preceding seven days 1,700,000 shells rained down on the German lines. Of the men who went over the top that Saturday, 68,000 had fought in the Salient or elsewhere in France, but some 90,000 were about to see action for the first time; most were the volunteers of Kitchener's New Army who responded to his recruiting call in the first months of the war. Now they carried, literally, a great burden. No infantry in any battle had ever been loaded with such heavy equipment. It was basically 30 lb, but was made heavier by the issue of picks or shovels strapped to the back of half the attackers, while others carried trench supports and even sledge-hammers. All this weight – borne under the rising sun of a July morning – forced the infantry to walk into action; they could not move quickly, nor throw themselves on the ground to avoid shell blast and hope to get up again and press forward.

As they waited to clamber out of the trenches, the crescendo of explosions reached 3,360 shells a minute along little more than 20 miles of Front. Some 200 miles away, the barrage could be heard by Londoners walking in Knighton Woods, at the southern tip of Epping Forest, and on Hampstead Heath, the rolling thunder breaking the tranquillity of a summer morning for more than half an hour. The climax came with the explosion of a huge mine in front of the village of Beaumont-Hamel at 7.20 a.m. Sixteen more mines were blown under German strong points in the following 10 minutes. At 7.30 a.m. the infantry went slowly into battle.

It was a day without precedent in British history. Before nightfall the attacking army lost 19,240 officers and men killed, with 2542 missing and 36,088 gravely wounded. Thirty-two battalions suffered more than 500 casualties during the day. The one battalion from an overseas dominion to go into action that morning – the 1st Newfoundland Regiment – was reduced from 810 officers and men to 68. Every officer in the battalion was killed or wounded within an hour and a half of going forward from the trenches. In all, German machine-gunners and field artillery killed 310 Newfoundlanders that day. Northern Ireland, like Newfoundland, suffered grievously: more than a quarter of the British dead that Saturday were Ulstermen.

The 'battle of the Somme' – in reality 12 interlocked battles – would continue for another 141 days. Men from Australia, Canada, New Zealand and South Africans were thrown into the attack, as also were battalions from every infantry regiment in the British army. The first 18 tanks, the 'caterpillars' mentioned earlier by Hankey and Haig, went into action on 15 September, 'prematurely', thought Churchill at the time. Mechanical problems led to breakdowns. Four tanks that crossed the enemy trenches caused havoc, enabling the infantry they supported to advance a mile. Haig was impressed and asked for 1,000 tanks to be made swiftly; they were to be modified so as to counter the mechanical problems and dispatched urgently. But when the first improved version joined the attack in November, the weather had broken, and the battlefield was deep in mud. The tanks' tracks and steering tails were soon clogged in the mire, unable to move forward or back. Their two 6-pounder naval guns made the tank a potentially formidable weapon, as Haig recognized, but the significance of the failure in the mud seems to have escaped him. On the night of 17–18 November the first snowfall of the winter effectively brought the battle to an end. By then 95,675 British and Empire troops had perished in the 'orgy of slaughter', together with 50,729 Frenchmen in the 11 divisions Joffre had spared from the struggle at Verdun. More than 170,000 Germans were killed in 21 weeks of fighting. The strategic gains were slight: the Germans were expelled from a strip of devastated countryside some 30 miles wide and, at one point, 7 miles deep: no major town fell and the only railway cut was the single-line track from Albert to Miraumont and Arras. In the end the Somme was an allied victory but one far from decisive and agonizingly slow to accomplish. On the last full day of battle the 51st Highland Division took the small town of Beaumont-Hamel, an objective the Fourth Army's Lancastrian and Yorkshire 'pals battalions' strove in vain to reach on the first day.

'In spite of the slaughter, the British army gained experience rather than discouragement,' Charles Cruttwell wrote in 1934, a point assessed in detail by Paddy Griffith 60 years later. 'Experience' stressed the need for closer collaboration and speedier communication between the Royal Flying Corps and the army staffs on the ground. Artillery tactics required modification, with more sophistication shown in the choice of targets. Haphazard shelling of forward lines should give way to the bombardment of support positions so as to isolate men in the trenches from reserves and supplies; there was a need to perfect the 'creeping barrage', keeping falling shells ahead of the advancing infantry while at the same time avoiding tragic mistakes that caused 'death by friendly fire'. Some tactical errors of the Somme were avoided on the Salient in the following year. Others were ignored or rendered impossible to attain by the nature of the terrain or the treacherous weather.

Every tactical success gained by the Germans on the Western Front in 1914–15 sprang in origin from surprise. After the Somme, this need for deception was recognized by British planners: it was practised by Plumer at Messines in early June and, on a grand scale, by the former Third Army commander, Allenby, in Palestine in September 1918. Haig, however, was slow to acknowledge the 'give-away' nature of long preliminary bombardments: he ordered the guns to open up 10 days before the scheduled Z-Day, an advance warning made even clearer to the enemy by a further six-day delay caused by the weather.[31] Haig had the misfortune to be a general on whom the sun rarely shone.

On 20 November, the day after the final assault on the Somme, the War Committee met in London to assess the needs of the Western Front now that the campaign was over. Before it was a paper from the Admiralty emphasizing that the Royal Navy lacked the destroyers and smaller ships needed for counter-submarine protection and pressing for land operations to deprive the Germans of their U-boat bases in Belgium. The minutes recorded, 'There is no operation of war to which the War Committee would attach greater importance than the successful occupation or at least the deprivation to the enemy of Ostend and especially Zeebrugge.'[32] To Haig's satisfaction 'the Belgian option' was again on the planners' table.

11

1917: 'THE VILLAGE HAS COMPLETELY DISAPPEARED'

Almost a million men, allied and German, perished on the Somme and at Verdun in 1916: Sir Martin Gilbert calculates that almost five men died for every minute the great battles continued.[1] Such heavy losses brought major military and political changes of leadership. Falkenhayn had already gone, discredited by his inability to break French resistance at Verdun, although he finally lost support from Kaiser Wilhelm over a far lesser issue, his failure to foresee the imminent adhesion of Romania to the allied cause. On 28 August, Hindenburg was appointed chief of the German general staff, with Ludendorff at his side as 'first quartermaster-general'. The French prime minister, Aristide Briand, waited until the two campaigns were over before unseating Papa Joffre at Chantilly on 12 December. He was made a marshal of France, the first baton bestowed by any French Republic – but with that honour came enforced retirement. General Lyautey became minister of war, and the energetic 58-year-old General Robert Nivelle, like Napoleon an artilleryman, was appointed to succeed Joffre as commander-in-chief.[2] During the last phase of Verdun, Nivelle had devised ways of combining infantry and artillery tactics more effectively than any previous general in the war. His fluency in English (his mother's native tongue) helped ensure that he 'made a very favourable impression' at Westminster, as Hankey observed.[3]

In Britain the principal change was political. An alliance of Unionists and radical Liberals backed Lloyd George as potentially a more dynamic war leader and on 7 December forced Asquith to resign after eight years in office. Lloyd George, the first Welshman to be prime minister, revolutionized the structure and character of government. He created a War Cabinet of five (himself, the Unionists' Bonar Law, Curzon, the imperial statesman Lord Milner and Labour's Arthur Henderson) with Maurice Hankey as secretary. The War Cabinet members held no departmental responsibilities; but both Arthur Balfour, who succeeded Grey as foreign secretary, and Lord Derby, the new war secretary, might attend cabinet meetings, if required. Derby was always sympathetic to the needs of the BEF and rarely took issue with the CIGS (Robertson) or with the commander-in-chief. Haig told his wife he was 'personally very sorry for poor old Squiff', as he 'seems to have had more capacity and more brain power than any of the others', but, he added, 'However, I expect less talk and more action is needed now.'[4] On Lloyd George's qualities of leadership he reserved judgement. They had met on several occasions, most recently on 25 November, and he was already uneasy over the new prime minister's predilection for 'sideshows', particularly in Italy and the Balkans. Lloyd George came into office determined to avoid further 'orgies of slaughter' like Loos and the Somme. Soon both Haig and the CIGS were viewing his forays into grand strategy with deep mistrust.

By mid-December 1916, Haig had been in command for 12 months and, as if to assure him of the government's confidence in his skills, the king appointed him a field marshal on the last day of the year. The BEF had expanded rapidly during 1916 and now comprised almost 1,600,000 men, including 106,000 Canadians and Newfoundlanders and 125,000 Australians and New Zealanders. No British commander had ever led so large an army in the field. Even so, the BEF remained far smaller than the French armies on the Western Front, shaken though they were by the demoralizing tragedy of Verdun.

Lloyd George wanted a morale-boosting allied victory achieved with the fewest possible casualties to British troops. He was prepared to seek it elsewhere than Flanders and France, though never doubting that, as he said, for Britain 'the West was the principal theatre of war'. Germany must be weakened by 'knocking away the props', he believed, by striking at her Austro-Hungarian, Ottoman and Bulgarian allies. He had hopes of the combined French, Serbian, Greek, British and Russian force with a foothold in the Balkans at Salonika, and he concurred in plans to go over to the offensive beyond the Suez Canal and carry the war against Turkey into Palestine and Syria. In the hope of galvanizing the Russians, he revived the idea of a mission to Petrograd, abandoned after Kitchener's death. Plans were perfected for Milner to sail for Archangel at the end of January 1917, with General Sir Henry Wilson as spokesman for the army. There was, however, little that could be done in Petrograd, and the Milner–Wilson mission achieved nothing. Both men returned home anticipating radical upheaval in Russia, but they failed to realize a revolution was imminent.

First, however, Lloyd George turned to Italy. On 2–3 January 1917 he travelled to Rome for a top-level conference, accompanied by Milner, Hankey and the CIGS. The Rome conference was also attended by Briand and Lyautey, and by the British and French commanding generals in Salonika as well as by Italy's military and political leaders. Again, little was achieved. Lloyd George was left with hopes of an effective advance into central Europe from Salonika in the spring, but he was deeply disappointed with General Cadorna, chief of staff of the Italian army, who did not think it possible to contemplate the capture of Trieste without assurance of reinforcement by both troops and heavy artillery from the Western Front.[5]

Lloyd George did not abandon his eventual hopes for the Italian Front but, in his frustration, he began to look with increasing favour at GQG's proposals for the spring. Nivelle wished the BEF to make a feint attack in the north, while 27 French divisions would be concentrated for a surprise assault on the German positions beyond the Aisne. By employing the tactics perfected in the last stage of Verdun, Nivelle claimed his army would 'rupture' the German line within 48 hours.[6]

Nivelle's plan ran counter to Haig's hopes for the coming year. Only a week before his fall from power Joffre had approved a combined operation, under British command, for the BEF, the French, the Belgians and the Royal Navy to 'capture the Belgian coast . . . This is practically the scheme at which I have aimed for the past twelve months,' a contented Haig wrote in his diary on 10 December.[7] Ten days later, however, Nivelle visited Haig and explained to him that he could not accept Joffre's final plan.

Fortunately the two commanders-in-chief had an amicable meeting and, over the following four weeks, agreed that the BEF would launch an offensive to absorb the German reserves at least a week before Nivelle struck on the Aisne. Haig found some comfort in the thought that, should Nivelle's master-stroke fail, he could count on French backing for operations in Flanders later in the year.[8] Meanwhile, planning continued on the proposed landing on the Belgian coast and its relationship to a general advance from Ypres on Roulers.[9]

During the next fortnight relations between Haig and Nivelle deteriorated. Haig argued that the over-stretched French railway system would not allow him to move his troops into the areas assigned to them so soon as 1 April, the day Nivelle required the BEF to open the diversionary offensive. Moreover, while he agreed with Nivelle's strategic ideas, he was unhappy at various tactical proposals, including a demand for a British assault attack on Vimy Ridge. Nivelle, for his part, thought Haig was prevaricating, and Lloyd George agreed with him. On 26 February, Haig was invited to meet Lloyd George and the CIGS at a conference in Calais where, he was informed, the logistical problems would be discussed with Nivelle, Briand and Lyautey. The transport difficulties were settled speedily, but Lloyd George then opened a general discussion on future policy. He stressed the need for a unified command and asked the French to put on paper their proposals for achieving that objective. Haig and Robertson were furious that so fundamental an issue should have been raised without prior consultation; they were far from mollified by assurances from the prime minister that 'the War Cabinet had decided last week' the British army must 'be placed under the French C-in-C's orders'. The generals complained that a unified command would mean the virtual absorption of the BEF in the French army. Haig subsequently sent a letter to King George V hinting he would resign rather than allow British troops to serve under French command. The king, who backed Haig up to the hilt, became in turn very angry when he realized his prime minister deliberately delayed sending him the minutes of the War Cabinet meeting at which the question of unified command was discussed. Moreover, the three Unionists in the War Cabinet considered Lloyd George was misrepresenting their views. The wrangle dragged on for several days, at one point the prime minister warning the king he might have to call for the dissolution of parliament and a general election to seek public backing for his conduct of the war. Eventually a face-saving compromise, devised by Hankey, limited Haig's subordination to Nivelle to the end of the offensive and gave him a right of appeal to the War Cabinet if he considered his orders endangered the BEF or the chances of victory.[10]

Milner and Derby believed the prime minister was plotting the downfall of both Haig and Robertson. On 7 March, Nivelle did indeed ask Lloyd George to replace Haig with the more compliant commander of the Fifth Army, Sir Hubert Gough.[11] Lloyd George hesitated, but in 1917 there still remained limits to the willingness of a British prime minister to accommodate the wishes of an allied partner in war, and no change was made. Haig co-operated loyally with Nivelle, although – like King Albert before him – he grumbled from time to time at the patronizing arrogance shown by some less senior French staff officers. On 14 March it was finally agreed that the British would 'continue to make all preparations' for an attack at the beginning of April in the Arras area, though Haig was still thinking primarily of reigniting the war in Flanders at the first opportunity.

Unfortunately the rift with Lloyd George broadened rather than narrowed as Nivelle's offensive drew closer. One of Nivelle's requests at Calais was for General Wilson to be appointed head of the British Mission at his headquarters in Beauvais. Over the following months the arch-intriguer was accepted by Lloyd George as his unofficial military adviser, groomed to succeed Robertson as CIGS when he was sure his position as head of government was secure to withstand any challenge from the Unionists or the Asquithian wing of his own party. These political activities exasperated Haig, but it was the prime minister's devious tactics at the Calais conference that rankled. In mid-July, Haig let Derby see how deeply he resented the way in which (as he saw it) 'our Government' provided 'almost unthinking support' to 'the Frenchman last January' while giving only grudging and belated backing to the plans for Third Ypres.[12]

The men in the trenches during the first quarter of 1917 knew nothing of these rivalries and disputes. Once again the weather was grim. An editorial in *The B.E.F. Times* (ex-*Wipers Times*) for 5 March claimed sardonically that a medical officer 'has noticed on several occasions lately the development of web-feet in some of his clientéle'. But, as in the first winter of war, it was the intense cold that caused most misery. Front-line troops were issued with woollen scarves and gauntlets, and with sheepskin coats to wear over their greatcoats. When the CO of the 1st battalion HAC was killed in February, the ground was frozen too hard for a grave to be dug. The subsequent thaw created the conditions so often associated with Flanders during 1917 – 'slimy yellowish-brown mud', as Gunner Philip Sylvester later recalled. 'The horses were up to their bellies in mud', Sylvester added. 'We had to shoot quite a number' who had 'sunk in over their fetlocks'.[13]

Further south, despite snow and solid ice covering the potholes of earlier shelling, the divisions still serving on the Somme kept the Germans on their mettle. Probing attacks were made in the second week of January and again in the third week of February. Then, unexpectedly, in mid-March the troops found relief from winter's grip, for the Germans suddenly abandoned the positions so heavily contested in the previous summer. On 16 March they began a three-day phased withdrawal to the *Siegfried-Stellung*, soon known to the allies as the Hindenburg Line. On paper they retreated some 20 miles along a front 65 miles long, from Arras down to St Quentin, and newspapers in London and Paris were jubilant. Yet, in reality, the Germans conceded little. Only two major towns were evacuated, Noyon and Peronne; mined streets, poisoned water wells, charred ruins of houses, barren fields and ruined railway tracks greeted the British and French as their troops filled the void. The operation was in fact a masterly strategic concept, generally attributed to Ludendorff, the first quartermaster-general. The Stellung, which had taken four months to build, comprised rectangular concrete blockhouses ('pillboxes') reinforced with steel, anti-tank ditches and barbed-wire barricades as well as deep zigzag trenches. All these defences were covered from the rear by two lines of artillery

The decision that Germany should stand on the defensive in the West during 1917 had been finally agreed at a conference of senior commanders convened at Cambrai on 15 January. It rested on three basic assumptions: the conviction that Russia was a spent force and close to collapse; the ability of the German Navy 'to bring England to her knees' by a ruthless U-boat campaign; the near certainty that Britain and France would take the initiative in Flanders and Picardy. If the allies threw raw divisions against hardened defenders in old bunkers, Germany could gain a land victory on the cheap. Details of the retirement were settled by General Kuhl, chief of staff to Crown Prince Rupprecht's Army Group, and Ludendorff warmly backed his proposals, convinced that Rupprecht could handle operations in Flanders throughout the year. The Kuhl–Ludendorff Plan – Operation Alberich – shortened by 30 miles the defensive line for which OHL had to find men and guns. Alberich freed 13 divisions and 50 batteries of heavy artillery, giving Rupprecht a strategic reserve to be employed in any sector threatened by a British or French offensive.[14]

There was as yet no comparable systematic line of defence within the Salient. The Germans had, however, erected between 1,500 and 2,000 pillboxes west of Ypres during 1916 and the early months of the following year. Many could be built speedily, by using prefabricated concrete blocks.[15] These pillboxes gave Rupprecht a defence in depth that had been missing during the fiercest fighting of First and Second Ypres. After Passchendaele, the original Hindenburg Line was extended northwards into Flanders and eastwards across Champagne, thus ensuring that by early 1918 a defensive shield covered 300 miles of German positions across the Western Front.

At the Cambrai staff conference, General Kuhl singled out Arras as the likely pivot of any Anglo-French offensive. The Germans were, therefore, not surprised when, amid sleet or heavy rain showers, ten British and four Canadian divisions launched attacks outside Arras on 9 April, Easter Monday. But the concentrated fire-power was far greater than they had anticipated: nearly 3,000 guns and 48 tanks supported the advancing troops. Allenby's Third Army and Horne's First Army made sensational gains on the first day. The Germans were pushed back at some points as far as 3 miles before nightfall and 9,000 prisoners taken for relatively few casualties, except at Vimy Ridge. The glorious achievement of the day was the rapidity with which the four Canadian divisions, fighting together for the first time, scaled and held 2 miles of German defences along Vimy Ridge, although at a cost of 3,598 lives. To many Canadians in the years ahead, Vimy Ridge was seen as the womb of the Dominion's nationhood.[16]

The triumphs of that first day at Arras could not be maintained. As in 1914–15 strict orders to halt for at least two hours of reassessment after gaining the first objective, inhibited initiative and enabled the Germans to rush the first reserves forward. Resistance stiffened on Tuesday, and by Wednesday (11 April) the impetus of the attack was irredeemably blunted. That night Australian veterans of the Somme made effective use of tanks to break entanglements of wire at Bullecourt, south of Arras. It was the last success of the battle and only temporary, for German reserves bore down on the Australian flanks, taking hundreds of prisoners. On Wednesday and Thursday battle casualties reached Somme proportions, with machine-guns and well-sited artillery again taking a heavy toll, particularly among the Australians. Although the fighting around Arras continued for six more weeks, Haig called a halt to the original attack on Sunday, 15 April. In six days the First and Third Armies suffered over 40,000 casualties in what had been intended as a strategic diversion.[17]

Some 60 miles south of Arras, Nivelle's offensive – known as the second battle of the Aisne – opened, belatedly, at dawn on 16 April. It proved a disaster. Despite Nivelle's repeated emphasis on the virtues of surprise, the Germans knew what to expect and where the blow would fall. Careless talk in London and Paris alerted them in the first instance; the discovery of detailed orders on captured officers in early March and again on 6 April confirmed all they suspected. The initial 'surprise' assault was heralded by heavy bombardment and launched by shivering Senegalese troops in heavy snow showers. Twenty-one German front-line divisions were ready to meet the challenge, with another 15 divisions poised to counter-attack. In vain General Mangin, commanding the French Sixth Army, poured battalion after battalion of supporting troops into the attack, including veterans of the crack XX Corps. In five days the French advanced 4 miles along 16 miles of Front, but no dent was made in the German defensive wall.[18]

French morale, high in expectation at Easter, plummeted rapidly. The 2nd battalion of the 18th Infantry Regiment, badly mauled on the first morning, was promised rest and recuperation. Instead, on 29 April the battalion was ordered back into the line.

The men refused to go. Their action triggered a series of bloodless mutinies that spread rapidly through Nivelle's disillusioned army. Within a month 54 divisions holding the line within 100 miles of Paris made it clear that they would not take part in further attacks.[19] Haig knew nothing of this widespread disaffection until 7 June. Fortunately, German intelligence, too, remained in the dark.

Nivelle, totally discredited, was dismissed as commander-in-chief on 15 May and sent to North Africa. General Pétain, saviour of Verdun, became chief of the general staff on 2 May and a fortnight later succeeded Nivelle; Foch took Pétain's place as chief of the general staff. The first task of the Pétain–Foch partnership was to restore discipline and fighting spirit in the army. Although Pétain was prepared to give limited support to his partners and encourage local attacks limited to specific objectives, the French would not take the offensive until July 1918, after Foch was appointed allied generalissimo. Thus throughout the second half of the year 1917 France and Germany both stood on the defensive in the West. The initiative lay with the BEF.

After Arras and the Aisne, Haig was more than ever convinced of the need to concentrate on Flanders. Already, early in April, he had chosen Sir Hubert Gough of the Fifth Army to command the vital northern sector of his projected offensive, including the landing operations to which Admiral Bacon had given great attention in the previous year. Gough had long basked in Haig's favour; he was a vigorous cavalry officer, at 47 considerably younger than most British generals. On 7 May, Haig summoned his five army commanders (Horne, Plumer, Allenby, Rawlinson and Gough) to a conference at Doullens where he expounded his plans for the summer: Plumer's Second Army would begin operations by taking the Messines–Wytschaete ridge at the south of the Salient, thereby protecting the right flank of the main advance, designed to clear the Belgian coast, with a line from Zeebrugge to Courtrai as the ultimate objective. As he was uncertain when units committed to the attack on Arras would return northwards, Haig assigned no specific date to this second phase of the battle; it would follow 'some weeks later'.[20] Not all the generals agreed with their commander-in-chief. Allenby's experience with tanks on the predominantly chalky soil around Vimy made him question their

employment in the water-logged Flanders plain. After the conference Haig decided to entrust the experienced Rawlinson rather
than the impetuous Gough with co-ordinating the amphibious
operation with Admiral Bacon. Detailed plans were completed by
early June. Rawlinson's Fourth Army would concentrate on the
coast, around Nieuport. His 1st Division – some 13,750 officers
and men – would make the landing on the beaches of Middelkerke.

Plumer planned the assault on Messines with meticulous attention to detail; Haig even thought him excessively cautious. He was
assigned II Anzac Corps (the New Zealand Division and 3rd
Australian), 16 (Irish) Division and 36 (Ulster) Division, and the
British 19, 23, 25, 41 and 47 Divisions. For over a year British and
Australian sappers had been digging 22 tunnels under German
strong points in a wide arc south of Ypres. One tunnel was
discovered by the enemy and blocked, but in the remainder nearly
500 tons of ammonal explosive were planted. For 17 days the
heavy guns maintained a constant bombardment of enemy positions in the front line and back towards Warneton. The Germans
never doubted that a Big Push was on hand, but they awaited the
attack with confidence, sure that the loose chain of blockhouses
and the tangled barbed-wire obstacles would repel the coming
assault as effectively as they had other attacks over the last two years.

The early hours of Tuesday, 7 June, were fine and clear. A
'wonderful summer night' with a full moon, a parish priest across
the valley from Wytschaete noted. Suddenly at 3.10 in the morning
a 'true volcano' of a 'firework . . . spewed fire' across the sky: 19 of
the 21 mines were exploded simultaneously. The subsequent shock
wave was felt as a violent tremor in Lille and the protracted rumble
heard in Westminster. On Hill 60 the crater was estimated at being
100 yards across and 45 feet deep, but the largest of all craters was at
Spanbroekmolen, halfway between Messines and Wytschaete, and
now a Pool of Peace; it is some 250 yards wide and 40 feet deep.
On that morning, Plumer's engineers had achieved the mightiest
man-made explosion on record at the time. It was not surpassed
until the testing of the atomic bomb 28 years later.

The infantry went forward while the earth was still shaking, with
tanks in support and under the thunderous roar of 2,230 guns and
howitzers firing high-explosive or gas shells. For the first time in

battle there was close methodically planned collaboration between the RFC and the troops, who had been issued with coloured identification drawings of 'friendly' planes and with flares to allow spotters to pinpoint their progress.[21] The New Zealanders took Messines village and Wytschaete fell to the Irish and Ulster Divisions, co-operating amicably despite the anguish caused in the previous year by the bloodshed of the Easter Rising. The Anzacs moved forward, to find craters and trenches filled with German dead; only a few isolated machine-gun nests survived, though from them would come deadly and unexpected bursts of fire until they were silenced by a trench mortar or hand grenades. During the day 7,000 prisoners were taken. Haig would have liked Plumer to press ahead and reach the Gheluvert plateau while the enemy was still reeling. Wisely, however, the Second Army commander would not endanger his gains by committing over-exuberant but tired troops to counter-attacks from German re-serves who had been spared the morning's bombardment. Haig was content: 'The operations today are probably the most successful I have yet undertaken,' he noted in his diary, after an afternoon drive of 50 miles from his chateau near Montreuil down to Second Army headquarters at Cassel. The commander-in-chief almost reached the front line on this his 'most successful' day; the nearest mine crater was little more than a dozen miles away. Next morning, General Harrington, Plumer's chief of staff, inspected the damage caused by the great explosion. He entered one concrete dug-out and 'found four German officers, sitting at a table – all dead, killed by the shock'. There was not a mark on any of them. 'They might have been playing bridge,' he observes.[22]

Improbably, amid all the upheaval of war, some Flemish families still sought to follow their normal way of life. The battle was fought on Corpus Christi Day and in a village church northwest of Wytschaete, Fr van Walleghem dutifully celebrated early Mass for 14 devout parishioners at an altar that 'trembled continuously'. Some parishioners returned later in the day for Evensong, with the guns at Dickebusch and Mount Kemmel continuing to pound the enemy. 'After Evensong we go up the Rodeberg for a view of the battlefield,' Fr van Walleghem recalled. 'The whole of Wytschaete is naked earth – the village has completely disappeared.'[23]

*   *   *

Seven weeks of fine summer days followed Plumer's victory, better campaigning weather than at any time in First or Second Ypres, but the BEF remained waiting in the trenches. The long delay in following up Messines has provoked the most serious sustained criticism of Haig's record as a general.[24] It gave the Germans an opportunity to reinforce Crown Prince Rupprecht's Army Group with fresh troops in mid-June, while at the same time General von Lossberg, the mastermind of fortification, became chief of staff of the Fourth Army, immediately ordering a strengthening of the defences along the crucial lines in the Gheluvert plateau. The Germans were also able to improvise an attack on Nieuport on 10 July, improving their positions at the mouth of the Yser. No great offensive in any war was ever so well advertised in advance to the enemy as Third Ypres.

The delay, however, did not spring entirely from a failure in command. Haig was under constant pressure from London, where Lloyd George swung back to the Italian option and wished to transfer heavy guns and material from the Western Front to Lombardy–Venetia. Even the CIGS privately urged Haig 'to support Italy with guns' when they met on 7 June, although he changed his mind five days later on hearing that Lloyd George was considering sending as many as 12 divisions and 300 heavy guns to the Italian Front.[25]

For over a week the commander-in-chief was in England arguing his case and attending meetings of the War Cabinet. After hearing Admiral Jellicoe's concern at the growing threat from U-boats, Haig was more than ever convinced of the need to clear the enemy from the Belgian coast and deprive the German navy of Zeebrugge and Ostend. But GQG was sceptical over the prospects for an amphibious operation. Pétain was personally sympathetic, and he assured Haig he was prepared for General Anthoine's First Army to participate in the proposed Flanders offensive. Foch, on the other hand, was far from sympathetic: he had told General Wilson on 2 June that he thought Haig's plan 'futile, fantastic and dangerous', a 'duck's march through the inundations to Ostend and Zeebrugge' and he saw no reason to change his mind.[26] The first battalions of Anthoine's troops relieved tired Belgians along 4 miles beside the Yser on 26 June, but it was clear to Haig that they would need careful training if they were to take part effectively in the coming offensive. Here lay yet another reason for delay.

The fine weather and good clear skies over England posed a further problem. On the morning of Wednesday, 13 June, 17 biplane twin-engine Gotha bombers took off from Gontrode and St Denis–Westrem airfields on the outskirts of Ghent and, unmolested, flew across the North Sea to bomb London in broad daylight. In all, 162 people were killed in the raid, among them 15 children at an infant school in the East End. Not a single German plane was destroyed. There was a public outcry and to protect London from further attacks two squadrons of RFC Sopwith Pups were withdrawn from the battle zone. Major-General Hugh Trenchard, the commander of the seven RFC Wings in France, reluctantly reassigned 66 Squadron to Calais and 56 Squadron to Kent, reducing the RFC's strength in a vital sector of the Front. A fortnight later 56 Squadron returned to Flanders, only for the Gothas to make a second raid on the following day. Once again Trenchard was deprived of some of his best pilots and planes, with 46 Squadron virtually inactive in England from 10 July to 30 August. Nevertheless on the eve of Third Ypres, the RFC and RNAS had 858 serviceable aircraft to employ on bombing raids, photographic reconnaissance, artillery spotting and meeting the challenge of the élite Richthofen 'Flying Circus', based on Marckebeeke, north of Courtrai. As a prologue to the coming drama, a major battle in the skies was fought out for over an hour on 27 July, when 59 RFC fighters were scrambled to attack 20 Albatros reconnaissance planes. Other German and British squadrons joined the fray, as well as some French aircraft. Two British planes were lost but nine Albatros destroyed. To the allied troops watching from the lines below, this success was heartening. On both sides, there was growing appreciation of the significance of air power in conjunction with land operations.[27]

As summer began to fade away, servicemen on leave and war-weary Londoners briefly enjoyed a tantalizing glance into a calmer future. At Lord's cricket ground on 14 July an English Army XI defeated an Australian Army XI in a 'sedate' match played 'in bright sunshine' on behalf of 'St Dunstan's Hostel for blinded soldiers and sailors', with Corporal Makepeace appropriately chosen to open for England. Batting honours were shared between Captain P. F. Warner of Middlesex and Corporal Tyldesley of Lancashire, but at the end of the day the 'not-out' batsman was Kent's Sergeant

Colin Blythe, a left-arm spin bowler who defied epilepsy to play in 19 Tests. Blythe went back to France where his unit, the Kent Fortress Engineers, was attached to the King's Own Yorkshire Light Infantry. Four months later 'the greatest Kent bowler of modern days' met his death as Passchendaele ended. Ten other Test players in the army teams left the Elysium of Lords on that July evening for the reality of France and Flanders. All were more fortunate than Blythe and survived.[28] Cricket metaphors abound in young officers' letters home to England: were images of green outfields and the unhurried rolling of wickets a natural optical escape from mud and desolation in the war-savaged landscape around them?

The preliminary bombardment for Third Ypres began two days after the cricket match at Lords. All preparations were well advanced. The ships and specially designed landing craft were ready for the amphibious operation and the Fourth Army highly trained for an enterprise that Bacon and Rawlinson were determined should not become a second Gallipoli. It was agreed that the tides would make 8 August the best morning for a dawn landing; Haig was sure that by then the Germans would be reeling from the impact of Fifth Army's initial advance.

Yet though Haig presented his plans for Third Ypres as early as 4 June, the War Policy Committee did not back proposals for operations in Flanders until 16 July and recommended that the offensive should end if it threatened to become a protracted battle like the Somme. Lloyd George still hesitated. He could see that there was no prospect of taking the enemy by surprise and, as a politician without a power base, he feared the demoralizing effect of long casualty lists on public opinion. Not until 21 July did Haig finally learn that he might go ahead with the offensive. Even so, the Cabinet insisted contingency plans be made to transfer troops to the Italian Front, in case the venture failed.[29] For Haig and his commanders, that was hardly a vote of confidence.

12

PASSCHENDAELE, 1917

Third Ypres, Passchendaele, remains the most harrowing victory in British military history. It is remembered as the battle that cut short the lives of 70,000 men from the United Kingdom and the overseas dominions. Many who had fallen already wounded were condemned to die in terrible agony, slowly drowned by rising water in the shell holes that pock-marked no man's land or choked by cloying mud from which they were too weak to struggle free. Contemporary paintings and photographs preserve images of a desolate landscape: broken tree-stumps; abandoned field guns and wallowing tanks too heavy to be hauled back from the morass. A disorderly mosaic of duck-boards and wooden planks twists a passage across ditches filled with sluggish water that would overflow and create yet another hazard, the greenish-black pools that no trench-maps could show. The monotonous empty scene conveys no impression of place or of purpose.

Historically, Third Ypres possesses a cohesive unity none of the participants could perceive at the time. The first attacks were launched on 31 July 1917, for the British the 1113th day of the war, and the fighting continued until the 1216th day. During those 16 weeks one broad-front battle was fought: Pilckem Ridge and the drive for Gheluvelt Plateau (31 July–10 August). It was followed by eight largely separate battles: Second Langemarck (16–18 August), Glencorse Wood (27 August), Menin Road Ridge (20–24 September), Polygon Wood (26 September–3 October), Broodseinde Ridge (4 October), Poelcapelle (9 October), First Passchendaele (12 October) and finally Second Passchendaele (26 October–10 November), with the ruined village that gave its name to the whole engagement falling to the Canadians on 6 November.[1] One battle, confidently anticipated by Haig as the offensive began, was never fought: no shells reached Roulers, 7 miles beyond Passchendaele and the first town on the road to Bruges and the Dutch frontier.

On the eve of battle Haig was buoyed up with optimism: 'Of 136 Tanks to be moved up . . . 133 are in position and all is well.'[2] The 'terrific bombardment' satisfied him; more than 3,000 guns – a gun for every 6 yards of battle front – pounded the German positions with high explosive and gas shells. Haig noted, however, that 'the bright weather expected by our weather prophet' is 'slower in its progress than expected'.[3] Junior officers shared both the C-in-C's optimism and his barometer-tapping concern. A few hours before going into action a 23-year-old captain in the Royal Field Artillery, John Wedderburn-Maxwell, wrote excitedly home to his father, himself a retired artillery officer: 'If you could only be here tonight *how* you would enjoy it! All the heavies that ever were will be firing from dark onwards . . . It should be great fun, provided the weather does not spoil it.'[4]

The 'fun' did not last. Plumer's Second Army supported Gough as his Fifth Army moved forward successfully towards Pilckem Ridge on the northern fringe of the Gheluvert Plateau, the main objective. This was familiar ground, fought over in 1915, and left broken by old bombardments. The morning was dry, and more than 130 tanks accompanied the troops without encountering problems with their tracks. All went deceptively well; the Liverpool Scottish advance from Wieltje across the Steenbeek stream following the lead of two tanks held high promise of a major outflanking movement. Ominously, however, gathering cloud frustrated RFC plans for reconnaissance from the air. The fighting grew tougher on the right flank, along the Menin Road. There the advance was checked in early afternoon by a fierce German counter-bombardment. At that moment, the rains came. By evening the craters caused by days of British shelling were filled with deep water, for all surface drainage had been destroyed. Tanks could not move; soon all wheeled traffic was halted. Even so, 6,000 prisoners and 25 guns were captured that day. Haig remained optimistic; but Crown Prince Rupprecht was well content too.

Overnight there was a constant heavy downpour. 'A terrible day of rain. The ground is like a bog,' Haig noted tersely. The famous photograph of seven men (see plate section) struggling through deep mud with a stretcher case was taken, not in the last phase of the battles, but on 1 August, little more than 24 hours after 'Passchendaele' began. That same day Guy Chapman MC, a junior officer in the 13th Royal Fusiliers, scribbled in his diary, 'There is no fighting. Hardly a gun is fired and the wretched soldiers crawl about in their shell holes sodden with rain. Unable to move – yet must die of exposure if they do not.'[5]

The unprecedented torrential rain continued for three days, churning up mud to a depth of 10 feet and forcing ground water to the surface. Gough called off the attack on Pilckem Ridge on 4 August, but Haig still had hopes of reaching the Gheluvert Plateau and encouraged Gough to await an improvement in the weather and then send his II Corps to press forward north of the Menin Road. On 10 August, Gough duly tried again, but precipitately and without adequate artillery preparation. The 25th Division took Westhoek village, but otherwise the gains were slight. Already more than 8,000 men were dead or missing, victims as much of flooded shell holes and the tenacious mud as of German shells and machine-guns. 'The attack was most satisfactory,' Haig noted, already showing that complacent contentment that runs through his diary pages for the next three months.[6]

Once the weather had forced the abandonment of the initial offensive there could, of course, be no question of an amphibious operation on 8 August. But greater attention had been given to detailed preparation for this aspect of the offensive than for any other. A top-security camp, technically an isolation hospital for troops in quarantine, was created at Le Clipon, east of La Panne. There the infantry received special assault training and tank crews practised driving up and over a sea-wall built to simulate any obstacle around Middelkerke. The Royal Navy responded with constructing a 600-foot long raft that, lashed with cable to two monitors, would convey tanks and guns to the beaches. In reading of these preparations there is a sense of looking forward to 1944 rather than back to 1914.[7] Haig witnessed a successful rehearsal of the landing in June and was loath to abandon the project. Dawn on 6 September was the next time when tidal conditions favoured a landing. Gough was therefore under pressure to make a third attempt at pushing ahead towards Roulers earlier than the condition of his men and guns warranted.[8]

On 16 August six divisions of the Fifth Army, supported on the left by two French divisions, attacked the German positions at Langemarck, where the student 'innocents' perished in October 1914. Weary troops, given no time for rest or preparation for the next challenge, were pitched against an enemy with carefully constructed bunkers and concentrated batteries and clusters of machine-guns. The small town, captured by the Germans in the initial gas attack of Second Ypres, was retaken, but at great cost. Although Gough's guns maintained a steady 'creeping barrage' in the morning, the terrible condition of the roads made it impossible to supply the shells and other equipment for a further advance. The 20th (Light) Division – recruited from Kitchener New Army volunteers – gained all its objectives, but the troops found that, in many places, they could only move forward 'in a series of small columns which wound their way in single file between the pools of mud and water'. With great courage the King's Own Yorkshire Light Infantry (KOYLI) and the Somerset Light Infantry stormed and took blockhouses west of Langemarck, an action in which Private William Edwards of the KOYLI won the Victoria Cross. Somehow, despite the mud and mire, the Light Division took more than 400 prisoners. On the right flank the London Territorials in the 56th Division were trapped in Glencorse Wood and Polygon Wood and virtually annihilated. At the best the Germans were pushed back 500 yards.[9]

Already more than 8,000 men were dead or missing, victims as much of flooded shell holes and the tenacious mud as of German shells, and Haig conferred again with General Rawlinson on 22 August. Rawlinson suggested his Fourth Army might make the landing independently of events on the main front, arguing that a surprise attack of this nature would draw off German troops and bring them to battle in the open rather than in their formidable entrenchments. He thought he could take Middelkerke and threaten Ostend, which might be attacked at the same time by monitors of the Dover Patrol. Haig rejected the suggestion, perhaps wisely: the German navy now had a Flanders Flotilla of torpedo boats and short-range U-boats that were augmented, over the following months, by eight destroyers, using both Zeebrugge and Bruges itself as bases.[10] Any amphibious operation could only be attempted behind powerful naval protection and in close co-ordination with an advancing army. Nevertheless, Haig was attracted by the possibility of a surprise night landing in early October, when suitable tides would coincide with a harvest moon.

On 25 August the commander-in-chief took the decisive step of transferring overall responsibility for the offensive from Gough and the Fifth Army to Plumer and the Second Army. The 'old man', as Haig invariably calls Plumer in his diary, had a more orderly, tactical mind, preferring carefully prepared attacks with limited and specific objectives. Two days after taking over command, Plumer sanctioned a small assault intended by his predecessor to complete unfinished business: another attempt to take Glencorse Wood. The weather was even worse than earlier in the month, with gale-force winds as well as heavy rain. By two o'clock in the afternoon the troops, knee deep in mud, could hardly stand up. When they sought to advance they were mown down by German machine-gun fire: so, too, were 16 prisoners, emerging from a pillbox with their hands up. A vivid account by an officer in the Warwickshire Regiment recounts how, as night fell, there came, from shell holes filling with water 'the groans and wails of wounded men: faint, long, sobbing moans of agony and despairing shrieks'.[11] Two farms were captured that day. Plumer immediately requested (and obtained) a three-week lull in operations to allow him to perfect his plans and to give the weary survivors of the long ordeal a respite.

In London, Lloyd George believed the sequence of events vindicated his doubts over the Western Front and its army commanders: 'Blood and mud, blood and mud — they can think of nothing better,' he complained. By contrast the news from Italy was encouraging: Cadorna, the Italian commander-in-chief, had (belatedly) opened an offensive three weeks later than Haig, and by 26 August a major victory seemed imminent. On 3 September, Lloyd George summoned Haig to London to discuss not the needs of the army in Flanders but ways to find 'surplus' guns and transfer them speedily from the BEF to boost Cadorna and 'knock away' Germany's Austrian 'prop'. Foch crossed to England to give his support to the Italian option. He spent two days conferring with the War Cabinet and with Haig and Robertson, both of whom vigorously resisted any weakening of artillery fire-power in France and Flanders. Eventually, Haig agreed to 'lend' a hundred guns on the understanding that they would be returned when he needed them again in Flanders. But the discussions revealed to him the deep divisions within the government. He sensed, correctly, that the prime minister would have liked to dismiss him (and Robertson too); only backing from Conservatives in the Coalition kept him in command. The tension lingered.[12]

For the next two months – weeks when Third Ypres reached the climax of Passchendaele – the commander-in-chief was inevitably also engaged in political infighting. Never once did he see for himself the condition of the terrain in which the Salient battles were fought, though he visited all Corps headquarters of the Second and Fifth Armies and spent several days 'at my house in Cassel'. Hearsay recounts that after the fighting was over Haig's chief of staff, General Kiggell, saw the battlefield below the ridge for the first time and broke down in tears exclaiming, 'Good God, did we send men to fight in *that*?' Doubt has been cast on the veracity of the tale, notably by John Terraine, and yet it rings true.[13] Haig and his staff dutifully studied reports from the Front, including aerial reconnaissance, and noted day by day each regiment's movements on maps with contours and place-names familiar from the battles of 1914 and 1915, but no assessment made in the tranquillity of a distant chateau could envisage the appalling transformation imposed by long bombardments and cruel weather. It is significant that a diary entry by Haig on 20 December suggests General Kiggell was close to a nervous breakdown.[14]

Plumer's pause puzzled the Germans. After a fortnight of relative quiet Crown Prince Rupprecht speculated that the offensive had been abandoned: ought some divisions to be relieved, he wondered?[15] But behind the British lines, there was constant activity. Selected assault troops received training on mock-ups of the defences that would face them. Haig inspected troops and watched field exercises, while Plumer briefed his Corps commanders thoroughly. The attacking infantry might expect a long, creeping barrage and were to advance, not in a broad wave, but grouped together to seize specific objectives. Once a battalion had fulfilled its task, a fresh battalion was to come forward to relieve it for the second assault; so the advance would continue. This leap-frog progression became a hallmark of Plumer's tactics.

For the first time infantry from Australia and South Africa were to play a major role at the centre of the Salient; they were joined later by New Zealanders, veterans of Messines. As the Australians came up from Poperinghe through Ypres the preliminary barrage greeted them: five days of shelling, even more intense than seven weeks earlier. The weather was astonishingly fine with an average seven hours' sunshine a day over the whole of September. Perversely, on the 19th, the eve of Plumer's renewal of the offensive, it rained steadily for the first time in more than a fortnight but by 5.40 a.m. the rain gave way to early-morning mist, favouring the attackers. The assault went ahead on an 8-mile front from Langemarck down to Hollebeke. Four British divisions in the Second Army were separated in the centre by two Australian divisions, with five more British divisions in the Fifth Army, south of the Menin Road. The northern flank brought the 3rd and 4th South African battalions into action, with two more battalions in support.[16]

The battle of the Menin Ridge developed according to plan. When the sun broke through, the RFC maintained constant air patrols, reporting on German movements and giving field headquarters a clearer appreciation of the battle than any earlier reconnaissance had offered. There was close co-ordination between the artillery and the advancing troops, enabling the guns to turn on incipient German counter-attacks with devastating effect. Leap-frogging carried the 1st and 2nd Australian Divisions through their first objectives within three hours, while the South African Springboks were even faster off the mark. The British infantry found that Plumer's tactics gave companies and even platoons opportunities for greater initiative, especially in forcing entries into the German bunkers, once their occupants were killed or dazed by the continuing shellfire. Menin Road Ridge became a morale-boosting victory – for those who survived. For, over the five days of fighting, the cost was heavy: 21,000 killed, missing, taken prisoner, or wounded; the South African brigade went into battle with 2,576 officers and men and lost 1,225 in killed, gravely wounded or missing within 36 hours.[17]

Similar tactics brought similar successes at Polygon Wood on 26 September and Broodseinde Ridge six days later. But again casualties were heavy: in Polygon Wood, 15,000 in all, with more than a third of them Australian. On the northern fringe of the wood, the 14th Australian Battalion showed indomitable courage in eliminating a line of pillboxes southeast of Zonnebeke. In the absence of more senior officers, the battalion was effectively led by Captain Albert Jacka, who had already won a Victoria Cross at Gallipoli and a Military Cross on the Somme. Jacka rallied the company commanders for an assault that many believed might have carried the battalion to Broodseinde Ridge if given adequate support. In all, however, no more than 4 square miles was taken that day.

At Broodseinde a thousand yards was gained on 2 October, and II Army took prisoner 100 officers and 4,000 men in a single day. The ridge was a valuable, strategic, observation platform, the incline on which the Commonwealth War Cemetery now stands; indeed it was during Broodseinde that Northumberland Fusiliers, seeing a resemblance between three German pillboxes facing them and cottages beside a familiar river, bestowed on them the immortal name 'Tyne Cot'. To Haig the day's achievements were a stepping-stone towards the higher crest on which Passchendaele stood. 'A very important success,' he noted in his diary. So confident was he of total victory along the ridges that he ordered Rawlinson to stand by to launch the amphibious operation.[18]

Already, however, there were warning signs: while the German gunners recovered their old accuracy, British artillery could not give the infantry sustained support. The guns were still being brought forward and were soon running short of ammunition. Nevertheless, the Anzac artillery was able to deliver a thunderous opening barrage, with shells falling on a German Guards Division as it prepared to mount a counter-attack; for Germany 'October 4th was a black day', as the official *Weltkrieg* history records. But there were heavy casualties among the British Imperial attackers, too: over 20,000 dead, wounded or missing, again with a third of them Australian. The New Zealand division advancing on Gravenstafel, slightly further to the north, lost 330 men killed and suffered 1,323 other casualties.[19] Yet the most ominous change from Plumer's two recent battles was in the weather: a steady drizzle became heavy rain by the afternoon.

Hindsight suggests Haig should have called a halt after Broodseinde before the weather finally broke and before Ludendorff, by now the effective decision maker at OLH, perfected plans to counter the new tactics. Both Plumer and Gough thought enough had been achieved. Haig, however, went ahead, still convinced a final thrust would bring the breakthrough, and once more Rawlinson was urged to keep the Fourth Army ready.

Only five days separate Broodseinde from Poelcapelle. 'A general attack' with 'very successful' results, was Haig's diary summary for 9 October; 'Something of a shambles' rightly comment his editors, even though they are generally sympathetic to the diarist.[20] As on 31 July the weather decided the fate of the battle, although on this occasion ahead of the opening barrage. Heavy rain throughout 7 and 8 October prevented the forward movement of the guns and, more important still, the arrival of supplies. All traffic, whether vehicular, equine or pedestrian, had to cope with flooded shell craters along the Menin Road. Some British troops – including newcomers from east Lancashire, in the 66th Division – took eight hours to march 4 miles through the rain to reach the points assigned for the assault. Frequently they were knee-deep in mud. The New Zealand Division remained in reserve that day.

Even before the battle, sickness, exhaustion and malingering reduced the 2nd Australian Division from a nominal strength of 12,000 officers and men to about 1,850. After heavy fighting throughout the day, the division was down to some 650 officers and men by dusk, when they were forced back to their starting line. In the small hours of the following morning these survivors were relieved. Wearily they trudged back for five hours to dug-outs and eventually to the scant shelter offered by ruined Ypres.[21]

Confused reports led Plumer and Haig to believe that the Australians had established themselves in a position from where they could make a bid for Passchendaele and the crest of the ridge, over a mile away. Haig therefore welcomed a proposal by General Godley, the New Zealander who commanded the II Anzac Corps, that the 3rd and 4th Australian Divisions and the New Zealand Division should press ahead with a new attack on 12 October. For the New Zealand Division First Passchendaele became a disaster, largely through the difficulty of maintaining contact with the artillery in such terrible weather. Early in the day a battalion commander was killed by 'friendly' artillery, but the shelling failed to cut a way through 50 yards of barbed-wire entanglement protecting concrete machine-gun nests on Bellevue Spur. Within a few hours the division lost almost 3,000 officers and other ranks. The Australians had similar experiences with an inadequate creeping barrage and untouched barbed wire, and they fared little better than the Kiwis. General Monash's 3rd Division had some 3,000 casualties and the neighbouring 4th Australian Division a thousand. Sadly, First Passchendaele achieved little, a gain of a few hundred yards and a haul of 600 equally weary German prisoners. That night Crown Prince Rupprecht wrote contentedly in his diary, 'Rain – our most effective ally'.[22]

By now Haig had reluctantly come to accept that there could be no thrust forward to Roulers before the year ended. On 15 October, Kiggell informed Admiral Bacon that 'Persistent ill-luck in weather conditions has delayed our advance so much that there is no possibility of our being ready for the combined operation this month,' and Rawlinson closed 1st Division's 'isolation camp' at Le Clipon seven days later.[23]

With his pet project of an amphibious landing ruled out and the prospect of rain continuing into the second half of the month, it would have been logical for Haig to call off the offensive before the casualty toll mounted even higher. He did not, for two main reasons: a need to secure a better defensive position, from which to mount an all-out attack in the spring, and a wish to pin down German troops in Flanders while General Byng's Third Army prepared a surprise attack with tanks across the chalky downs west of Cambrai. Only a raid in strength was contemplated but the project increasingly held the commander-in-chief's attention. Not that planning for Second Passchendaele was neglected. Haig needed fresh troops, in divisions with a leavening of veterans and under an experienced commander. He turned to Lieutenant-General Sir Arthur Currie and the Canadian Corps.[24]

Currie had seen action at Ypres in 1915 and was reluctant to return to the Salient. The Canadians felt they had been badly used by General Gough at the Somme and did not wish to serve in his Fifth Army. Currie, knowing he had strong backing in Ottawa, agreed to relieve the Anzacs on condition that the Corps was attached to Plumer's Second Army and that he was given time to site the supporting artillery with care. He wished the assault made in stages rather than by a leap forward in a single action. Plumer agreed with him. Although British troops were in action on 22 October, seeking to root out specific machine-gun nests, a fortnight passed with no major battle. During this relative lull, plans for the Canadian Corps and for six British divisions were carefully integrated. In contrast to Poelcapelle and First Passchendaele, the final assault on the ridge was well rehearsed.

Second Passchendaele began at 5.40 a.m. on 26 October, in autumn mist that soon turned to heavy rain. The Hood battalion of the Royal Naval Division, whose baptism of fire had come at Antwerp in the third month of the war, made some progress on the left of the line, but the defences and the driving rain checked the five other British divisions. In the centre the Canadians advanced astride the Gravenstafel–Mosselmarkt road. They found the Ravebeek, normally a small stream, flooding the fields and creating a swamp through which progress could be made only slowly along narrow 'paths', all too easily covered by German machine-gunners. The Bellevue Spur pillboxes and machine-gun nests that had taken such a toll of the Australians during the earlier battle again proved formidable. In the ultimately successful assault on the spur Lieutenant Robert Shankland and Captain Christopher O'Kelly gained the Victoria Cross in separate actions. A third VC was won by Thomas Holmes, a young private in the Mounted Rifles, who with three Mills bombs single handed destroyed a machine-gun post and captured a pillbox at a vital point on the edge of Wolf Copse. On that Friday the Canadians gained almost all the positions assigned them in Currie's orders.

Over the weekend mule tracks of wooden planks were formed, to allow ammunition and supplies to reach the forward posts. Monday (30th) was a day free from rain and the Canadian divisions resumed their advance, with support on their left from the Royal Naval Division and the 50th Northumbrian Division. Further small gains were made on 3 November, but it was not until Tuesday, 6 November, that the Canadian 2nd Division cleared the eastern fringe of the ridge and entered the smoking red-brick ruin that was once Passchendaele village. A final assault to consolidate the position and make it defensible was made four days later. The casualty lists of British, Canadian and Australian troops made as grim reading as in the later months of the Somme. During their relatively short experience of the Passchendaele fighting the Canadian Corps alone lost 15,634 killed or wounded.

Third Ypres was over. In 16 weeks the apex of the Salient was pushed forward up the ridge some 6 miles towards Roulers, although along the Menin Road the advance was no more than 2,500 yards. The principal vantage points dominating the eastern approaches to Ypres were taken. The battles allegedly shielded the most vulnerable sectors of the French front from attack until Pétain could restore order, and morale was boosted by the coming of the first American troops. For these gains, however, nearly 70,000 of Haig's troops perished on the battlefields and 170,000 were seriously wounded. If French and Belgian losses along the Yser are added to these figures, the total cost to the allied armies rises to over a quarter of a million men. German losses remain in dispute:[25] they cannot have been so high as the 400,000 estimate given by Sir James Edmonds in the British official history; John Terraine was probably on safer ground with a figure of 260,400 dead and wounded.[26] No statistics, however terrible they read on the page, can convey the sorrow that enveloped so many families in four continents as they approached the fourth Christmas of war.

13

'EVERYONE INTO BATTLE'

Beyond Flanders, Europe had changed dramatically during the 16 weeks of Third Ypres. When the first guns opened up on Pilckem Ridge, Russia's armies were still in the field, fighting in Galicia and at Riga. On the day after Passchendaele fell, the Bolsheviks seized power in Petrograd, with Lenin calling on 'all warring peoples' to seek 'a just and democratic peace'. From another ally good news had come as late as 18 August, the day the battle of Langemarck ended: General Cadorna reported his troops had pushed the Austrians back 5 miles in the eleventh battle of the Isonzo. But Lloyd George's hopes for a breakthrough south of the Alps were soon to fade. On 24 October – as the Canadians completed preparations for Second Passchendaele – a predominantly German army attacked high in the mountains, in terrain where no commander had ever contemplated a major offensive. Before nightfall, the prettily scenic town of Caporetto was in German hands – and so, too, were 15,000 prisoners, a hundred guns and some 15 miles of the upper Isonzo valley.[1]

Within two days an Italian retreat became a rout. Cadorna urgently sought help. Foch at once ordered two divisions sent to Italy and set out for Cadorna's headquarters in Treviso himself four days after the first Germans entered Caporetto. For three critical weeks the chief of the French general staff remained in Italy, strengthening the nation's will to stay in the war. Lloyd George, too, responded to Cadorna's plea: he insisted that the CIGS dispatch two more divisions to Italy and follow Foch to Treviso. Another three divisions would soon be on their way south. To Haig's dismay on the day after the Canadians entered Passchendaele he was ordered to send Plumer, the soundest of his generals, to command the British troops south of the Alps. Plumer was away from Flanders for the next four months.

Lloyd George used the Italian crisis to secure greater inter-allied cohesion and a co-ordinated general strategy for the war as a whole. He backed French proposals for a Supreme War Council, breaking the news of his decision to a sceptical Haig in Paris on 4 November. Then accompanied by General Smuts, the South African soldier and statesman he co-opted to serve in the War Cabinet, Hankey and Sir Henry Wilson (who strongly supported the French proposal) Lloyd George travelled to Rapallo for a conference that kindled some fighting spirit in Italy's political leaders and took practical steps to halt the retreat on the Piave river. It was at Rapallo, in the improbable setting of the New Casino Hotel, that a Supreme War Council came into being, though the council's headquarters were the Trianon Palace in Versailles.[2] The prime ministers of Britain, France and Italy served as council members, each appointing a military representative; Lloyd George chose General Wilson. Robertson remained hostile to the whole concept, not least because he saw in the military representative a likely and eager successor to his post as CIGS.

By 14 November, Lloyd George was back at Westminster. He found Londoners indignant at 'inadequate' defences that failed to prevent four successive nights of air raids, with incendiary bombs dropped on the capital, an alarming novelty. Yet, unexpectedly, ten days later church bells across England could ring out to celebrate a victory for the first time in the war. At Cambrai, on 20 November, 374 tanks led almost a quarter of a million British and Canadian troops to break through a 6-mile weakly held sector of the Hindenburg Line. As there was no artillery preparation, Byng's Third Army took the Germans completely by surprise. The tanks penetrated wire entanglements of three defence lines and at some points penetrated as deeply as 4 miles. More ground was won in six hours than around Ypres in six months. George Samuel, a captain in the Royal Field Artillery, wrote to his wife that evening, 'Since the 8th . . . I have . . . not had my boots off for several nights at a time. We have done all our marching by night and hidden ourselves by day . . . But it's been worth it. The six hours pure joy we have had today have repaid every bit – and I am confident that we shall go further when we want to!'[3]

Alas! the prospect of decisive victory soon receded. Haig and Byng had not expected such dramatic success; no plans existed for exploiting what was intended as a raid in strength. Two cavalry divisions held in reserve were never ordered to advance, and by dusk on the first day 65 tanks were destroyed in action; 109 others had broken down. A week of hesitancy followed the triumphs of the opening day. The Germans brought up fresh infantry regiments and a mass of artillery for a counter-attack. By the end of the month all the land gained on 20–21 November had been lost, apart from two small villages. Another 45,000 names were added to the casualty lists. Confidence in Haig's overall strategy fell to a low ebb, although much criticism at Westminster and in the news-papers centred on GHQ and the structure of command rather than on the C-in-C personally.

Lloyd George would have liked to replace both Haig and Robertson[4] but both officers could still count on firm support from the Unionists and from the king. It was, however, agreed that GHQ needed a shake-up. To Haig's regret, he lost both his chief-of-staff, General Kiggell, and his chief intelligence officer, Briga-dier-General Charteris, whom Lloyd George blamed for giving wrong estimates of the German numbers before Cambrai. Haig was pleased by an improvement in relations between GHQ and GQG, and he welcomed the resolute spirit that followed appointment of Georges Clemenceau as French prime minister in late November. But it was with great reluctance that he accepted a request from the Supreme War Council at Versailles to take over a further 28-mile sector of the Front from the French. Already a shortage of trained men had induced the War Office to change the composition of an army corps, cutting each of them from four battalions to three, but by early February the BEF was ready to assume responsibility for 123 miles of the line, from the Yser in the north down to the Oise. Inevitably the new sector, assigned to General Gough's Fifth Army, was behind its neighbours in trench construction.

Haig told the War Cabinet early in January that the best way of frustrating German plans was to resume the offensive in Flanders; he still had faith in the value and importance of cavalry. Curzon, with recent experience in mind, icily observed that 'the character of warfare in the ensuing months would present few opportunities for the use of cavalry'.[5] With regret Haig concentrated on improving defences of the troops in the Salient and, with less urgency, across the old frontier and down to the Somme. Third Ypres had shown the value to the Germans of trench defence in depth. By mid-January when, at Lloyd George's request, Smuts and Hankey crossed to France to inspect the defences, the British lines had gained a string of advanced outposts a mile ahead of the main network of trenches. The outposts were served by concealed 'alleys' that ran back in some places for two and a half miles. The visitors were impressed. The prime minister had also asked Smuts and Hankey to look for a younger commander who might fittingly replace Haig. They could find no suitable candidate: the C-in-C retained their confidence, but Hankey returned to London uneasy over morale. In a private note, he warned Lloyd George: 'The army is tired of the war and there is a general feeling that peace is not very distant.'[6]

OHL's plans for 1918 were already well advanced. As early as 11 November 1917, Ludendorff and Hindenburg summoned the generals in the West and their principal staff officers to a conference at Mons.[7] Closure of the Eastern Front allowed a major change of policy in Flanders and France, Ludendorff told them: it was essential to abandon the defensive strategy of the past year and seek a swift and final victory before men and material from America bolstered 'the Entente Powers'. Several options were considered, even a renewal of the Verdun offensive. Ludendorff's chief of the operations department Lieutenant-Colonel Wetzell, presented a plan for a two-stage offensive, with a feint attack in the Verdun sector or between Arras and St Quentin masking the main assault, one that was designed to force the British to sue for peace by striking around Ypres. Wetzell proposed that the first objective should be, not Ypres itself, but the key railway junction of Hazebrouck, whose capture would isolate the troops in the Salient from the main allied army in France and enable the advance to continue and take Dunkirk, Calais and Boulogne.

After the battle of Cambrai, however, Ludendorff rejected any plans for attacking at Verdun or in Flanders. His preference was an all-out offensive across the Somme in a bid for Paris. To him there were lessons in both recent battles. Cambrai had shown the value of tanks; bigger 'land battleships' must be speedily developed, with the technical knowledge acquired from captured British models. The victory at Caporetto confirmed the importance of secrecy and surprise: all forward movements in the coming offensive should therefore be made at night; by day, camouflage must conceal the massing of artillery from prying reconnaissance aircraft. The specialist storm-troopers, developed by Falkenhayn, were to train in collaboration with equally specialized artillery units and with 'assault troops'. They should move forward quickly and carry on advancing rather than pause to consolidate initial gains. Behind the lines, there was intensive training and rehearsals throughout February – a month when with characteristic perversity the weather remained fine that winter.

Meanwhile, Germany's enemies consumed much time in inter-allied conferences and, among the British, in civil–military political bickering. Lloyd George out-manoeuvred Robertson when he sought to preserve the independent authority of the CIGS, and Robertson resigned his post – making way, almost inevitably, for Sir Henry Wilson.[8] Outwardly, Haig was quietly confident of defeating any Spring Offensive by Ludendorff. On 2 March he told his assembled senior generals that he was so impressed by all he had seen of their preparations that his only fear now was that Germany might hesitate to launch an offensive.[9] If it came, he was convinced the blow would fall once again in Flanders, and he retained six divisions in reserve, to cover the Channel ports. Sir Herbert Gough, whose Fifth Army was thinly spread along the most southerly sector, argued that the enemy would make a strike for Amiens, seeking a breakthrough at the point where the Fifth Army's new positions bordered the most northern French outposts. The Fifth Army comprised only 12 under-strength infantry divisions and three cavalry; they were expected to hold 42 miles of the Front. To placate Gough, Haig spared him two reserve divisions.

As late as Saturday, 16 March, the restructured intelligence at GHQ reported that no build-up 'south of the Bapaume–Cambrai road' could be detected.[10] That night 47 German divisions were on the march southwards to join 28 divisions already at the Front. The movement continued through the hours of darkness on Sunday, Monday and Tuesday. Shortly before midnight on Wednesday, heavy fog enveloped the lines, muffling all sound through the small hours of Thursday, 21 March. Then, at 4.40 a.m., 'Operation

Michael' began. Some 6,000 guns and 3,500 mortars bombarded 40 miles of Front between the River Scarpe, near Arras and St Quentin.

There had been no barrage like it in any previous offensive. High-velocity howitzers targeted railway stations and sidings at some points 25 miles away. In the front line, high-explosive, gas and shrapnel shells fell on the Fifth Army trenches. There was, too, an innovative Blue Cross shell, two-thirds explosive and one-third diphenylchloroarsine, an irritant gas that incapacitated a victim by constant sneezing. By 8.40 a.m. when the assault infantry went forward fog, smoke and gas had thrown a hideous blanket over a vast battlefield. The sun did not begin to break through until early afternoon. By then General von Hutier's 18th German Army had taken all their prescribed objectives. By dusk Hutier's forward troops were 5 miles into the defences. The British losses that day were appalling: more than 7,000 dead and 21,000 captured. Overnight a deeply perplexed General Gough ordered the Fifth Army to fall back beyond the Crozat canal. On Monday afternoon (25th March) the Third Army was ordered back to a line along the Ancre, close to the Somme battlefields: the BEF's second great retreat of the war had begun. 'During the whole of this dreadful march we were shelled, shelled, shelled,' wrote D. J. Polley, a machine-gunner in the Royal Naval Division. 'If there can be monotony in the expectation of death, then the very din of battle became monotonous.'[11]

The German troops were elated. Second Lieutenant Herbert Sulzbach, a gunner, wrote in his diary: 'This day must be the greatest in the history of the world. The last night of the four years of static warfare passed . . . in the greatest possible excitement. The impossible thing has been achieved: the break-through has succeeded!'[12] The first OHL war communiqué told the German people the battle 'was under the personal leadership of His Majesty the Emperor'. This statement was almost as exaggerated as Sulzbach's enthusiasm; the kaiser spent fully nine hours that day with the military paladins at their headquarters in Avesnes. The patriotic *Kölnische Zeitung*, dutifully following OHL's lead, called the offensive 'Die Kaiserschlacht' (The Emperor's Battle), and the name stuck. It was a burdensome honour to bear. The Napoleonic mantle condemned Wilhelm to success; failure would irreparably damage the prestige of the dynasty.[13]

Despite the euphoria, Ludendorff was far from content with the first day's achievements. As reports reached him at Avesnes it became clear that casualties were high: over 10,000 dead and almost 29,000 wounded. Moreover in the north he had looked for encirclement of General Byng's Third Army at Arras but the dry, chalky fields were spared the fog that arose from the marshes to the south. The RFC could not get airborne and direct the guns for a British counter-bombardment. In consequence, General von Below's 17th Army made none of the progress shown by the 18th Army.

So it was to be for the next 16 days, with holding operations in the north while the 18th Army swept ahead, across the old Somme battlefield. One day Gutier's troops advanced 10 miles and on the next, 12. In alarm the allied commanders, together with Clemenceau and President Poincaré, hurriedly conferred at Doullens on 26 March and agreed to entrust Foch with responsibility for co-ordinating the activities of all the allied armies on the Western Front. He was accepted as a Supreme Commander, a generalissimo in all but name, a status confirmed ten days later.[14]

Yet at first it seemed as if military co-ordination came too late. Morale in Paris had been badly shaken when two shells fell in the heart of the city on the first Saturday of the offensive. Three days after the Doullens conference a shell hit the church of St Gervais during Mass on Good Friday, killing 88 worshippers. It was difficult to convince Parisians that the enemy was not at the gates of the capital, but could fire from a hidden site 75 miles away. Another 300 shells fell on Paris over the next three months, a constant reminder of German strength and the power of Krupps artillery.[15]

All remained quiet within the Ypres Salient. To Haig's satisfaction, Plumer had returned from Italy and resumed command of the Second Army; he was even prepared to spare troops to go south-wards, as reinforcements for threatened positions around Amiens. Although the BEF's stubborn resistance blunted the penetrative power of Hutier's troops, on 28 March they came within 10 miles of Amiens. A week later, in the same sector, the indomitable Australians launched a successful counter-attack. Ludendorff was a realist, at least over military affairs: on 5 April he recognized that his troops needed rest and reinforcement. Operation Michael came to an end; the allied dead and gravely wounded were as yet unknown, but some 70,000 French and British troops passed into prisoner-of-war camps and more than a thousand guns were captured. German losses too were heavy, perhaps as high as a quarter of a million men killed, gravely wounded or taken prisoner. By the end of the first week in April, some German divisions could muster no more than 2,000 men.[16]

Almost immediately, Ludendorff reverted to a variation on the plan Wetzell had advocated at the Mons conference. 'Operation Georgette' would be launched in Flanders, striking not in the first instance for Ypres but for the railway junction of Hazebrouck, 19 miles from the German front south of Armentières. As a second objective Crown Prince Rupprecht's Army Group was to gain Mont Cassel, the highest point in the hills along the Franco-Flemish border.

This sector of the British line was weakly held. General Horne's First Army was over-stretched: on average his divisions were each responsible for slightly more than five and a half miles of front. Among his forward troops were four brigades of the 2nd Portuguese Division, due to be relieved on 10 April. Although the British had anticipated an attack in Flanders in the year, the timing and the choice of battleground took them by surprise. On 8 April a German airman inadvertently revealed to his French captors that troops were massing in front of the Arras to Armentières sector, but the news cannot have reached British headquarters more than 12 hours before 'Georgette's' guns opened up.

The countryside between the La Bassée canal and the River Lys was flat and marshy and, as on 21 March, the Germans were assisted by a clinging mist, in places as dense as fog. The full weight of a barrage from the German Sixth Army's guns, firing gas and high-explosive shells, fell on the unfortunate Portuguese.[17] At least one battalion did not wait to see the infantry emerging from the cloud. The 'pork-and-beans', as they were nicknamed by the Tommies, ran like frightened rabbits: 'I don't believe that some of them have stopped running yet,' Lieutenant Arthur Preston White of the neighbouring 1st Northamptonshires wrote six weeks later in a letter from hospital.[18] Other fugitives stole any bicycles they found and were seen pedalling desperately in the general direction of Le Havre. Most of the Portuguese brigades were simply overwhelmed by the onslaught: 6,000 men ended up in prisoner-of-war camps. There is no precise record of their losses, but one in seven of the Portuguese Expeditionary Force perished on the Western Front, and 9 April was their grimmest day of battle: the death toll that day must have been considerable. So intense was the fighting that the 7th Gordon Highlanders, seeking to plug the gap, lost some 700 officers and men killed, seriously wounded or taken prisoner.

Within three hours the Germans were through the thin British line. To the right, Territorials in the 55th West Lancashire Division held the village of Givenchy, already heavily fortified. They were still defying the enemy when relieved five days later. To the left of the gap the 2nd Worcesters checked the advance in the village of Neuve Eglise. But a new danger arose: on 10 April the German Fourth Army struck north of Armentières, drawing Plumer's Second Army into the battle and bringing the fighting back once again to the Messines–Wytschaete ridge. And on this occasion Plumer had neither the manpower nor the guns to check the German thrust. For fear of encirclement Plumer felt forced to evacuate the ridges east of Ypres. In the course of 48 hours almost all the gains made in 1917 were lost, including Messines and even Passchendaele.[19]

Over the following days the Germans pushed forward up the Menin Road as far as Hellfire Corner, the crossroads only a mile east of the Menin Gate. Here they were checked by the original fall-back defences strengthened during Second Ypres and by continued resistance on Pilckem Ridge that threatened their left flank. The danger for the city was greater than in either October and November 1914 or in the following spring. Haig was extremely worried. He pressed the French to prepare plans for flooding the low-lying land between the Flanders heights and Dunkirk, but his immediate concern remained the shortage of well-trained troops. On the first day of 'Georgette' he saw Foch and sought French help. None was forthcoming: Foch needed every division he could find to protect Paris and meet the attack Pétain anticipated in Champagne. Late in the evening of 10 April, Foch and Weygand again met Haig, however, and agreed to press ahead with plans for an advance northwards from the Somme. This threat to Ludendorff's communications would release British,

Australian and Canadian troops and give Haig the reserve force he desperately sought.[20]

Next morning the C-in-C wrote out personally the famous Order of the Day, addressed to the First and Second Armies: 'There must be no retirement. With our backs to the wall and believing in the justice of our cause each one of us must fight on to the end.'[21] Haig did not mention the Order in his diary entry for 11 April, and there is no evidence that it stiffened the sinews of any of the weary troops to whom it was addressed, nor indeed that many of them knew of it until after the battle. Brigadier-General Freyberg VC, visiting the Hampshire Regiment near Bailleul an hour before dawn next day, 'found the whole battalion asleep, lying in every kind of position'. Later Freyberg came across another 'snoring company'. The men were extra-ordinarily resilient. 'It is all fearfully thrilling and everyone is in the best spirits,' Lieutenant-Colonel Murray of 15th Brigade Royal Horse Artillery assured his family: 'It doesn't matter losing ground if we make it as expensive as we have been doing.'[22] Was Haig's rallying call of 11 April intended as much to boost morale at home as to hearten the troops in the fields?

Yet, in what is generally called the Battle of the Lys, there were several instances of magnificent defiance. Most notable was the determination of the 4th Brigade of the 31st (Guards) Division to counter the German threat to Hazebrouck. In four hours of hand-to-hand fighting along almost a mile of the hurriedly constructed lines south of the town one company of 250 Grenadiers was completely destroyed, another was reduced to 20 men and a third to only six. But Hazebrouck, the hub of the strategic railway network, was never captured.

Ludendorff's plans were again frustrated. He turned instead to the North, with the two armies once again engaged at Langemarck on 17 April. An attempt to force a way through the Belgian lines along the Yser was repelled that day in the fortified village of Kippe. Four Belgian infantry regiments fought throughout the day with courage and tenacity. They took 800 prisoners, a great fillip to Belgian trench morale.

Finally, Ludendorff looked again longingly towards the Channel ports and massed three and a half divisions to oust six newly arrived French regiments from Mount Kemmel, the 500-foot high vantage point commanding the route to Dunkirk. Hindenburg flattered the geographical contours of Flanders by assigning the task of conquering the mount to the Alpine Corps, veterans of attacks along the Serb-Greek frontier as well as in the Carpathians and northern Italy. Their assault on 25 April was preceded by an intense artillery bombardment with mustard gas and phosgene. The French troops found their respirators offered insufficient protection. They fled down the northern slopes of the mount ahead of the Alpine Corps, showing Portuguese alacrity. Some 800 French were taken prisoner at the crest of the mount and another 1600 in Kemmel village.[23]

It was, however, Georgette's last fling. Ludendorff, like Falkenhayn in the same region during the autumn of 1914, was alarmed at the extended and exposed position of his troops, many of them the best-trained battalions still available to him. The Army Group commanders, especially Crown Prince Rupprecht, warned him of falling morale and battle weariness. His overall strategy of springing surprises by mounting concurrent attacks in isolated sectors was proving a drain on manpower and resources. OHL could no longer control more than one battle at a time. Ludendorff had to choose between making a final drive for Paris or pushing ahead for the Channel ports. At this moment he was unexpectedly confronted with a new problem. Already, on two occasions, OHL was alerted by reports of increased naval activity in the Channel. Were the British contemplating amphibious operations?

Admiral Sir Roger Keyes had succeeded Admiral Bacon in command of the Dover Patrol the previous December. Keyes was highly critical of the discarded plans for an amphibious landing. The Admiralty, however, was alarmed at the prospect of destroyers based on Zeebrugge and Ostend joining the smaller U-boats in breaking through the protective barrage and causing havoc among the cross-Channel transports that sustained the BEF. Keyes accordingly spent the first three months of the year perfecting plans to seal the two Belgian ports with block-ships. Twice in mid-April an armada of more than a hundred small vessels and the old cruiser HMS *Vindictive* set out from Dover, only to run into difficulties and return to port. On 22–23 April, Keyes tried again, flying his flag in the destroyer, HMS *Warwick*. Shortly after midnight, as his ships approached the Belgian coast, Keyes greeted the coming of St George's Day with the signal 'St George for England'. From the

Vindictive came the response, 'And may we give the dragon's tail a damned good twist.'[24]

The raid did not achieve all Keyes had hoped. At Zeebrugge the block-ships trapped the destroyers but the smaller U-boats soon found a channel to avoid them. At Ostend two block-ships ran aground on a sandbank short of their objective: the *Vindictive* was herself used as a block-ship in a second raid there a fortnight later. During the raid on Zeebrugge, the *Vindictive* transported a large body of men, equipped with weapons tried and tested in the trenches – flame-throwers, mortars, machine-guns and even howitzers. The marines attacked the German garrison on the Mole with great courage: eight Victoria Crosses were won at Zeebrugge, two at Ostend. Casualties, however, were heavy: 200 dead and 400 wounded. In Britain the highly dramatic raids lifted morale at one of the low points of the war. They also had considerable influence on Ludendorff, particularly the equipment assigned to the marines. He now had to reckon with a possible landing behind his lines. Six days after the Zeebrugge Raid, Ludendorff ordered the Fourth and Sixth Armies to end their advance and consolidate. St George may not have knotted the dragon's tail but Georgette caught a decisive blow from the swirl of the twist.

Over the next six months, the outcome of the war still seemed in the balance to the public at home. Good news came from outside Europe with successful offensives in Palestine, Mesopotamia and eventually in the Balkans, too.[25] American troops had crossed to France at the end of June 1917 and in mid-January 1918 took over a sector of the Front on the Meuse. But it was not until the spring of 1918 that their commander, General Pershing, could begin building up a formidable US army in Europe. During the six weeks of Germany's Michael and Georgette offensives 158,000 Americans landed at Brest; another 245,000 followed in May. Ludendorff had to act swiftly and decisively before the newcomers were 'acclimatized' and ready for action.

To the surprise of Foch, Pétain and Haig the Germans were able to launch their third major offensive in ten weeks on Monday, 27 May. Ludendorff amassed guns and storm-troopers along a 45-mile sector of the Chemin des Dames and, in the initial advance, broke easily through the French Sixth Army. By Tuesday night a salient

15 miles deep pointed directly towards Paris. Place-names last in
the spotlight 45 months ago returned to the headlines. By Thursday
the Germans were back on the River Marne, east of Chateau-
Thierry, little more than 40 miles from the capital.[26]

If the ground were familiar, so too was Ludendorff's strategy. He
pushed forward too far too fast, and he had to halt in order for
supplies to catch up. On this occasion roads, railways and troops
passing through the towns were subject to bombing from the skies,
both by the French and by the Royal Air Force (the RAF, created
on 1 April by the amalgamation of the RFC and the RNAS to
form a separate service, independent of both the War Office and
the Admiralty). General Franchet d'Esperey, who had shown such
verve in 1914, commanded Army Group North and, in consultation with Pétain, concentrated his troops east of the Marne
between Chateau-Thierry and Rheims. For three weeks in June,
Army Group North and the US 1st and 3rd Divisions held the
Germans in check. Foch wished to launch an immediate counter-
attack but was prepared to wait until Ludendorff exhausted his
forces.

On 14–15 July a terrifying artillery duel was fought out west of
Rheims as Ludendorff sought to envelop his enemies by striking
south-westwards. Foch parried the subsequent attack, with support
not only from the Americans but also from an Italian division. In
three days the Germans lost 50,000 men, though allied casualties
were also high, mainly from the initial bombardment. On 18 July,
Foch at last struck, with General Mangin's Tenth Army threatening
the vital lateral supply route, the road from Soissons to Chateau-
Thierry. After another three days of battle, the threat to Paris was
finally removed. Ludendorff kept his operations staff at work on
further projects, the most advanced being a renewed attack in
Flanders, to cross the Yser and swing northwards, cutting off the
Belgians and reaching the coast in the vicinity of La Panne. But all
such plans were little more than war games. On 22 July, Hindenburg had to report to the All Highest War Lord that the Kaiserschlacht was ending in total failure.

On 8 August – to become for Ludendorff 'the Black Day of the
German Army' – Haig joined the offensive. Elaborate deception,
including great activity by two Canadian battalions in the Flanders
hills, convinced German observers that most Dominion troops

were in the Mount Kemmel area. Bogus wireless messages, duly
intercepted by the Germans, also suggested the imminence of an
offensive in Flanders; even King Albert learnt of the bogus
messages, and was puzzled and aggrieved that neither Foch nor
Haig had consulted him. But all attention was focused once more
on the Somme. Together with the Australians, the Canadian Corps
formed the spearhead of an attack launched by Haig that day finally
to clear the threat to Amiens and, if possible, force the Germans
away from the Somme and back to the Hindenburg Line. The
allied gains led to a series of conferences, in which Haig and the
more cautious Pétain successfully curbed Foch's propensity for
frontal assaults. On 15 August, Foch (newly created a marshal of
France) accepted a strategy of carefully timed thrusts up the line.
'*Tout le monde á la bataille*' ('Everyone into battle') was his rallying
call, and *tout le monde* responded. By 30 August a confident headline
in *The Times* could welcome 'The Flowing Tide' of victory.
Among brigades and battalions back to lines left in April was
the 15th Royal Horse Artillery. 'It is curious to look back to those
dark days in April when we were hanging on to Ypres by our
eyelids,' Colonel Murray wrote home on 1 September; 'Who
would have thought then that in four months we should be chasing
him [Ludendorff] back thoroughly beaten?'[27]

In London the War Cabinet remained suspicious: optimistic
predictions from the BEF commanders-in-chief had so often
proved ill-founded; the Hindenburg Line had yet to be breached,
and there was concern that bakingly hot weather in July and early
August was giving way to thunderstorms, conjuring up visions of
another ghastly assault through churned-up mud. As CIGS, Sir
Henry Wilson gave Haig more loyal support than the C-in-C had
expected, but he too warned him against massed frontal attacks.
Haig was angered by such sustained criticism, not least because the
war had at last become mobile and, as a cavalryman, his strategic
instincts were sound – at times more far-sighted than those of
Foch.[28]

Command of the northern sector of the Front, from the Ypres–
Poperinghe Road to the coast was accorded to King Albert, with
11 Belgian divisions and six French. To his right, Plumer remained
in command of the British Second Army, down to the south of
Armentières. Fighting in Flanders flared up again at the end of

August, as the Germans began to pull back from their own exposed salient around Kemmel. The British 38th Division regained Mount Kemmel on 31 August. A fortnight earlier, the US 27th and 30th Divisions took over a sector of the line at the foot of Kemmel. From 31 August to 4 September the Americans were engaged in heavy fighting, during which they advanced for more than a mile and captured the villages of Vierstraat and Voormezele, incurring more than 2,000 casualties. But the main American theatre of war lay far to the east on the Meuse south of Verdun, around St Miel, where the 'doughboys' gained their first victory in Europe.

In the Belgian trenches officers had for some time been concerned at what they regarded as subversive activities by the Flemish Front movement, pressing to secure full self-government for Flanders in post-war Belgium.[29] In June the Front leaders called on Flamingant Dutch-speakers in the trenches to defend themselves against enemy attack but avoid being needlessly slaughtered – a curious distinction, seen by King Albert's French-speaking staff officers as discouraging participation in any drive against the enemy. The Flemish Front leaders believed they could count on 50,000 'militant Flamingant soldiers' but they misunderstood the mood of their compatriots. The men might resent Francophone supremacy, but they loathed German occupation of towns and villages even more intensely. When the opportunity to free the homeland from the invader arose, they stood at one behind their royal commander-in-chief. The Flemish Front leaders were arrested and imprisoned – a rash move, perhaps, for it made them martyrs for their cause.

Yet when the main offensive by King Albert's Flanders Army Group began at dawn on 28 September there was no sign of treasonable disaffection. The Belgians were supported by French and British troops. Across crater-pocked ridges and the wasteland of old trenches the advancing troops met surprisingly little resistance as they took Poelcapelle, Gravenstafel and Passchendaele; by now the most reliable German regiments were holding the Hindenburg Line. It was there that on 29 September the 46th Division – mainly Shropshire lads, together with the Sherwood Foresters – broke into the German defences across the St Quentin canal, taking 2,400 prisoners and capturing 70 guns.[30] In Flanders that day the Belgians found the German defences in the forest of Houthulst more formidable, and they suffered heavy losses. As so often in this sector, the weather intervened. By 2 October the attackers were again impeded by heavy mud. The old prize of Roulers still eluded them.

Meanwhile, Plumer's troops had thrust forward up the Menin Road beyond Hooge, recovering land lost in April and the earlier battles. The greatest change of all, however, came on 3 October in Ypres itself. Not a shell struck the town or the ruined villages clustering around it on that Thursday. An eerie silence suffused the streets. After four years the town was beyond the reach of German guns and the noise of battle receded into a distant rumble. Within a fortnight, VADs, the women who had volunteered for front-line nursing with the Voluntary Aid Detachment, were tending the wounded in Ypres's improvised hospitals.

Gradually the Germans pulled back across Belgium. As early as 3 October the navy ordered 31 serviceable destroyers, torpedo-boats and U-boats to leave Ostend, Zeebrugge and the Bruges canal for the safety of home ports. At last, on the morning of 17 October, a British aeroplane flying over Ostend reported that the Germans had pulled out of the town. That afternoon Sir Roger Keyes welcomed King Albert and Queen Elisabeth aboard the destroyer HMS *Termagant* at Dunkirk. With the black, red and gold standard of Belgium flying above the White Ensign the *Termagant* made a surprise entry into Ostend harbour, to the delight of the townsfolk. 'A wonderful trip,' King Albert wrote to Lord Curzon. 'It was a great day for us to enter our first reconquered town after 4 years.'[31]

Two days later Belgian troops liberated Bruges and Zeebrugge and reached the Dutch frontier outside Sluis: the coast was cleared. The Flanders Army Group was poised to press forward on Ghent, Brussels, and Charleroi with Plumer's Second Army between the rivers Lys and Scheldt, two French corps supporting the Belgian drive on Roulers and Courtrai, and the mass of the Belgian army to the north and east.

Europe's future, however, was being shaped elsewhere, in a valley of pine and birch on the fringe of the Belgian Ardennes. OHL's headquarters were in the Hotel Britannique at Spa. There the news reaching Hindenburg and Ludendorff was uniformly bad: the defences in the West were crumbling; the allied armies based on Salonika had forced Germany's smallest ally, Bulgaria, to seek peace terms; the multinational Habsburg and Ottoman empires were close to disintegration, and 'red cells' of Bolshevik trouble-makers were reportedly agitating in the fleet and the munition factories. The military paladins thought peace and constitutional reforms essential for Germany if the Reich was not to suffer the fate of Russia; Kaiser Wilhelm recognized the logic behind their arguments, though reluctantly and with reservations. In a letter to the Crown Council in Berlin, dated 4 October, Hindenburg pressed the need for the 'immediate despatch' of a peace offer: 'Owing to the breakdown on the Macedonian Front . . . weakening our reserves in the West' and 'the impossibility of making good our very heavy losses in the battles of the last few days . . . it is imperative to stop fighting . . . in order to spare further useless sacrifices,' he explained, 'Every day lost costs thousands of brave soldiers' lives.'[32] Through Swiss mediation, contact was made with President Woodrow Wilson in Washington on 4 October.

Despite the urgency of Hindenburg's plea, the conflict continued for five more weeks: the allied governments were divided over the terms to be offered to the enemy, with influential figures in France, Britain and America arguing for the war to be carried into Germany as an act of preventive retribution.[33] At times the fighting reached an even greater intensity. Some German positions were fanatically defended by individual regiments or battalions – Prussian, Bavarian or Saxon – frustrated by the sudden transition from near victory to imminent defeat. Conversely, Herbert Sulzbach thought the French shelling a week before the Armistice was the heaviest of the war: 'It isn't a barrage any more, it isn't even a hurricane of fire, it's a typhoon of fire!', he wrote in his diary on 4 November.[34] During the last hundred days of the war in the West the British took 188,000 prisoners, the French 140,000, the Americans 44,000 and the Belgians 14,000.

After the liberation of Bruges, the pace of the left flank of the Flanders Army Group slackened, in part because of delicate political negotiations between emissaries from the capital and King Albert; the Belgians were still in the western outskirts of Ghent when the war ended. On the Scheldt the British Second Army reached Marlborough's old battlefield of Oudenarde. Further south the reconstituted Fifth Army had crossed from Lille into the province of Hainaut at the end of October; attached to the Fifth were the Portuguese, with the same liaison officer, Captain

Dartford, attached, as during the March débâcle; he noted that their reintegration was supervised by 'a strong personality . . . Col. B. L. Montgomery'.[35] By 10 November the Fifth Army was near Tournai. Slightly over half of Belgium was still under German occupation.

On Thursday, 7 November, there were rumours in London and Washington that an armistice had been signed. In reality, a German delegation was at last on its way to meet Marshal Foch in his headquarters Pullman train at Réthondes, in the forest of Compiègne; there would be no more negotiations but the delegates had to seek final authority to sign the proffered terms from Spa – and it was still possible that Germany would fight on. Expectancy in the trenches ran high over the weekend when, on Saturday evening, it was confirmed that Kaiser Wilhelm had abdicated and was said to be seeking sanctuary in Holland. Soon after five in the morning of Monday, 11 November, the Armistice was signed in Foch's railway-saloon office. 'Hostilities will cease at 11 A.M. today,' Foch informed all commanders in the field at ten minutes to seven. Fittingly, on the previous afternoon, Canadians and British had entered Mons, where for the BEF it all began.

14

THE PILGRIM TRAIL

It took Captain Herbert Sulzbach's regiment 12 days to cover 200 miles from the Armistice line to Bonn, where they were 'cheered like anything' and marched proudly past their commanding general at the bridge over the Rhine. As they pulled back through the Belgian villages they 'kept meeting small or large parties of French or British prisoners moving west on their way home'. Yet, though Sulzbach reflected sadly 'on the splendid mood they must be in compared to us', he commented more than once on the conviction of his compatriots, soldiers and civilians alike, that 'we are undefeated and unconquerable'.[1] Dangerous legends were already in the making.

Throughout the second half of November 1918 and into December the armies were on the march again, back to the old frontier and beyond. The Armistice terms stipulated that allied and associated troops should occupy all western Germany as far as the Rhine. The French were to have a bridgehead across the river at Mainz, the British at Cologne and the Americans at Coblenz. No sector was specifically allocated to the Belgians, but it was subsequently agreed they would press northeastwards, as far as Duisburg. Despite political disorder in many German cities and pillaging in Brussels by one disaffected unit, the withdrawal from Belgium proceeded in good order and with impeccable discipline. The Dutch allowed as many as 70,000 Germans who had served in Flanders to pass through their province of Limburg and make their way home free of any restraints imposed by their enemies, a concession that infuriated the victors. But the armies further south rigidly followed a prescribed programme of retreat.

Two days after the guns ceased firing King Albert and Queen Elisabeth were welcomed in Ghent, although delicate political discussions delayed the king's entry into his capital at the head of the army until Friday, 22 November. King George V's second son, Prince Albert, represented his father at the celebrations in Brussels and, wearing RAF khaki, rode beside the Belgian king from the Port de Flandre to the Place de la Nation in autumn sunshine, among happy crowds whose cheers were often choked with emotion. General Plumer was among the allied commanders who, along with Belgium's political and religious leaders, greeted the king in the Chamber of Deputies. There the monarch delivered a speech from the throne promising major reforms including universal male suffrage, an equal status for the two national languages and the establishment of a specifically Flemish university in Ghent. Although Belgian women had to wait until 1946 before they could vote, this speech foreshadowed radical changes in the structure of Belgian society, particularly in the relationship between Flemings and Walloons.[2]

The victorious Salient veterans began their advance on 17 November, the Sunday following the Armistice. At first the British Second Army moved forward at no more than 6 miles (10 km) a day, in order to give the enemy time to retire ahead of them. By Friday, however, some of the cavalry were riding once more beside the fields of Waterloo. The first troops arrived at the German frontier as early as 24 November and concentrated around Aachen, regrouping before continuing their march to the Rhine. The date of 13 December became the day of proudest satisfaction, for soon after nine o'clock that morning the British reached the Hohenzollern Bridge across the great river and entered Cologne, the 9th (Scottish) Division at their head, followed by the 29th Division, the Gallipoli veterans who had fought so tenaciously at St Julien during Third Ypres. Above them, the equestrian statue of the fallen kaiser in martial pose looked out towards the lands his armies failed to hold. Three days later Haig arrived in Cologne and was received by Plumer with a guard of honour outside the railway station. In the years ahead many ex-servicemen, reflecting on the sudden change of fortune in the autumn of 1918, remembered the day of crossing the Rhine and entering Prussia's second largest city as the moment they could finally accept the reality of victory.

As so often during the past 33 months the most famous of trench magazines reflected the mood of the day. The *Wipers Times* had changed its name on five occasions, to keep up with the movements of the 24th Division, and when in December 1918 the twenty-third and final copy appeared it carried a long and involved letterhead: 'The *Better Times* with which are incorporated the Wipers Times, the New Church Times, the Kemmel Times, the Somme Times and the B.E.F. Times.' But, whatever the title, its 12 pages retained the familiar medley of simple jokes, dry irony and sentimentality that lifted morale in the darkest days. Readers were, for example, warned of 'the horrors of peace', their attention drawn to the attack 'the redcaps' began on 11 November when a 'barrage of paper fell right on our trenches, and mixed with the H.E. was gas in enormous quantities'. But the editorial struck a more serious note:

> One cannot but remark on the absolute apathy with which the end was received over here. England seems to have had a jollification, but here one saw nothing but a disinterested interest in passing events. Perhaps that was because the end came without the expected culminative crash, and the decisive battle was spread over many months and so became an indefinite action and not a 'show'. Anyway though some may be sorry it's over, there is little doubt that the line men are not, as most of us have been cured of any little illusions we may have had about the pomp and glory of war, and know it for the vilest disaster that can befall mankind.[3]

Back in Wipers itself, there was still a strong British presence. A makeshift hospital remained open, caring both for the men struck down by Spanish flu and for those wounded by the explosive debris of war that littered the fields and the streets. The search for live shells and grenades began, and so too did the systematic registering of graves, under the supervision of the Imperial War Graves Commission and the inspired leadership of Major Fabian Ware, who had set up the first Graves Registration Commission as early as March 1915. Shell holes were filled in, sometimes by German prisoners of war but also by 'coolies' from the Chinese Labour Corps, who remained encamped near Poperinghe for ten months after the Armistice. Progress was slow, not least because of heavy snowfalls in February 1919 that covered the city's wounds with a white frozen sheet. After the thaw the fields remained sodden, bringing back to the surface that 'Flemish porridge' so familiar to all who had survived Passchendaele. Life remained hard for Belgians across the kingdom: only food relief from the British and Americans staved off a famine and a combination of war damage and German confiscations hampered industrial recovery. Before the end of the year four out of every five Belgian workers could not find steady employment either in the factories or the fields.

For several months after the war decisions on the immediate future of Ypres continued to be imposed by the town-major, Lieutenant-Colonel Beckles Willson, a Canadian. He was a fanatical advocate of preserving the ruins of the city as 'an eternal memorial to British valour', and he wrote: 'What Jerusalem is to the Jewish race, what Mecca is to the Mohammedan Ypres must always be to the millions who have lost a husband, son or brother, slain in its defence, and now sleeping their eternal sleep within sight of its silent belfry.' Until he was demobilized in October 1919, Willson used his authority to advance his ideas, even forbidding the start of work on rebuilding homes and shops around the Grand Place. 'This is Holy Ground! No stone of this fabric to be taken away. It is a heritage for all civilised people' ran a notice placed over the rubble of the Cloth Hall. After demobilization Willson played a major role in setting up the Ypres League, the association of Salient veterans, under the active presidency of Field Marshal Viscount Plumer of Messines and Bilton (the title taken by the former Second Army commander when, in 1919, he was raised to the peerage).

In London, Churchill, who returned to the Cabinet as Lloyd George's secretary of state for war and air in January 1919, recognized the force of Beckles Willson's arguments. 'I should like us to acquire the whole of the ruins of Ypres,' Churchill told the Imperial War Graves Commission a week after taking up office: 'A more sacred place for the British race does not exist in the world,' he proclaimed. Many in London agreed with him, to establish a protected zone of pilgrimage appealed to popular sentiment. But it was a curiously possessive idea; it ignored Belgian national feeling and the pride of the Yprians in their historic past. In the immediate aftermath of war too little thought was given to the long-term needs of 'brave little Belgium'. It was fortunate that within the Cabinet Lord Curzon, ever sympathetic to King Albert, consistently countered the more extreme proposals with sound common sense. Ypres was singled out for honour with the award of the Military Cross in 1921, more than a year after President Poincaré bestowed the Croix de Guerre on the city. Practical aid came from the Agricultural Relief of Allies Committee, a body in which its patron, King George V, took a personal interest. Once the fields were cleared fertilizers, seeds, cattle and chickens were sent across the Channel to help Flemish farmers.[4] King George and Queen Mary saw Ypres and the Salient battlefields for themselves in May 1922, during an eight-day state visit to Belgium.

The government in Brussels – a ten-man coalition in which half the ministers were francophone Catholics – was inclined to allow preservation of the devastated Cloth Hall and the cathedral church of St Martin. The ministers also considered preserving Dixmude in its ruined state as a similar tribute to the Belgians killed in the Yser battles. But before the war West Flanders had become one of Belgium's most fertile agricultural areas; it was too vibrant a province to have towns fossilized as archaeological sites. More than 50 villages in the Salient and along the Yser had been levelled during the four years of shelling and hand-to-hand fighting. The Belgian government instituted a Service for Devastated Regions as soon as the guns fell silent but little could be achieved during the winter months. Some farmers took the initiative, recruited temporary labourers themselves and cleared the fields, subsequently seeking reimbursement by the state, but to undertake a major rebuilding programme was beyond their means.

By spring 1919 almost a third of the Flemish peasant refugees had come back in search of what remained of their homes – and found in most cases that they had to improvise shelters, sometimes taking advantage of the old German bunkers. The Belgian authorities hurriedly purchased some of the many British Nissen huts still in the Salient and promised the home-comers 'Albert Houses' – temporary wooden bungalows, provided from a fund sponsored by the king. The Albert Houses were slow to arrive. They could be erected speedily, but they proved extremely cramped: a family's needs were met either with three rooms, covering an area of 65 square feet, or by two squeezed into just over 40 square feet.[5] Although a high royal commissioner was appointed in April 1919 to co-ordinate planning, by midsummer the leading Dutch-language newspaper was complaining of 'the government's shameful neglect of the Flemish people'.[6] This apparent muddle over reconstruction made good propaganda for the Flemish national movement, already a powerful influence across the Yser basin.

The initiative was taken, not by the high royal commissioner, but by a clear-minded, vigorous burgomaster whom the Yprians were fortunate to have presiding over their municipal affairs. Long before the Armistice was signed René Colaert voiced his opposition to preserving the ruins: Ypres should be rebuilt and recover its rightful place as one of Belgium's historic cities. The burgomaster was supported by Jules Coomans, whose work on modernizing Ypres had been nearing completion when the war began, and also by a younger architect, Eugène Dhuicque, who had remained in Ypres and supervised the erection of emergency buttresses to support the outer shell of the Cloth Hall after the great bombardment. Colaert toured the kingdom to collect money for rebuilding the Cloth Hall and to make certain that Flemish Ypres, no less than Louvain in Brabant, was remembered as one of Belgium's 'martyred cities'. Meanwhile, with municipal backing, the townsfolk set about the task of reconstruction independent of any formal plan. Work began on the totally wrecked railway station. The Place de la Gare – or as most locals called it the Stationsplein – was cleared of debris; the centre of the square was filled with flower-beds and shrubs that came as a gift from England; young trees were planted along what had been the Boulevard Malou, making a pleasant contrast to the Nissen hut shanties of the first months of peace. By 1923 a new station was complete and hotels opened for visitors in the square as well as along the northern side of the Grand Place and the western end of the Menin Road. René Colaert remained the most influential figure in Ypres until he became terminally ill in 1927. The Stationsplein was renamed in his honour.

The British attachment to the sacred ruins remained an embarrassing problem. In spring 1920, Colaert had suggested that the most suitable memorial to the British dead would be the rebuilding of the Cloth Hall in their honour, but this proposal was unacceptable to the British government, not least on financial grounds.

A few months later Colaert did, however, succeed in accommodating the wishes of a newly constituted National Battlefield
Memorials Committee, headed by Lord Midleton, to the needs
of the city. It was agreed that the Midleton Committee should
abandon the idea of a memorial in the centre of Ypres and consider
replacing the wrecked Menin Gate that had stood at the head of the
road along which so many thousands had marched into battle: Hell
Fire Corner was barely a mile (just over 1 km) away. In June 1921
the Midleton Committee and the War Graves Commission
authorized Sir Reginald Blomfield to design a memorial that would
both honour the long struggle of King George V's armies in the
Salient and commemorate by name the 'missing' dead.

Blomfield chose to create a new and grandiose Menin Gate,
where before the war there had been a mere passageway through
Vauban's ramparts. Work began in spring 1923. It immediately ran
into difficulties that might perhaps have been foreseen, for beneath
the surface clay came a layer of shifting sand. Blomfield had to sink
a virtual carpet of concrete piles 36 feet into the ground to support
the massive arch he envisaged. The Scottish sculptor William Reid
Dick, himself a veteran of the Western Front, designed a lion, alert
and brooding rather than poised to roar; it surmounts the eastern
entry to the arch and looks out towards the eastern ridges between
Gheluvert and Passchendaele. Beneath the lion, and beneath the
sarcophagus with which Blomfield crowned the western entrance
to the arch, was inscribed the dedication: 'To the armies of the
British Empire who stood here from 1914 to 1918 and to those of
their dead who have no known grave.'

The inauguration of the Menin Gate was planned to mark the
tenth anniversary of Third Ypres. Characteristically the weather
threatened to delay completion. Heavy rain swept in from the
northeast as the painters worked to engrave the last of the 54,900
names of officers and men with no known grave on the panels of
the interior of the arch or beside the steps and in the loggias. But
the gate was completed on time, and on Sunday, 24 July 1927,
Field Marshal Viscount Plumer unveiled the memorial in the
presence of King Albert and several thousand relatives of the dead.
Buglers from the Somerset Light Infantry were the first to sound
the Last Post beneath the arch. Pipers from the Scots Guards played
'The Flowers of the Forest', and Lord Plumer sought to hearten the

bereaved: 'Now it can be said of each one in whose honour we are assembled here today, "He is not missing. He is here."' King Albert also spoke, emphasizing that for four years the city of Ypres had stood at the very threshold of the British Empire. The novelty of radio allowed the occasion to be relayed to London by the one-year-old British Broadcasting Corporation. Monday's *Times*, as well as reporting the deeply moving ceremony in full, commented, 'In view of the difficulties, the reception was good.'[7]

The reception accorded Blomfield's masterpiece was, however, mixed. Thousands of bereaved relatives, sweethearts and close friends present that Sunday shed tears of anguished pride on seeing the name of a loved one incised on the panels. So did many other visitors who made individual pilgrimages to Ypres during the summer of 1927, when for two months after the unveiling the Last Post rang out each evening from beneath the arch. But some veterans were deeply unhappy. Many found their reflective memory rekindled only by the cemeteries and poppies. Siegfried Sassoon, who attended the ceremony on 24 July, went angrily back to Brussels and in a powerful poem deplored the consecrating of this 'sepulchre of crime'.[8] Others were affronted by what they considered the pompous grandeur of the memorial itself, feeling it was out of character with the rebuilt town that lay behind it.

There was criticism, too, at the failure to provide enough panels in the Menin Gate to include the full roll of 90,000 'no known grave' names. For the United Kingdom dead, the panels showed only those killed before 15 August 1917. Some 34,000 further names of United Kingdom victims of the last 15 months of battle were inscribed on Sir Herbert Baker's memorial boundary wall at Tyne Cot. Unlike the Canadians, the South Africans and Australians, the New Zealand government preferred to honour all of the Dominion's 'missing' names with memorials close to where they fell, notably at Polygon Wood, Messines, Tyne Cot and neighbouring Gravenstafel.[9]

A year after the unveiling – on 8 August 1928 – the British Legion, the charity for ex-servicemen for which Earl Haig had worked tirelessly until his death in the previous January, organized the first, great, national pilgrimage to Ypres and the arc of surrounding cemeteries. It was a five-day event with 11,000 participants and culminated in a Sunday service at the Menin Gate attended by 20,000 people, which was again broadcast across the Channel. The Legion's pilgrims included the Prince of Wales.

By now the craftsmen and gardeners of the Imperial War Graves Commission were bringing peace and dignity to the battle cemeteries created during the war itself. Uniform headstones, designed by Sir Edwin Lutyens and given slightly curved tops to relieve their severity, replaced the temporary wooden crosses of wartime; carefully trimmed lawns set among shrubs and plants suggested the serenity of an English country garden. A white Cross of Sacrifice, designed by Blomfield and bearing a bronze sword of salvation, presided over each cemetery. Some headstones showed the emblems of other faiths, notably the Star of David. 'There are more than 150 burial places, 169 to be exact, within an area of less than 140 square kilometres or 54 square miles,' Dr Marc Derez estimates. 'One cemetery per square kilometre or three at least per square mile.'[10] One of the smallest cemeteries, dating back to the earliest fighting, was on Ypres's ramparts, shaded by trees above the waters of Vauban's moat. The largest of British cemeteries in any theatre of war was on Tyne Cot, where Baker included three surviving German pillboxes in his colonnaded memorial wall. No lion was depicted here, as on the Menin Gate: instead, sculpted kneeling angels surmount the twin pavilions at either end of the wall, in mourning for the dead of Passchendaele.

In July 1931, Albert's son, the future King Leopold III, inaugurated a memorial to the missing in the Armentières sector of the Front at Ploegsteert, only a short distance from the Franco-Belgian border. On it were inscribed more than 11,000 names, commemorating not only those killed around Ploegsteert but also some of the dead with no known grave from Loos, Aubers Ridge and Hazebrouck. These battlefields were well across the frontier; their dead were buried in Belgian Flanders because the authorities in Paris would allow the British only four memorials on French soil. Sir Gilbert Ledward's open-rotunda design for the Ploegsteert Memorial made an interesting contrast to Baker's classicism.

In central Ypres, northwest of the cathedral, one further shrine of remembrance for the war dead of the United Kingdom and the Dominions was completed more than a decade after the fighting ended. St George's Memorial Church, designed by Blomfield in unmistakably Anglican style, was built in response to an appeal from Viscount French, made shortly before his death in May 1925, and warmly backed by the Ypres League. Lord Plumer laid the foundation stone immediately after unveiling the Menin Gate, and St George's was dedicated on Good Friday, 1929. Soon brass plaques covered the walls or were inserted discreetly into the floor, commemorating by name the contribution of outstanding individuals and the tenacity of battalions, regiments or divisions. Fading regimental-colours standards hung above the outer aisles like banners of an order of chivalry. A new 'must' was added to the British pilgrim trail.

Despite the chronic uncertainties of the Irish problem between the wars, the province of Cork presented Ypres with a Celtic cross monument to the dead of the Munster Regiment, which was placed uniquely in the centre of the city, outside St Martin's Cathedral. Not until 1998 did a single memorial commemorate the 'thousands of young men from all parts of Ireland . . . who fought a common enemy'. On the eightieth anniversary of the Armistice, Queen Elizabeth II and President Mary McAleese unveiled a stone Peace Tower in a specially created park on Messines Ridge, and Catholics and Protestants alike solemnly repudiated 'violence, aggression, intimidation, threats and un-friendly behaviour'. But another world war had been fought and Northern Ireland wracked by almost 30 years of bloodshed before such a pledge of peace could be made.

Apart from a Belgian war cemetery at Zonnebeke and a French cemetery south of Wieltje, most final burial places for other nationalities lay some distance from Ypres, making less impact on the prevailing landscape than did the British. The largest Belgian cemetery was set in the forest of Houthulst, some 7 miles north of Poelcapelle and east of Dixmude. There is also an attractively wooded cemetery at Keim, north of Dixmude, and others near Poperinghe and at Ramscapelle. Soldiers from the United States killed in August and September 1918 were buried in the Flanders Field American Cemetery at Waregem, beneath the first slopes of Mount Kemmel. The main French national cemetery at Kemmel dates from the early 1920s, but it was not until 1932 that Marshal Pétain unveiled the impressive winged figure that fronts the column on the hill above it. The French were slower at caring for graves in foreign fields than remembering the dead of their homeland; Pétain had inaugurated the massive and macabre Thiaumont Ossuaire on the ridge north of Verdun five years earlier, within weeks of the unveiling of the Menin Gate.

At first the German dead – more than 100,000 across Flanders – posed problems for the diplomats. In 1925, however, the Belgians agreed that the authorities in Berlin should assume responsibility for almost 700 small cemeteries in West Flanders. Work began on concentrating the burials at Langemarck and at Vladslo, some 3 miles east of Dixmude, or out at Menin, which with nearly 48,000 burials became the largest German cemetery. Hooglede, where only some 8,250 were interred, remained almost unchanged.

The legend of heroic sacrifice made by student volunteers in October 1914 gave Langemarck a special place in Nazi mythology, and when the enlarged cemetery was rededicated in 1932 brown-shirted SA were present in noisy numbers. Despite flowering shrubs and the colourful insignia of the German universities, Langemarck remains a sombre resting place, shaded by oaks. A mass grave holds the bones of 25,000 victims of the early fighting. Concrete from a German pillbox, dating back to 1916, was incorporated in the north wall. At the far end of the cemetery four sculptured figures stand at attention, mourning silhouettes against the western sky.

Belgian restrictions on the amount of land that might be covered by cemeteries for the vanquished made them necessarily compact. Even at Langemarck in some instances eight exhumed bodies were reburied in a single grave, with the names and rank of the dead (when known) recorded on a flat-stone marker shared with a second grave. Among the dead at Vladslo is 18-year-old Musketeer Peter Kollwitz, the son of a doctor and a sculptress from Berlin, who was killed on 23 October 1914 in a Belgian attack near neighbouring Esen; Kollwitz's name is inscribed on a stone alongside 19 others. Originally he was buried in the small graveyard at Esen, but in 1956 the remains of all interred there were transferred to the larger cemetery. His mother's tragically beautiful memorial, showing two parents on their knees in grief, was completed for Esen in 1932 but moved to its present site at the same time as the reburial.[11] While the angels of Tyne Cot and the statuesque mourners of Langemarck pay tribute to soldiers who died fulfilling their sense of duty, Käthe Kollwitz's creation perpetuates the human tragedy of families called to sacrifice the joys of parenthood and plunged thereafter into questioning sorrow over the futility of war.

Inevitably the spread of memorials and war cemeteries changed the character of Ypres. Gradually old landmarks were restored: St Martin's Cathedral was ready by 1930, the city's skyline improved by an elegant spire above what, in old photographs, always looks an unfinished tower. Work began in earnest on the Cloth Hall in 1928, and the belfry was unveiled in 1934, although it was another 33 years before the scaffolding finally came down around the Nieuwerk.

Post-war Ypres remained a market town, bustling with activity on Saturday mornings. But the most profitable industry was now a restrained tourism that, at least between the wars, avoided vulgarity. The devaluation of the Belgian franc in 1926, leading to a revised exchange rate favouring sterling, attracted more and more English visitors, at least until the slump of 1931; a further devaluation by 28 per cent in 1935 led to a second influx. The emphasis was focused on remembrance. From May 1929 the sounding of the Last Post by buglers under the Menin Gate became a nightly ceremony that was to continue until six days before the German army returned 11 years later. A Salient Museum opened in the basement of what had once been the Butcher's Hall. Visitors who might have patronized a Belgian company were assured that only 'bona-fide British ex-servicemen' were employed as drivers and guides for the cars and charabancs of Blue Queens excursions. The Blue Queens were ambitious: they sought to boost Ypres's hotels as centres for Belgium as a whole by offering daily excursions to Brussels, Antwerp, Ghent and Bruges and every Thursday to Middelburg market, on the Dutch island of Walcheren. For purely holiday tourists, however, Ypres could never compete with the long line of resorts along the coast.[12] Within the Salient the Blue Queens had as rivals Wipers Auto Services, also run by veterans, while other ex-officers were ready to drive visitors to particular battle-sites or cemeteries at 10 guineas for each journey – payable, no doubt, in sterling.

Most visitors came, however, as day trippers, whisked in by coach from Ostend and Blankenberge, Heist or Knokke. They saw the Menin Gate, watched the restoration of the Cloth Hall and were taken out to Tyne Cot cemetery and Hill 60, the most frequented battle-site. In the 1930s the coaches paused at Diksmuide (the Dutch name for wartime Dixmude) during their journey from the coast to remind their passengers of what many felt was the forgotten sector of the Western Front.

The French had honoured the Yser battles as early as January 1920, when the ruined town received the Croix de Guerre at the same time as Ypres. But political tension between Dutch-speakers and French-speakers delayed commemoration of the heroic struggle by the government in Brussels. At last, ten years after the Armistice, a Calvary dedicated to soldiers and civilians killed during the war was erected on the far side of the river south of Dixmude. Belgians from all parts of the kingdom travelled to the Calvary and knelt in prayer at a religious shrine blessed by the Catholic Church.

Flemish nationalists – most of them lower-middle-class Dutch-speakers from the smaller towns and villages – were far from satisfied. Even while the war was in progress, gravestones with specifically Flemish markings were replaced by standard stones with French inscriptions, a practice intensified after the return of peace. Resentment at continued discrimination against Flanders induced Dutch-speaking sympathizers to raise a large sum for the erection in 1930 of the IJzertoren, a 165-foot tower half a mile west of Dixmude. Architecturally the tower was a striking symbol, a huge Celtic-style cross solidly expressionist, anti-militarist in conception and dedicated to the Flemish war dead; the bodies of eight Flemish heroes were interred in the crypt. High on the IJzertoren the letters AVV–VVK stood out boldly: they comprised the initials of the nationalists' fundamental pledge, 'All for Flanders: Flanders for Christ'. Anyone heading down the N35 to Ypres could not fail to be impressed. Pan-Belgian pilgrimages to the Calvary declined. Each August, Flemish ex-servicemen's associations gathered at the tower for ceremonies that began as tributes to the war dead but increasingly became strident protests at the failure of the government in Brussels to satisfy Flanders's needs or defend Flemish interests.

The Flemish Question, particularly the language issue, plagued Belgian politics throughout the inter-war years. It was voiced more often at demonstrations or in the press than in parliament; Flemish nationalists, sitting under various labels, remained a fringe group in the chamber. Concessions were gradually wrung from a succession of 18 coalition governments, all except two headed by Catholic leaders. As early as 1921, Dutch alone was recognized as the language of administration in the Flemish provinces although, since the schooling of most civil servants had been in French, the law was difficult to enforce. The University of Ghent did indeed become fully Dutch speaking, as King Albert had promised in his speech from the throne, but not until 1930. Proposals for separate Dutch-speaking and francophone armies were abandoned, as inoperable and potentially divisive. At last in 1931–2 revised legislation clarified the status of Dutch as the recognized language of the Flemish provinces: in the old Salient, Ypres thereafter officially became Ieper, Passchendaele Passendale, the Menin Gate the Menenpoort and the Lille Gate the Rijselsepoort.

Despite his undoubted respect for democracy, King Albert kept a tight hold on foreign affairs and defence, although, in 1924, Flemish nationalists thwarted a proposed commercial treaty he favoured with France. In 1918–19 he was incensed with the Dutch over their relations with Germany during and after the war; he backed a bid by his foreign minister, Paul Hymans, to induce the victorious Great Powers to force Holland to cede the Dutch province of Limburg and the left bank of the Scheldt down to the sea in a general readjustment of frontiers. This policy was unrealistic: both Hymans and his king hoped to benefit from the adulation heaped on Albert and his suffering subjects in the first months of war. But there is no place in diplomacy for gratitude or sentiment. The realism of the Paris peacemakers came as a shock. 'Has England forgotten August 1914?' ran a banner of protest at a demonstration in Brussels.[13] By the Treaty of Versailles, Belgium's sole gains from the Great War were 400 sq miles of heavily forested land around Eupen and Malmédy, a mandate over Ruanda–Urundi (formerly in German East Africa) and a far smaller sum in reparations than Albert thought his kingdom merited. It was not finally paid for another six years.

Both the king and Hymans – foreign minister eight times down to March 1935 – were ready to jettison the old concept of neutrality, convinced that it had failed the nation in the pre-war crisis. Despite Albert's lingering suspicion of France, the Belgians sought security by attachment to the new alliance system the French were building up in Europe, and in September 1920 a military agreement was concluded, remaining secret for more than a year. When, in 1923, Germany lagged behind in payment of Reparations, Belgian troops supported the French decision to occupy the Ruhr. Such close co-operation was always highly unpopular within Flanders. The policy came under severe strain after 1929 once the French began to build fortifications as a barrier against German aggression, for the proposed Maginot Line stopped short at the Belgian-Luxembourg frontier. Many Belgians argued that the new, purely defensive, role of the French army invited Germany at some future date to strike once more through their kingdom to outflank the Maginot Line. The anger of demonstrators on the Yser pilgrimage — anti-French, anti-militarist, anti-Brussels — reached such a pitch that it attracted attention abroad: was Belgium moving towards partition?

The king's prestige continued to bind the nation together, but, in February 1934, Albert slipped and fell to his death while rock-climbing near Namur. He was succeeded by his eldest son, 32-year-old Leopold III, carefully groomed for the past 20 years for the responsibilities awaiting him but lacking his father's worldly intelligence and moral courage. For most of the Great War, Prince Leopold had remained with his mother, brother and sister at the Villa Maskens in La Panne, less than 15 miles from the Yser Front. When he was 14 he was formally 'presented' in uniform to the 12th Infantry Regiment and crossed to England in 1917 to further his education at Eton, joining the Officers Training Corps at the college. A happy marriage in 1926 to the beautiful Princess Astrid of Sweden helped Leopold conquer a diffidence he showed in these early years, and the couple were popular in Brussels and Wallonia. Tragedy struck on 29 August 1935, a mere 17 months into the reign, while they were on holiday in Switzerland: Leopold was driving his car beside Lake Lucerne near Küssnacht when he apparently misjudged a bend in the road and crashed, killing Queen Astrid.

On recovering from his injuries the grief-stricken king buried himself in official duties, but he became increasingly dependent for advice on his military aide-de-camp, General Raoul van Over-straeten, who in 1917–18 had served on Albert's staff at Furnes. In

1940, General Sir Alan Brooke thought Overstraeten an evil influence on the king, and General Montgomery agreed with him.[14] In 1936, however, Overstraeten's views seemed to Leopold to make good sense. Flemish nationalists, and the growing number of Catholic politicians shocked by the leftward swing of Paris politics, would be placated by cancellation of the 1920 agreement with France. Leopold could then commit Belgium to a treaty-free neutrality, and in relief parliament would accept increased taxes to complete the new, proudly Belgian, defensive line of hopefully impregnable forts, west of Maastricht, begun in Albert's later years; Eben Emael, the key concrete and steel fortress, covering three vital bridges over the Albert canal north of Liège, already bristled with well-protected artillery. The end of the military accord with France was publicly announced on 6 March 1936. Significantly next morning Hitler defied the Treaty of Versailles and sent the German army eastwards into the demilitarized Rhineland.

In May a general election showed a swing to the right, with a newly formed fascist party receiving almost an eighth of the votes cast nation-wide. The chief of staff General Édouard van den Bergen, a Francophile at heart, still hoped to keep in touch with the French Ministry of War, but for the moment Overstraeten's star was in the ascendant, and little heed was given to van den Bergen's views. The king pressed ahead with the policy inaugurated earlier in the year. In a speech in October 1936 he looked back to the situation in 1914: he declared it was now time for Belgium to prepare, not for a coalition war against Germany, but for crises in which powerful defences would let the kingdom remain as 'unflinchingly' neutral as 'the Netherlands and Switzerland'.[15] Two months later military conscription was extended from 12 to 17 months, and work was speeded up on the Albert canal defence line. The Brialmont doctrine was, it seemed, back in favour.

On 13 October 1937, Germany gave an assurance to Brussels that the Führer would respect Belgium's neutrality. King Leopold believed his Belgium could serve Europe as a neutral arbitrator, a role he strove personally to assert in the last month of peace and again after the conquest and partition of Poland a few weeks later, on both occasions with no success. Less sanguine observers of German policy in Paris and London suspected a resurrection of the original Schlieffen Plan and in January 1939 suggested informal talks to settle a policy should the Netherlands be invaded, but the response from Brussels was adamant: no French troops would be allowed passage through Belgium whatever happened in the north. Mobilization of the Belgian army began on 25 August 1939; by now it included two embryonic motorized cavalry divisions, but no more than 10 tanks. Ten days later King Leopold assumed the responsibilities of commander-in-chief, having approved a declaration of neutrality on the previous day. After inspecting the defences he was as confident of Eben Emael's impregnability as were the French generals of the Maginot Line.

Others shared their king's confidence. Three months earlier, on Whitsunday afternoon, a veteran of the Yser battles fell into conversation with an Englishman and his 12-year-old son on the seafront at Ostend. The Belgian recalled the water-logged trenches around Dixmude and the grim fighting across the river in 1918. 'But it won't happen again,' he said proudly. 'We've fine forts along the canal behind our frontier. If they come next time, they'll never get through.'

15

EPILOGUE: 'THE WAR HAD NEVER STOPPED'

A mere 25 years elapsed between the retreat from Mons and the Anglo-French declaration of war on Hitler's Germany, as short a time span as separated the invasion of the Falklands from the last months of the Blair government. The majority of adults in Britain and France retained clear memories of the earlier conflict, and there was a widespread feeling that the new clash of arms arose from a need to resolve business left unfinished by the Armistice of exhaustion welcomed in November 1918.

Most Great War commanders and statesmen had died before 1939, but some familiar names were soon back in the headlines. On the day war was declared Winston Churchill returned to the Admiralty as first lord, the post he held in 1914. Across the Channel the 73-year old Marshal Pétain was still active, serving as France's ambassador to Franco's Spain, and General Weygand, Foch's wartime 'shadow', was fetched out of retirement to command France's armies in mandated Syria and Lebanon, with his headquarters in Beirut. One survivor from the early Great War battles held even higher office. General Maurice Gamelin, Joffre's head of operational planning at the Marne, was chief of the general staff; he automatically assumed command of French land forces on the coming of war. Gamelin, once an enterprising innovator, was now aged 67, and he seemed cautiously conservative, looking back for inspiration to Joffre the Imperturbable. It was his misfortune to recall the problems of 1914 all too clearly, refighting in his mind a campaign that had come close to defeat. Although King Leopold insisted on observing strict neutrality, Gamelin assumed from the outset that soon there would again be heavy fighting in Belgium, and ways to advance across western Flanders to the rivers Scheldt and Dyle dominated his strategic planning in the first months of the war.[1]

A British Field Force began crossing the Channel on 4 September 1939, the day after war was declared. Before the end of the week it was renamed the British Expeditionary Force at the instigation of King George VI, who believed his subjects would find the familiar name heartening, as he did himself. Within three weeks 152,000 officers and men were in France, with General Viscount Gort VC as the latter-day Sir John French and Sir John Dill and Sir Alan Brooke as corps commanders. Field Force was, perhaps, a more appropriate name than Expeditionary Force, for the second BEF unlike its predecessor was essentially defensive in character. Although boosted in the new year by eight Territorial divisions and eventually including more than 300 tanks, at first the BEF lacked any armour and could count on only 12 squadrons of aircraft in support. Gort's troops were, however, integral to Gamelin's plans. He proposed they should be ready to advance as far forward as Louvain as soon as Hitler invaded Belgium. Meanwhile, true to Joffre's belief that *les Anglais* should be kept well away from the sea and from home, the BEF was concentrated around Lille, sandwiched between the French 7th Army by the coast and the 1st Army between Valenciennes and Maubeuge.

This was familiar ground to many veterans. Men recalled to the colours or volunteering once more from a sense of duty indeed felt they were taking the stage for Act Two of an unfinished drama. Among regular officers was Major-General Sir Bernard Montgomery, commanding 3rd Division: he had been present at the liberation of Lille, after serving on Plumer's staff in 1917 and ten years later brought four fledgling subalterns from his old regiment to hear him expound his views on the Ypres battlefields. General Sir Alan Brooke, too, recalled that earlier war, with mixed feelings of nostalgia and dismay. On 13 October he wrote in his diary, 'Had tea in Sir John French's old billet' at St Omer. Three weeks later Brooke saw 'the window I used to look out of at headquarters during the battle of Vimy. It brought back floods of memories, and made me feel that the war had never stopped. It had only been interrupted by a happy dream of 20 years.'[2]

The first winter of war was the coldest in Europe for many years;

there was little fighting along the Western Front. Hitler, however, insisted that the Army General Staff (OKH) should prepare for an early offensive, designed to knock out France and force 'England' to sue for peace. The first plan, 'Fall Gelb' (Operation Yellow), was a variation on the original Schlieffen theme, including a march through the Netherlands. A series of postponements, due mainly to the weather, gave General von Manstein, an Army Group chief of staff, the opportunity to put forward drastic changes, in effect combining the 1914 strategic concepts of Moltke and of Falken-hayn. While the offensive would still begin with an invasion of Belgium and Holland, Manstein proposed that the most powerful assault would be made by armoured panzer divisions advancing through the forested Ardennes, now no longer seen as an obstacle to modern tanks and providing an opportunity of outflanking France's Maginot Line forts. The armoured divisions would go forward swiftly around Sedan. One group would then wheel northwards across Artois in a dash for the Channel ports, encircling the allied northern armies in Belgium. The second panzer group would strike due westwards down the Somme to Amiens and Abbeville, sub-sequently descending on Paris, which, it was assumed, would be defended by weaker forces. Hitler approved this 'sickle slice' plan on 20 February 1940. With minor changes it provided the key to the astonishing German victory in the West three months later.[3]

Meanwhile, by chance, the Belgian General Staff had gained details of OKH's original Operation Yellow. On 9 January a small plane ferrying a German major to a conference in Cologne was carried off-course and crashed in deep snow at Mechelen, just across the Belgian frontier. Partially burned papers carried by the major alerted Belgian intelligence to German intentions to march on Paris through the Low Countries.[4] The Dutch and the French were duly warned. Gamelin took the revelations so seriously that he modified his plans. He now proposed that when the Low Countries were invaded no less than 30 French divisions, together with the BEF, should pour into Belgium. The motorized columns of the French 7th Army would then speed across Flanders and into the Netherlands north of Antwerp, with Breda as their objective. Once established at Breda they would bolster Dutch defence before the German right flank could wheel down to the coast and envelop King Leopold's army. This 'Breda Variant' was incorporated in France's operational plans on 10 March. Had the German high command closely followed the pre-1914 Schlieffen Plan, Gamelin's strategy might have checked the invaders and saved Antwerp and all of Flanders from occupation. But it was already out of date. Hitler had given his approval to the 'sickle slice' project 19 days earlier.

War returned to Belgium in the small hours of Friday, 10 May. Heavy air attacks were made on airfields in the Low Countries and northern France, and 16,000 airborne troops parachuted into The Hague, Rotterdam and Leiden. Some 100 picked troops, intensively trained for the operation, landed silently in eleven gliders near Belgium's Albert canal and seized the vital bridges. As dawn broke, paratroopers landed on the roof of Eben Emael, rated the most formidable modern citadel in the world. They brought with them explosive charges, which were dropped down apertures under the outer steel shell or, in two instances, lodged in the barrels of guns projecting from the turrets. Airborne assault was a military innovation as unexpected and as revolutionary as the coming of tanks in the Great War: it was the one eventuality the builders of the fort had failed to consider. Throughout the Friday and on into Saturday the Belgian garrison held out in Eben Emael and the neighbouring defences along the canal. But at noon the survivors were forced to surrender. The protective shield on which Belgians had confidently counted to prevent 'it happening again' was in the invader's hands. Hitler is said to have hugged himself with delight on hearing Eben Emael had fallen.

The allied troops duly moved forward in fulfilment of Gamelin's plan. The French mechanized division reached Breda in record time but no contact was made with the Dutch army, for what remained of its best divisions had swung northwards away from Breda and the Scheldt, desperately seeking to defend Rotterdam. By Saturday evening Gamelin's hopes for the Netherlands were shattered. The mechanized division, woefully short of fuel and with no arrangements made for replenishment, pulled back across the Belgian border to the far from adequate defensive line along the Dyle. That night the BEF completed their planned advance from Lille to Louvain. As General Brooke reached his new headquarters east of Brussels he ended his diary with the ominous comment, 'A day of ceaseless alarming rumours of Belgians giving way!'[5]

During the next fortnight the rumours multiplied. Too often they were found to be true. The Belgian army was soon demoralized, with the fragile bonds linking Dutch-speakers and francophones beginning to wear thin. On Sunday, 12 May, the Germans struck their decisive blow. General Heinz Guderian, the foremost German advocate of armoured warfare, had massed the tanks of his crack XIX Corps in the Ardennes. They now emerged from the reputedly 'unpenetrable' forests and, backed by hundreds of Stuka dive-bombers, secured bridgeheads across the Meuse over the following three days.[6] A French counter-attack failed, and the breach in the allied line broadened into a German corridor 60 miles wide. The BEF began pulling back through Brussels to the Charleroi canal, its commanders already alarmed by the mounting German threat on both flanks. In Paris the prime minister, Paul Reynaud, turned in despair to two First World War 'saviours'. Marshal Pétain reached the capital early on 18 May, to enter Reynaud's government as vice-premier. Even earlier on that Saturday, General Weygand set out by air from Beirut, summoned home to replace the discredited Gamelin as commander-in-chief.[7]

During the 30-hour flight Weygand jotted down notes of possible military options, based upon experience of the earlier war for he knew nothing of what was happening in the current battle. Most comments were generalities, echoes of Foch at his pinnacle of power, but the notes are more specific over the needs of Belgium, where Weygand had spent much of a mysterious boyhood, with his parentage unknown but the Boulevard Waterloo in Brussels registered as his place of birth. High among his priorities was the need for King Leopold's army to maintain contact with the French and the BEF, defending Flanders and the coast, though ready to open once more the sluice gates and fall back on a line of defence behind the Yser.[8]

By Sunday afternoon (19th), when Weygand reached central Paris, such thoughts were largely academic. That afternoon Guderian's panzers were crossing the old battlefield of the Somme, fighting off a series of persistent incursions by tanks of the French 4th Armoured Division, commanded by a General de Gaulle, a name as yet unknown to the public. Next day the panzers leapt forward another 60 miles, entering Abbeville in the evening, with an Austrian tank battalion reaching the Channel coast. Weygand found this 'lightning warfare' as puzzling to comprehend as the first months of the Great War had seemed to Kitchener but, within 30 hours of arriving in Paris, he was in the air again, making a courageous flight across the new panzer corridor to an airfield near Béthune and on to Calais.[9] He was determined to confer with King Leopold, General Gort and General Billotte, commander of the French Army Group. From Calais, Weygand was driven to Ypres, down 60 miles of road crammed with refugee columns, as in the dark days of 1914. By 3 p.m. he was in the town hall, looking out across the Grand Place at the still incomplete restoration of buildings levelled by the shells of that earlier war. Leopold, with General van Overstraeten at his side, reached Ypres three-quarters of an hour later. The congested roads delayed Billotte even longer, while Gort did not arrive until 8 p.m. That was an hour after Weygand, angered by his absence, had set out for Dunkirk and a hazardous voyage to Cherbourg by motor torpedo-boat.

The Ypres conference on 21 May was not a success.[10] Weygand elaborated his plan: the Belgians must pull back from their current positions on the Scheldt and establish a line along the Yser and the Lys, to protect the rear of a southward thrust by Billotte's First Army intended to link up, around Bapaume, with a counter-attack launched by General Georges northwards from the Somme; the panzer corridor would thus be sealed. King Leopold, unlike his father on such occasions, said little: he left Overstraeten to explain that 'after the forced marches the army had made, it was too weary' to retreat back to the Yser: 'at least two days of rest' were needed. Leopold went so far as to tell Weygand that he 'would think it over' (*réfléchirait*). Billotte was more positive, although he admitted that the fighting had thrown the French First Army into confusion. Weygand's proposed southward thrust would, he thought, have to be undertaken primarily by the British. The French and Belgians thus downloaded responsibility for cutting off the panzers on to the absent commander of the BEF.

It is small wonder that when Gort arrived he treated Billotte's proposals with considerable reservation. One reason for his absence from the afternoon session was that he had been co-ordinating a counter-attack launched on that Tuesday southwest of Arras. Some 83 tanks in General Martel's 50th Division penetrated 10 miles into the panzer corridor, with their further progress checked by the failure of the French First Army to provide the flank cover on which Gort had counted. He pointed out to Billotte that the BEF's reserves were already committed to battle, and he doubted if a major attack could be made for another three or four days. When the Ypres meeting broke up only Billotte retained any confidence in Weygand's plan. Overstraeten's account of the conference ends on a note of hopeless despair.[11]

A few hours later General Billotte was fatally injured when the car in which he was travelling skidded in heavy rain outside Ypres and in the black-out was hit by a lorry. For 48 critical hours the French Army Group was left without a C-in-C. The BEF was by now for the most part back on the starting line the troops had left ten days previously. Gort's Corps commanders were convinced the Belgians were about to drop out of the battle: 'Nothing but a miracle can save the BEF now, and the end cannot be far off,' Brooke wrote in his diary at Armentières on 23 May. During that Thursday the Germans entered Boulogne. Next morning they were attacking Hazebrouck and closing in on Calais.[12]

As late as noon on 25 May, Gort still hoped to send his 3rd Corps southwards to cut through the panzer corridor, but by the evening he realized such action would court disaster: some 14 German armoured divisions and at least a dozen infantry divisions packed the corridor. He was alarmed too by the claws of the two German army corps threatening to encircle his battle-weary 11 divisions and cut them off from the sea. On 26 May, Gort ordered the BEF to head for the coast and embark: 'all guns, vehicles, stores etc. would be abandoned'.[13] There was no possibility of retaining a foothold in Belgium.

General Brooke sought to establish a perimeter line protecting Dunkirk, running from Gravelines through Ypres to Nieuport, where he hoped the Belgian army might still be capable of checking the advance of German forces coming down from the north. Momentarily it seemed as if the Belgians might rally. On 25 May a proclamation in King Leopold's name called on his troops to wage war 'with all our power and energy on the same ground on which we victoriously faced the enemy in 1914'. There were instances of courageous resistance, notably at Hill 60, where the Belgians put to good use trenches preserved in memory of the earlier clash of arms. But both Gort and Brooke recognized that the king felt little commitment to the common cause.

On the morning of 26 May, General Brooke drove through Ploegsteert and into Ypres. No Belgian troops were to be seen in the familiar streets; the only French soldiers were postal clerks overlooked in the general exodus. British sappers stood by to demolish the bridges, on one occasion almost leaving their corps commander on the wrong side of the canal. From the eastern ridges, beyond the Menin Road, artillery fire gave warning of a German approach. General Martel was ordered to prepare for a delaying action if the Germans mounted an all-out assault on Ypres itself, and General Montgomery, whose 3rd Division still lay southwest of Lille, was assigned a night march of some 30 miles to take up positions along the Yserlee canal northwards from Boesinghe through Steenstraat to Dixmude.

No sooner had Montgomery reached the Yserlee, early on 2 May, than he learnt that King Leopold had accepted German demands for Belgian capitulation. The army was ordered to end all resistance. The king personally surrendered his sword, choosing to remain with his people. He believed that even as a prisoner of war he might find means to lighten his subjects' burden. The Belgian ministers dissociated themselves from their sovereign's action and maintained a government in exile.

The immediate effect of the capitulation was to open a gap in the northern fringe of Dunkirk's outer perimeter of defence. Hurriedly, Brooke and Montgomery improvised a force to hold the line of the Yser down to Nieuport and the sea. No attempts were made to open the sluice gates.

Most towns on either side of the border were by now being heavily bombed, Poperinghe and Armentières in particular, but central Ypres remained unscathed. Brooke visited Martel again on 28 May, when the silence of the streets was broken by the sound of shells exploding on the outer suburbs. Later that day the last troops left Ypres along the road and railway route to Poperinghe, where fires still raged from the recent bombing. Ahead lay 'the deliverance of Dunkirk' when, between 27 May and 4 June, 338,000 British and allied troops were brought across to England from Dunkirk harbour and the 15 miles of beaches running northwards to La Panne.[14]

* * *

In the first week of June, even before the opening of the second phase of the battle that brought Germany victory over France, Hitler visited Ypres. His Mercedes paused at the Menin Gate and then drove out to Langemarck, where he paid homage to the 'innocents' mowed down in 1914. He returned for a longer visit to the Salient after the French capitulation on 24 June, accompanied on this occasion by two of his wartime comrades. They toured the battlefields they had known – Gheluvert, Comines, Wytschaete, Messines – as well as again honouring the dead of Langemarck. Few Belgians saw them or were aware of Hitler's presence.[15]

Ypres, Poperinghe and the surrounding villages remained under German occupation for more than four years. Many families had their younger and fitter menfolk taken to Germany as forced labourers. The shadow of the Gestapo was present everywhere. Local dignitaries, lawyers, high-school teachers and other 'intellectuals' were at first arrested. Most were soon released after questioning. Many subsequently supported the Resistance, secretly or passively, but the Germans also played on Flemish Francophobes to recruit collaborators: even before the close of 1940 some Flemish nationalists enlisted in the Westland Regiment of the Waffen-SS Germania Division.

The Jewish community in this region of Flanders was small but, as elsewhere in Belgium, Jews were rounded up and detained in holding camps while their business affairs were investigated before confiscation of their property. Brialmont's Fort Breendonck, on the road from Malines to Antwerp, became a concentration camp to which non-Jews, too, were sent for 'punishment'. The guards became notorious for their sadistic practices. After the war 16 Belgians who had collaborated with the Nazis at Breendonck were executed, shot with their backs to the firing squad as a sign of their infamy. By midsummer 1942 the Final Solution, that appalling crime of genocide, was sending Jewish survivors eastwards to the gas chambers of Auschwitz. At least 25,000 Belgian Jews perished in the Holocaust.

Throughout the occupation the Commonwealth war cemeteries were treated with respect, though specifically anti-German inscriptions were erased from plaques and monuments. The most treasured fittings of St George's Memorial Church in Ypres were removed for safe keeping by regular members of the congregation before the town fell. During the occupation German Protestants occasionally held services in the church, fatigue parties having unscrewed commemorative brass plaques on the chairs in advance: all were returned after the war.

At Poperinghe the contents of Talbot House were hidden by a group of friends before the German authorities requisitioned the building and its outhouses as billets for a predominantly Austrian regiment. Other units moved in for periods of recuperation until in 1941 it served for several months as a discreetly managed brothel for officers of the German navy. Respectability returned before the end of the year with Talbot House becoming the residence of the senior local German commander. The chapel in the Upper Room remained inviolate.[16]

The 3rd Polish Armoured Division, attached to Field Marshal Montgomery's Second Army, liberated both Poperinghe and Ypres on the same day, 6 September 1944. A bugler is said to have sounded the Last Post that evening under the Menin Gate while firing could still be heard coming from across the canal. Three days earlier allied troops had entered Brussels, and there were hopes the war would end rapidly as in 1918, but the enemy resistance stiffened. In mid-December an unexpected German offensive in the Ardennes momentarily raised fears of a break-through to Antwerp and the lower Scheldt. A pincer movement by Montgomery and the American general, George C. Patton, won 'the Battle of the Bulge' in the new year. By the end of January 1945 the kingdom was clear of Hitler's armies.

In post-war Belgium the public mood was angry, as in so many lands where the Resistance hunted down alleged collaborators. The most dramatic act occurred in March 1946 when extremists opposed to Flemish nationalism blew up the original IJzertoren at Dixmude – only for it to be replaced 19 years later by the present, even higher, peace monument. King Leopold III, whom the Germans had kept under virtual house arrest at the palace of Laeken for the first four years of the occupation, was widely unpopular. He was deported to Germany in the late summer of 1944 with his family including his second wife, the Princess de Rethy. It was all too easy to make him a scapegoat for Belgium's misfortunes in 1940, and he was alleged, unfairly, to have collaborated with Hitler. Leopold settled in Switzerland, his brother Charles serving as regent. In 1950 a referendum showed 57 per cent of voters favoured Leopold's return. Although he came back to Brussels, the parties of the left remained hostile. There were serious riots, and in July 1951 he abdicated in favour of his elder son by Queen Astrid, Baudouin I. On Baudouin's death in 1992, Leopold's second son acceded as Albert II.

This acrimonious public debate over the monarchy was waged against a background of economic and constitutional change that continued through four decades. There was a dichotomy in Belgian political life. Externally, positive statesmanship brought the kingdom more and more into Europe, with interdependence offering a profitable substitute for strict neutrality. Internally, the chronic language disputes ensured that the emphasis in domestic legislation was on devolution. In 1958, the year in which Brussels staged a world fair and the city skyline gained the Atomium, the Belgian capital also welcomed the European Economic Community, while in 1967 NATO headquarters moved from Fontainebleau in France to the Brussels suburb of Evere. But during the EEC's first years, the local language question brought Flemish radicals out on the streets of Brussels and several other towns. Three constitutional amendments during Baudouin's reign ceded the control of education and cultural affairs to regional governments. Finally, soon after Albert II's accession, Belgium became a federal monarchy, with five community assemblies, each with its own minister president (prime minister).

In theory the person of the king has served to unite a polyphonic nation, as in the opening months of the Great War. Old tensions, however, come readily to the surface. Thus, in August 2006, Yves Leterme, minister-president of the Flemish community, gave an interview to a Parisian newspaper in which he dismissed the concept of a Belgian nation. Belgium, he claimed, was ' an accident of history': it was little more than 'the king, the national football team and certain brands of beer'. He ridiculed 'the difficulties francophone leaders, and even the king of this country, have in speaking fluent Dutch'.[17] Significantly the interview coincided with the annual IJzer Pilgrimage, four days in which passions over past struggles tend to run as high as in the Apprentice Boys parades of Northern Ireland.

Fewer tourists crossed to Flanders from Britain after the Second World War than in the 1930s: they had more recent battlefields to visit, and the purchase of foreign currency was restricted. Numbers picked up again in the late 1950s and 1960s. There were several reasons for this revival of interest. The availability of new source material encouraged scholars with experience of modern soldiering to reassess the Great War critically, though retaining admiration for the heroism and endurance of the troops: two best-sellers, Leon Wolff's *In Flanders Fields* (1958) and Alan Clark's *The Donkeys* (1961) were devoted to the Salient and northwest France. Clark provoked controversy by his contempt for brass-hat leadership. So, too, did the sustained irreverence of Joan Littlewood's satirical *Oh! What a Lovely War* (1963). The public's rediscovery of Wilfred Owen's poetry, both through Britten's *War Requiem* (1961) and Cecil Day-Lewis's edition of his collected poems in 1963, broadened the cultural search for understanding the men of the trenches; a definitive edition of Siegfried Sassoon's collected poems had appeared two years earlier, in 1961. Greatest influence of all, however, was the impact of television. The BBC's *Great War* series (1964) projected images of Grandad's war into the sitting room and in many instances prompted ageing survivors to download long repressed memories. The personal immediacy of their tales of living history gripped a younger generation, an experience to be repeated at the change of the century through interviews with the last veterans.

Contemporary Ypres, though a lively market town with attractive walks along the old ramparts, is no longer the slumbering city whose medieval grandeur charmed Francis Bumpus a century ago. Poperinghe continues to brew fine beer, and out at Passchendaele there is an annual cheese festival, but along familiar roads radiating from Ypres are factory pig-farms and business ventures, some benefiting from the silicon-chip revolution. The town has absorbed surrounding villages, while to the north an industrial park covers old trench lines at Boesinghe. But the Salient has not receded into a remote past. German bunkers and pillboxes remain on farmland where ploughing may be halted by the discovery of unexploded shells, grenades or parts of weapons. An army disposal unit, based at Houthulst, regularly garners the yield of this 'Iron Harvest'. Battlefield archaeologists and licensed amateur 'diggers' have worked on sites where building contractors unearth the relics of war, including human remains and shreds of uniforms, notably at Boesinghe.[18] A soldier's identity is rarely established. Occasionally the discoveries are reported in the daily newspapers or feature in television programmes, keeping the Salient topically in the news.

Modern battle bears little resemblance to the fighting in Flanders. The campaigns against the Ottoman Empire afford more relevance to today's conflicts than the war on the Western Front. There was trench warfare in Korea in 1952–3 and during the Iran–Iraq conflict of the early 1980s, when Iraqi defence lines repelled waves of infantry as fanatical as the German assault on Langemarck in October 1914. For the most part technological innovation has ruled out calls for cannon fodder. Strategic planning for major conflicts seeks swift and decisive results from precision-guided missiles, the ultimate artillery barrage perfected by other means. It is not surprising that Yprians readily identify themselves with the people of historic towns that have suffered bombardment and partial destruction, notably Mostar and Dubrovnik.

For many of us war is abhorrent with whatever weapon it is fought. It remains 'vile wicked folly and a barbarism', as Churchill once declared. The silent message of the panels on the Menin Gate and the ranks of gravestones on parade at Tyne Cot is the need to strive patiently for reconciliation between peoples and nations. Some who come to the Salient today find hope and inspiration in the Island of Ireland Peace Tower and Park on Messines Ridge or the Pool of Peace created from the mine crater at Spanbroekmolen. It matters little where one gains the inner calm that brings reflective understanding. There can be no one visiting Ypres for any length of time who fails to sense the heart lifting with pride and pity at the courage of those who diced with death as shells fell among them while they trudged the long roads of Flanders or endured the horrors of trench warfare in Flanders fields.

NOTES

2 'Unequalled in Grandeur'

1 *The Times,* 9 August 1914, p. 4.
2 McKisack, *The Fourteenth Century*, p. 432.
3 Churchill, *Marlborough*, vol. 2, pp. 92–125, 180–81, 570–71.
4 For Ypres's general setting, see the stimulating chapter by Marc Derez in Liddle (ed.), *Passchendaele in Perspective*, pp. 437–58.
5 Kossmann, *The Low Countries*, pp. 503, 712, 719.
6 Bumpus, *The Cathedrals and Churches of Belgium*, p. 116, quoted by Marc Derez in Liddle (ed.), op. cit., pp. 437–8.
7 Baedeker's *Belgium and Holland*, pp. 29–31.
8 For an informative map of railways at Ypres in 1918: Gilbert, *Routledge Atlas of the First World War*, p. 22.
9 Strachan, *First World War,* vol. 1, p. 209. See also J. Stengers on Belgium in Wilson (ed.), *Decisions for War*, pp. 151–6.

3 Plans and Illusions

1 Macdonald, *Voices and Images of the Great War*, pp. 6–9, including an extract from the diary of Henri Desagneux in Paris; Brown, *1914*, p. 101; C. A. Macartney to the author in conversation, December 1964.
2 Text of the memorandum in Ritter, *The Schlieffen Plan*, pp. 134–8. On Ritter's study see L. C. F. Turner in Kennedy (ed.), *The War Plans of the Great Powers*, pp. 199–217.
3 Strachan, *The First World War,* vol. 1, pp. 176–9 and 207, for analysis of strength of invading army.
4 On Joffre and Plan 17, Strachan, op. cit., pp. 191–8. For the evolution of Joffre's strategy, S. R. Williamson in Kennedy (ed.), op. cit., pp. 133–53.
5 Grey, *Twenty Five Years*, vol. 1, ch. 6. Hargreaves article on the 'Origin of the Anglo-French Military Conversations'. J. McDermott, 'The Revolution in British Military Thinking' in Kennedy, op. cit., pp. 99–112. Howard, *The Continental Commitment*.

6 Ottley to first sea lord, Gooch and Temperley, *British Documents on the Origins of the War*, vol. 3, p. 186.

7 Grey to Lord Tweedmouth, Gooch and Temperley, ibid, p. 203.

8 The Barnardiston–Ducarne talks and plans can be followed in Gooch and Temperly, ibid, pp.187–201.

9 See two articles in the *Journal of Modern History*: Helmreich 'British concern over Neutrality and British Intervention'; Thomas, 'Anglo-Belgian military relations and the Congo Question, 1911–13'.

10 Dubail–Wilson agreement: Gooch and Temperley, op. cit., vol. 7, no. 640; Callwell, *Sir Henry Wilson*, 1, pp. 98–9.

11 Minutes of CID meeting, 23 August 1911, NA, Cab. 38/19/49. Churchill, *World Crisis*, vol. 1, pp. 329–42.

12 Hankey's comments: Hankey, *The Supreme Command*, vol. 1, pp. 81–2.

13 Williamson, *The Politics of Grand Strategy*, pp. 167–204. F. A. Johnson's pioneer study of the CID, *Defence by Committee* is critically analysed in Mackintosh's article 'The role of the Committee of Imperial Defence'. Ch. 6 of Holmes's biography of French, *The Little Field Marshal*, admirably assesses the impact of the Ulster crisis on the army commanders, but the fullest study of the Curragh affair is Beckett (ed.), *The Army and the Curragh Incident*. See also Keith Jeffery on Wilson, *Oxford Dictionary of National Biography (ODNB)*.

14 Brock and Brock (eds), *Asquith: Letters*, 24 July 1914, p. 123.

15 Grey, op. cit., vol. 1, p. 315; Churchill, *World Crisis*, vol. 1, p. 159; Brock and Brock, ibid, 26 July 1914, pp. 125–6.

16 Churchill, *World Crisis*, vol. 1, pp. 163–4.

17 Gilbert, *Churchill*, vol. 3, pp. 8–13.

18 Chandler (ed.), *The Oxford Illustrated History of the British Army*, pp. 206–11, 242–5.

19 Roskill, *Hankey*, vol. 1, pp. 107–8.

20 For eve-of-war cabinet discussions see Hazlehurst, *Politicians at War*, with ch. 5 assessing views of the non-interventionists.

21 Hazlehurst may be supplemented by Brock in Evans and Strandmann (eds), *The Coming of the First World War*, pp. 145–78.

22 Brown, *1914*, pp. 50–51.

23 Cassar, *Kitchener*, pp. 172–7; Palmer, *Victory 1918*, pp. 1–3; Pollock, *Kitchener*, pp. 372–3.

24 Brock and Brock (eds), op. cit., 5 August 1914, p. 157; Cassar, ibid, pp. 174–86.

25 Churchill, *World Crisis*, vol. 1, pp. 188–9; Grey, op. cit., vol. 2, pp. 63–7; Hankey's notes, N A Cab, 41/22/1; Blake (ed.), *The Private Papers*, pp. 68–9; Holmes, op. cit., pp. 196–8.

26 Interestingly, in his diary Haig twice comments on the report that Holland had been invaded; Sheffield and Bourne (eds), *Douglas Haig*, pp. 53 and 54.

27 Ibid, p. 55.

28 Ibid, p. 56.

29 Cassar, op. cit., pp. 185–90; Simkins, *Kitchener's Army*, and his chapter in Chandler (ed.), op. cit., pp. 241–54.

30 Pollock, op. cit., p. 386.

31 Terraine, *Mons*, pp. 27–8.
32 Childs, *Episodes and Reflections*, p. 117.
33 Terraine, *Mons*, pp. 17–18.
34 Kitchener's battle orders are reprinted from Edmonds's official *History of the Great War*, vol. 1, pp. 442–3, as appendix 1 of Sheffield and Bourne (eds), op. cit., pp. 512–13.
35 Terraine, *Mons*, pp. 30–32; Barker, *The RFC in France*, vol. 1, pp. 29–30; O'Connor, *Airfields and Aircraft*, pp. 14–19.
36 Macdonald, *1914*, p. 66; Brown, *1914*, pp. 68–72.
37 No one has discovered the reason for the original rift between French and Smith-Dorrien. In his *ODNB* entry on 'Dorrien' (*sic*) Stephen Badsby mentions contemporary speculation of mischief-making by Wilson. For ramifications of the rift see Beckett (ed.), *The Judgement of History*.
38 Marshall-Cornwall, *Foch*, p. 59.

4 The Mobile War

1 Macdonald, *1914*, pp. 82–5.
2 Edmonds, *Military Operations: France and Belgium, 1914*, vol. 1, pp. 64–6.
3 Terraine, *Mons*, p. 91.
4 Ibid, pp. 108–11.
5 Holmes, *The Little Field Marshal*, p. 220.
6 Sir George Arthur, *Life of Lord Kitchener*, vol. 3, pp. 55–61.
7 Terraine, *Mons*, p. 211; Edmonds, *Military Operations: France and Belgium, 1914*, vol. 1, p. 494.
8 Reminiscences in Macdonald, *1914*, pp. 228–36, and Brown, *The Western Front*, pp. 14–18.
9 J. French, *1914*, pp.79–80; Cruttwell, *History of the Great War*, pp. 79–80; Holmes, op. cit., p. 223. Brock and Brock (eds), *Asquith: Letters*, p 207.
10 Gliddon, *VCs of the First World War*, pp. 67–79.
11 Spears, *Liaison, 1914*, pp. 314, 336–7; Brock and Brock (eds), op. cit., pp. 213, 214, 217; Terraine, *Mons*, pp. 186–91.
12 Spears, ibid, pp. 366–71; Strachan, *First World War*, vol. 1, pp. 226–7.
13 Passingham, *All the Kaiser's Men*, pp. 24–7, on German response to the long march.
14 Bloem, *The Advance from Mons*, p. 110.
15 Macdonald, *1914*, pp. 206–7; Gibbs, *The Pageant of the Years*, p. 111.
16 Anon, *History of The Times*, vol. 4 (i), p. 220.
17 Chandler (ed.), *Oxford Illustrated History of the British Army*, pp. 204–5, on Boer War casualties.
18 Brock and Brock (eds), op. cit., p. 209, and fn 4, p. 210; *History of the Times*, vol. 4 (i), pp. 222–7.
19 Brock and Brock (eds), ibid, p. 217; Chandler (ed.), op. cit., p. 245.
20 Hatcher, *Laurence Binyon*, pp. 142–3. The book is both a biography and a literary assessment.

21 Keegan, *The First World War*, pp. 118–25.
22 Spears, *Liaison, 1914*, pp. 388–90, 394.
23 The best study of the Marne remains Tyng, *The Campaign of the Marne*, published more than 70 years ago; see also Isserlin, *The Battle of the Marne*.
24 Müller, *Die Sendung von Oberleutnant Hentsch*, pp. 13–21; Volkmann, *Am Tor der neuen Zeit*, pp. 47–83; Barnett, *The Swordbearers*, pp. 100–101.
25 Terraine, *Mons*, p. 217.
26 Marshall-Cornwall, *Foch*, pp. 104–5; Brown, *1914*, p. 127.
27 Sheffield and Bourne (eds), *Douglas Haig*, p. 69.
28 Keegan, op. cit., p. 136; Macdonald, *1914*, pp. 297–8.
29 Mason, 'The Aisne', pp. 289–90.
30 Holmes, op. cit., p. 240.
31 Reichsarchiv, *Weltkrieg*, vol. 5, pp. 3–25.
32 Görlitz (ed.), *The Kaiser and his Court*, pp. 35–6.
33 Holmes, op. cit., p. 242.

5 Antwerp and Beyond: 'A truer Hell'

1 A biography of Brialmont by P. Crockaert was published in Brussels in 1925. For his political ideas see Kossmann, *The Low Countries*, p. 356. For developments after Brialmont's death see Bitsch, *La Belgique entre la France et l'Allemagne*.
2 The fullest maps of the forts at Liège, Namur and Antwerp are in Banks, *Military Atlas of the First World War*, pp. 28–9.
3 Duffy, 'The Siege of Antwerp', p. 376.
4 Ibid, p. 377; Beckett, *Ypres*, pp. 17–18.
5 Roskill, *Hankey*, vol. 1, p. 142; Churchill, *The World Crisis*, vol. 1, pp. 263–4.
6 Tuchman, *The Guns of August*, pp. 433–4 and 539–40.
7 Churchill, *The World Crisis*, vol. 1, p. 264.
8 Gilbert, *Churchill*, vol. 3, pp. 98–9.
9 Ibid, pp. 65, 67–8, 74; Churchill, *The World Crisis*, vol. 1, pp. 268–72.
10 Churchill, *The World Crisis*, vol. 1, p. 273; Gilbert, *Churchill*, vol. 3, p. 73. See also opening ch. of Keith-Falconer, *The Oxfordshire Hussars in the Great War*.
11 Gilbert, *Churchill*, vol. 3, p. 74, 22 September. This section of the letter is omitted from the Brocks's *Asquith: Letters*.
12 Duffy, op. cit., pp. 378–82; *The Times*, 1 October 1914.
13 Churchill, *The World Crisis*, vol. l, pp. 299, 302.
14 Kitchener's reluctance to send the 7th Division is clear from Churchill's narrative: ibid, pp. 303 ff. See also, for creation of the division, the first ch. of Atkinson, *The Seventh Division*.
15 Holmes, *The Little Field Marshal*, pp. 242–3.
16 Gilbert, *Churchill,* vol. 3, pp. 103–19.
17 The conflict between King Albert and his government is well illustrated in Thielemans (ed.), *Albert 1er*, notably on pp. 40–41.

18 Gilbert, *Churchill*, vol. 3, *Companion*, pt 1, pp. 156–7.

19 Ibid, p. 163; Brock and Brock (eds), *Asquith: Letters*, p. 262, with fns 2 and 3.

20 On the creation of the Royal Naval Division (RND) see Gilbert, *Churchill*, vol. 3, pp. 47–52, with presence at Antwerp covered on pp. 107–25 *passim*. For a critical assessment of Churchill's mission and the value of the naval brigades see Strachan, *The First World War*, vol. 1, p. 272.

21 For the war council: Thielemans (ed.), op. cit., p. 41; Gilbert, ibid, p. 118; Churchill, *World Crisis*, vol. 1, pp. 321–2.

22 Hassall, *Rupert Brooke*, p. 466.

23 For Londoners' reactions to Belgian refugees see Palmer, *The East End*, p. 117.

24 Brown, *1914*, p. 179.

25 Deguise's account (1921), Duffy, op. cit., p. 380. Galet, *Albert*, pp. 247–53, criticizes Deguise, suggesting he could have held out longer.

26 For the changing moods at Charleville see Görlitz (ed.), *The Kaiser and his Court*, pp. 35–56; for Paterson's comments on the Aisne: Brown, *1914*, p. 159; Alexander Powell's report on German entry is quoted in Gilbert, *The First World War*, pp. 87–8.

27 The photograph of the Germans on the captured bus is reproduced from *The Times History of the War* by Sir Martin Gilbert in his *Churchill*, vol. 3, as illustration 9.

6 Armies in Collision

1 Fr C. Delaere in Macdonald, *1914*, pp. 344–5; Coombs, *Before Endeavours Fade*, p. 26.

2 Strachan, *The First World War*, pp. 270–72.

3 Macdonald, *1914*, pp. 351–2.

4 Gunner Burrows's diary cited in Macdonald, ibid, p. 353.

5 Foch, *Memoirs*, pp. 142–3; J. French, *1914*, pp. 199–205.

6 Hamilton, *Monty*, vol. 1, pp. 82–4.

7 Macdonald, *1914*, p. 354.

8 Holmes, *The Little Field Marshal*, p. 127.

9 Macdonald, *1914*, p. 357.

10 Maria van Asche of Passchendaele village's reminiscence in Macdonald, *1914*, p. 358.

11 Blake (ed.), *Private Papers*, p. 74; Sheffield and Bourne (eds), *Douglas Haig*, p. 73.

12 Statistics on German Fourth Army from Reichsarchiv, *Der Weltkrieg*, vol. 5, pp. 282, 593.

13 Falkenhayn to Albrecht, 10 October 1914, ibid, p. 279.

14 Thielemans (ed.), *Albert 1er*, pp. 175–8; Galet, *Albert*, p. 265.

15 Ronarc'h and the French Marine Fusiliers: Beckett, *Ypres*, p. 22.

16 Strachan, *The First World War*, vol. 1, p. 275.

17 Reichsarchiv, *Der Weltkrieg*, vol. 5, p. 302; Gilbert, *Churchill*, vol. 3, p. 135; Churchill, *The World Crisis*, vol. 1, pp. 335–9.

18 Banks, *Military Atlas of the First World War*, pp. 67–71, has maps of the battle of the Yser, diagrams of the sluices and shows the inundated region in detail. Thielemans (ed.), op. cit., p. 43; Cammaerts, *Albert of Belgium*, pp. 196–9; Beckett, *Ypres*, pp. 86–7.

19 For a critical German commentary on the fall of Dixmude see Unruh, *Langemarck*, pp. 124–7.

20 Sheffield and Bourne (eds), op. cit., pp. 73–4 (a fuller entry than in Blake, op. cit., pp. 74–5).

21 Sheffield and Bourne (eds), ibid.

22 French's diary quoted by Holmes, op. cit., p. 246.

23 Edmonds, *Military Operations: France and Belgium, 1914*, vol. 2, p. 168.

24 Holmes, op. cit., p. 246.

25 Hyndson, *From Mons to the First Battle of Ypres*, p. 80.

26 Corporal Letyford of the Royal Engineers, cited in Macdonald, *1914*, p. 361.

27 Beckett, *Ypres*, p. 80, citing Dillon's letter in IWM Dillon Mss 82/25/1.

28 Sulzbach, *With the German Guns*, p. 37.

29 Unruh, *Langemarck*, p. 9.

30 Binding, *A Fatalist at War*, p. 19.

31 See Fox, 'The myths of Langemarck', pp. 13–25; cf. Strachan, op. cit., vol. 1, p. 274.

32 Private Knight, cited in Beckett, *Ypres*, p. 95.

33 Atkinson, *The Seventh Division*, pp. 51–6.

34 Reichsarchiv, *Der Weltkrieg*, vol. 5, p. 317.

35 Beckett, *Ypres*, p. 93.

36 Sheffield and Bourne (eds), op. cit., p.75.

37 Beckett, *Ypres*, p. 94.

38 Reichsarchiv, *Der Weltkrieg*, vol. 5, p. 338

39 Strachan, op. cit., calculates two to one (p. 276); Cruttwell, *A History of the Great War*, suggests 'six to one in all arms' (p. 103).

40 Edmonds, *Military Operations: France and Belgium, 1914*, vol. 2, p. 282.

7 Days of Crisis

1 Beckett, *Ypres*, pp. 114, 116. Dr Beckett's detailed analysis of these critical days is far superior to any other on the British role in this unusually far-flung battle. The maps in the official history (Edmonds, *Military Operations: France and Belgium, 1914*, vol. 2) are good and informative.

2 Kershaw, *Hitler*, pp. 90, 663, makes use of Hitler's surviving letters, taken from A. Joachimsthaler, *Korrektur eine Bibliographie: Adolf Hitler* (Munich, 1989).

3 See the accounts from civilians used by Macdonald in *1914*, pp. 370–71.

4 Holmes, *The Little Field Marshal*, p. 248. Marshall-Cornwall, *Foch*, p. 136. Dr Beckett (*Ypres*, p. 120) gives the impression that French wrote to Churchill on that day saying he hoped to be at Bruges and Ostend within a week, but the letter was dated four days earlier; see *Asquith: Letters*, p. 247, n. 7.

5 Beckett, ibid, pp. 123–4.

6 Foch, *Memoirs*, p. 156; earliest account by Meunier-Surcouf in Puaux, *Marshal Foch*, pp. 145–6; Anon, *Armées Françaises*, pt 4, annexe 4, p. 322; J. French, *1914*, p. 245; Callwell, *Sir Henry Wilson*, vol. 1, p. 185.

7 Farrar-Hockley, *Death of an Army*, p. 153; Görlitz (ed.), *The Kaiser and his Court*, p. 41.

8 See, in general, Lindsay, *The London Scottish in the Great War*. For Ronald Colman see the biography by J. B. Colman, *Ronald Colman*, pp. 6–13. On Basil Rathbone, the entry in *ODNB* by Sheridan Morley. Rathbone was later commissioned in the Liverpool Scottish and received the Military Cross.

9 Accounts of the day's fighting, based on memoirs and diaries, have been used by Beckett (*Ypres*, pp. 124–30) and by Macdonald (*1914*, pp. 388–95). See also Edmonds, *Military Operations: France and Belgium, 1914*, vol. 2, pp. 346–50, and the article by Goldsmith, 'Territorial Vanguard', pp. 230–38.

10 Beckett, ibid, p. 133

11 Macdonald, *1914*, p. 384, here makes good use of Gunner Burrows's diary.

12 In his *History of the Great War* (p. 104) Cruttwell credits General Fitzclarence with bringing the 2nd Worcesters into the line, but Dr Beckett, *Ypres*, p. 134, using Imperial War Museum archives, has shown that, while Fitzclarence took rapid action to check the German incursion, the pooling of reserves had been agreed by the divisional commanders on the previous evening. There is a good account of the counter-attack in Stacke, *The Worcestershire Regiment in the Great War*, pp. 32–5. See also Brown's *1914*, pp. 185–8, with map on p. 190.

13 On the Hooge disaster, Beckett, ibid, p. 135; Wyrall, *History of the Second Division*, pp. 136–7.

14 Sheffield and Bourne (eds), *Douglas Haig*, pp. 22–3; Gardner, *Trial by Fire*, pp. 220–21; Hussey, 'A hard day at First Ypres', pp. 75–89.

15 Beckett, *Ypres*, p. 137 (assessing approach of the official historian as shown by the Liddell Hart papers).

16 The comment on the Worcesters was made in February 1915: Bodleian Library, Selborne MSS, 73. For J. French's account of his activities on 31 October see his *1914*, pp. 252–60; cf. Holmes, op. cit., pp. 251–2. For the two versions of Haig's diary, Sheffield and Bourne (eds), op. cit, p. 76. An early, and reliable, eye-witness account in Charteris, *At GHQ*, pp. 52–3.

17 Weygand, *Foch*, p. 87; General Weygand was writing as late as 1947. Foch's *Memoirs* (pp. 157–8) also recall French's fatalistic gloom. French himself, *1914*, p. 260, merely says, 'We all went thoroughly into the situation.'!

18 Edmonds, *Military Operations: France and Belgium, 1914*, vol. 2, pp. 342–3; Anon, *Armées Françaises*, vol. 1, pt 4, p. 353, and annexe 4, pp. 386–9.

19 Haig's diary, 31 October 1914, Sheffield and Bourne (eds), op. cit., p. 76.

20 Edmonds, *Military Operations; France and Belgium, 1914*, vol. 2, p. 340.

21 Dauzet, *La Bataille de Flandres*, p. 114. This was one of the few occasions when Haig formally thanked the French for their support (Beckett, *Ypres*, p. 144).

22 Goldsmith. 'Territorial vanguard', pp. 231–8; Beckett, *Ypres*, p. 149; Gough, *The Fifth Army*, pp. 68–9.

23 Beckett, *Ypres*, p. 149.

24 For the Irish Guards at Zillebeke, Kipling, *The Irish Guards in the Great War*, pp. 38–9; for the cavalry charge, G. Arthur, *The Story of the Household Cavalry*, vol. 3, pp. 111–12.

25 Görlitz (ed.), op. cit., pp. 41–2.

26 Lyn Macdonald makes highly effective use of Gunner Burrows's diary in her lovingly researched *1914*. The entries quoted here are from pp. 406, 407 and 408.

27 Haig's diary, 11 November 1914, Sheffield and Bourne (eds), op. cit., p. 79; Holbrook in Macdonald, *1914*, p. 411.

28 Beckett, *Ypres*, pp. 168–9.

29 Edmonds, *Military Operations: France and Belgium, 1914*, vol. 2, pp. 439–41.

30 Roberts, *Waterloo*, p. 107.

31 Mockler-Ferryman, *The Oxfordshire and Buckinghamshire Light Infantry Chronicle*, pp. 202–3. A vivid account of the action in Nonneboschen wood by Colonel Baines, taken from his papers in the Imperial War Museum, is in Brown, *1914*, p. 200.

32 For Fitzclarence's death the main source is Craster, *Fifteen Rounds a Minute*, pp. 151–2. For this phase of the battle in general: Beckett, *Ypres*, pp. 170–71.

33 Gliddon, *VCs of the First World War*, pp. 155–63.

34 Oxford reminiscences I noted in 1944 seem confirmed by Brittain's *Testament of Youth*, p. 111. For the Lille meteorological figures see the research of Phillip Griffiths cited by John Hussey in Liddle (ed.), *Passchendaele in Perspective*, p. 155, n. 12.

35 Sergeant William Edginton in Brown, *The Western Front*, p. 52.

36 Roynon (ed.), *Massacre of the Innocents*, p. 28.

37 Lord Tennyson's obituary, *Wisden Cricketer's Almanack*, 1952, pp. 963–4; Brown, *1914*, p. 199.

38 Anon, *Ypres*, p. 124; 25 November orders, Reichsarchiv, *Weltkrieg*, vol. 6, pp. 372, 398–404; Rupprecht von Bayern (ed. W. Frauendiest), *Mein Kriegstagebuch*, vol. 1, pp. 258–61.

39 German explanation in Anon, *Ypres*, op. cit., p. 15.

40 Sister Marguerite-Marie, B. Bryan, *The Irish Nuns at Ypres*, p. 76. For the town under bombardment see also Dendooven and Dewilde, *The Reconstruction of Ieper*, p. 51. My attention was drawn to these last three books by Ian Beckett's use of them as sources for his ch. 7.

41 Particularly good prints of Antony of Ypres's photographs illustrate Roynon's *Massacre of the Innocents*, pp. 43–4.

8 Deadlock in the Trenches

1 Cruttwell, *History of the Great War*, p. 106. For Falkenhayn's 'broken instrument' metaphor see Ritter, *Staatskunst und Kriegshandwerk*, vol. 3, p. 63. For Kitchener's remark on war as he understood it, Grey, *Twenty Five Years*, vol. 2, pp. 68–9.

2 Definitive casualties remain elusive. Those given here are based on the official history: Edmonds, *Military Operations: France and Belgium, 1914*, vol. 2, pp. 276–7, 465; see also Beckett, *Ypres*, pp. 176–7. The figures include the 8th Division, which did not reach the trenches until 13 November. For the 7th Division see Cruttwell, *History of the Great War*, and the divisional history by Atkinson.

3 For Kitchener's strategic views at this time, Cassar, *Kitchener*, especially pp. 268–70, and David French, *British Strategy and War Aims*. On the New Armies and their employment: Simkins, *Kitchener's Army*; Blake (ed.), *Private Papers*, p. 84; see the contemporary account of life in their ranks by Hay, *The First Hundred Thousand*.

4 Jacques Weygand, *Weygand, mon Père*, p. 99.

5 Brittain, *Testament of Youth*, p. 113. Breakfast cartoon in *Punch*, 9 December 1914, p. 481. Partridge drawing, *Punch*, 23 December 1914, p. 519.

6 Fleming's letter and Churchill's observation to his wife: Gilbert, *Churchill*, vol. 3, *Companion*, pt 1, pp. 273–4.

7 Colonel Lord Loch, cited from IWM documents by Brown, *1914*, p. 263. This aspect of the war is carefully documented in Brown and Seaton, *Christmas Truce*.

8 Anne Williamson, *Henry Williamson*, pp. 35–6; Williamson's novel, *A Fox under my Cloak*, ch. 3, 'Heilige Nacht'. The extracts given here are from Williamson's contribution to *Purnell's History of the First World War*, vol. 2, no. 4, pp. 552–6. For the comments of others, see Brown's *1914*, pp. 263–74.

9 Roynon (ed.), *Massacre of the Innocents*, p. 108 (4 January 1915). Roynon includes a facsimile of French's 'snorter', p. 109.

10 Kershaw, *Hitler: Hubris*, p. 93, citing a dossier in A. Joachimsthaler, *Korrektur eine Bibliographie: Adolf Hitler* (Munich, 1989). For German Army Order of the Day, see Passingham, *All the Kaiser's Men*, p. 48.

11 *Daily Sketch*, 9 January 1915, pp. 1–2, 6–7, facsimile in Williams (ed.), *Newspapers of the First World War*.

12 Churchill to Asquith, 29 December 1914: Gilbert, *Churchill*, vol. 3, *Companion*, pt 1, pp. 343–5.

13 All three memoranda are printed in Gilbert, ibid: Hankey, pp. 337–43; Churchill, pp. 347–9; Lloyd George, pp. 350–56. The companion includes the minutes of the War Councils, with the session of 13 January 1915 on pp. 391–6; for Churchill's reference to the 'coast game' see p. 375. On Hankey: his *Supreme Command*, vol. 1, pp. 244–50; Roskill, *Hankey*, pp. 149–50. On Lloyd George see his *War Memoirs*, vol. 1, pp. 219–24, and Grigg, *Lloyd George*, p. 180, for his visit to the BEF; pp. 195–9 for the memorandum and its aftermath. The search for alternative battle fronts is treated with greater detail than here in Palmer, *Victory 1918*, pp. 15–17, 318.

14 Blake (ed.), *Private Papers*, p. 84; Marder, *Dreadnought to Scapa Flow*, vol. 2, pp 197–8; Thielemans (ed.), *Albert 1er*, p. 46; Gilbert, *Churchill*, vol. 3, *Companion*, pt 1, p. 334; for French to Kitchener on 26 December 1914, pp. 444–6, 469.

15 Lieutenant Neame VC, who served as a lieutenant-general in the Western Desert in 1941, wrote an autobiography, *Playing with Strife,* after being captured by the Italians. The book narrates an adventurous military career from Flanders and France in one world war to the Apennines in the other.

16 Facsimile in Roynon, op. cit., p. 170.

17 Sir John Keegan (*The First World War,* p. 209) suggests the German defenders 'were about one-seventh the strength of their assailants', but his figures seem to include the BEF's back-up battalions while limiting the Germans to 'two infantry regiments and a Jäger battalion'. Sir John's account of the battle (pp. 208–13) is highly instructive and provides a clear analysis of the 'functional and structural' problems that 'were to bedevil success in trench offensives'.

18 Ibid, pp. 208–13.

19 Oldham, *Messines Ridge,* pp. 36–7.

20 Ibid, pp. 32, 35.

21 Chaney's biography of Barrie: *Hide and Seek with Angels,* pp. 307–9.

22 Cave, *Hill 60,* ch. 3, has much technical detail on mining operations; pp. 81–92 for April 1915.

23 Roynon, op. cit., pp. 198, 203–4.

24 Cave, *Hill 60,* pp. 20–31. Cave's compact study is a masterly, detailed narrative.

25 Ibid, pp. 42–7, with Woolley's own account.

26 Ibid, pp. 20–24, cites Johnston's comments from the Bedfordshires' regimental history.

27 Smith-Dorrien, *Forty-Eight Years' Service,* p. 281.

9 Weapons of Terror

1 Private Alfred Broomfield in Max Arthur, *Forgotten Voices of the Great War,* p. 77.

2 Ibid, pp. 79–80 (Underwood), and p. 82 (Dorgan). Lieutenant Strange's report: Strange, *Recollections,* pp. 111–12; Willson, *Ypres,* pp. 71–2.

3 Falkenhayn, *Die Oberste Heeresleitung,* pp. 83–4.

4 Blake (ed.), *Private Papers,* p. 87. For Dundonald project in Crimean War: Palmer, *The Banner of Battle,* p. 74.

5 German Pioneer Regiment: Lieutenant Hahn in Macdonald, *Voices and Images of the Great War,* pp. 81–2.

6 Alan Clark's *The Donkeys,* pp. 76–80, gives a succinct account of the battle with emphasis on the role of the Canadian division. For intelligence warnings of gas, see his appendix 2, pp. 190–91, and for the Robertson to and from Smith-Dorrien correspondence his appendix 3, pp. 192–5.

7 The account of the first stage of Second Ypres is based on the official history: Edmonds, *Military Operations: France and Belgium, 1915,* vol. 1, pp. 251–65. See also the article on Second Ypres by Swinson, pp. 827–37, especially for the dismissal of Smith-Dorrien. Cruttwell's account (*History of the Great War,* pp. 152–8) is particularly interesting as he was serving in the Ypres trenches at the time.

8 Edmonds, ibid, pp. 288–9; Cave, *Hill 60*, pp. 52–5.

9 Cave, ibid, pp. 59–71, prints Greg's graphic account of the fighting, from the Cheshire Regiment's history.

10 Edmonds, *Military Operations: France and Belgium, 1915*, vol. 1, p. 397; see also Clark, *The Donkeys*, appendix 3.

11 In addition to the references above, Smithers, *The Man Who Disobeyed*, pp. 252–6.

12 These paragraphs are based on the official history by Edmonds and on Cruttwell's account but see also Roynon's *Massacre of the Innocents*, pp. 238–44 and 354.

13 'Into Battle' is in many anthologies, including Philip Larkin's 1973 edition of *The Oxford Book of Twentieth Century Verse*, pp. 226–6.

14 Haig's diary, 30 April 1915, in Sheffield and Bourne, *Douglas Haig*, p.110.

15 Edmonds, *Military Operations: France and Belgium, 1915*, vol. 2, pp. 40–41, on Aubers Ridge.

16 *The Times*, 14 May 1915, p. 8. For Lloyd George and the problem of munitions, Grigg, *Lloyd George*, pp. 240, 248–82.

17 Lucy, *There's a Devil in the Drum,* cited by Nigel Cave in his comprehensive *Sanctuary Wood and Hooge*, p. 33.

18 Schofield, *Wavell*, with the events of 1915 covered on pp. 58–9. See also the diary of Captain Billy Congreve in Fraser and Thornton, *The Congreves*, p. 269.

19 O'Connor, *Airfields and Airmen*, pp. 49–51.

20 Cave, *Sanctuary Wood and Hooge*, p. 52.

21 See the long extract from Pollard, *Fire-Eater*, cited under that title by Cave, ibid, pp. 32–5.

22 The battalion commander's report is in Cave, ibid, pp. 66–9.

23 Crofton's diary for 5 June 1915, Roynon, op. cit., p. 264.

24 Ibid, p. 265.

25 These paragraphs are based primarily on: Holmes, *The Little Field Marshal*, pp. 300–305; Sheffield and Bourne, op. cit., pp. 149–62; Heinz, *Loretto*, pp. 163–8, and the analysis by Cruttwell (a participant) in his *History of the Great War*, pp. 165–9.

26 Brittain, *Testament of Youth*, pp. 235–43.

27 Macdonald, *Voices and Images of the Great War*, pp. 116–17.

10 'Orgy of Slaughter'

1 Charteris, *At GHQ*, p. 116.

2 Holmes, *The Little Field Marshal*, p. 305.

3 *The Times* of 2 November 1915 made the dispatch public.

4 Haig's diary in Sheffield and Bourne (eds), *Douglas Haig*, pp. 130–31 (14 July), pp. 166–7 (24 October). For the king's opinions of French and Haig and his influence on the change of command see Rose, *King George V*, pp. 192–3.

5 Alistair Horne's classic study *The Price of Glory* summarizes Falkenhayn's memorandum, pp. 42–5.

6 Haig's diary, 26 December 1915, Blake (ed.), *The Private Papers*, p. 120. Sheffield and Bourne (eds), op. cit., include no diary entries between 14 December and 1 January.

7 For preparations for the Somme see Gilbert, *Somme,* pp. 11–30.

8 The talks at Dover and with Kitchener are more fully covered in Blake (ed.), op. cit., pp. 132–4 than in Sheffield and Bourne (eds), op. cit., pp. 181–2.

9 Oldham, *Messines Ridge*, pp. 43–54.

10 Williams, *Byng of Vimy*, pp. 128–9.

11 D. J. Goodspeed, 'Prelude to the Somme, Mount Sorrel, June 1916' in Cross and Bothwell (eds), *Policy by Other Means*, pp. 147–61.

12 For Churchill in Flanders, Gilbert, *Winston S. Churchill*, vol. 3, pp. 648–760, supplemented by the companion vol. 3, pt 2, pp. 1278–1502.

13 Holts, *Battlefield Guide*, p. 190, reproduces Hitler's painting of the Sunken Road at Croonaert beside a photograph of the same scene today.

14 H. H. Morell recalling The Fancies in Roberts and Pearson (eds), *The Wipers Times*, p. 333.

15 See *The Wipers Times* (as above), the complete series of the 'famous wartime trench newspaper' repr. 2006 in book form, with intro. by Malcolm Brown and excellent notes by Patrick Beaver.

16 Ibid, p. 5.

17 Blunden, *Undertones of War*, p. 122. For Eliane Cossey and her sisters see also Holts, op. cit., pp. 164–5 (invaluable for anyone visiting Poperinghe today).

18 Chapman, *A Haven in Hell*, p. 14. (At Pusey House, Oxford, books and the provision of places to read them stimulated and sustained a meditative Anglo-Catholicism centred on Eucharistic worship.)

19 Ibid, p. 76. Paul Chapman's book contains many extracts from Clayton's letters and reminiscences.

20 Putowski and Sykes, *Shot at Dawn*, pp. 316–42, includes analytical tables listing the executions.

21 Kossmann, *The Low Countries*, p. 543.

22 Ibid (p. 533) is informative on Cardinal Mercier but, strangely, ignores the popular hero, Burgomaster Max.

23 Thielemans (ed.), *Albert Ier*: Foch and Gamelin, 20 January 1916, pp. 243–4; Haig and Curzon, 7 February, pp. 248–9; Maglinse, 5 December, p. 294.

24 Ibid, pp. 62, 102, 169, 256.

25 See Albert's diary entry for 7 February 1916, Thielemans (ed.), op. cit., p. 248. Fischer, *Germany's Aims in the First World War*, pp. 216–23, examines the Toerring–Waxweiler conversations.

26 See Thielemans (ed.), op. cit., pp. 266–7, for Albert's account of Foch's visit on 11 May.

27 Gilbert, *Somme*, pp. 23–6; Roskill, *Hankey*, pp. 266 and 268; Palmer, *Victory 1918*, p. 62.

28 Sheffield and Bourne (eds), op. cit., p. 188.

29 Cassar, *Kitchener*, pp. 476–80; for 'pained hush' see *Daily Mirror*, 7 June 1916, p. 5.

30 The following paragraphs are based on: Gilbert, *Somme*; Middlebrook, *First Day on the Somme;* Terraine, *The Smoke and the Fire*; Prior and Wilson, *The Somme*; Edmonds, *Military Operations: France and Belgium, 1916.*

31 Cruttwell, *A History of the Great War,* p. 277; Griffith, *Battle Tactics of the Western Front, passim.*

32 NA PRO CAB 42/24/13, Minutes of the War Committee, 20 November 1916, cited by D. French, *The Strategy of the Lloyd George Coalition,* p. 51.

11 1917: 'The village has completely disappeared'

1 Gilbert, *Somme*, pp. 244–5.

2 For the infighting that brought down Joffre see Dutton, 'The Fall of General Joffre', pp. 338–51.

3 Hankey's diary, 15 January 1917: Roskill, *Hankey,* p. 361.

4 Sheffield and Bourne (eds), *Douglas Haig,* p. 259. Replacement of Asquith by Lloyd George: Grigg, *Lloyd George,* pp. 435–74; Jenkins, *Asquith,* pp. 479–519; Hankey, *Supreme Command,* vol. 2, pp. 553–70.

5 For the Rome conference: Roskill, *Hankey,* pp. 350–52; Robertson, *Soldiers and Statesmen,* vol. 2, pp. 135–7; Bonham-Carter, *Soldier True,* pp. 200–203; Lloyd George, *War Memoirs,* vol. 2, pp. 838–50. Milner's Russian mission: Wrench, *Alfred, Lord Milner,* pp. 322–6. For Salonika: Palmer, *The Gardeners of Salonika,* pp. 108–31, supplemented by Nicol, *Uncle George,* pp. 118–20. Palmer, *Victory 1918,* pp. 16–284, recounts Lloyd George's Italian, Balkan and Middle Eastern alternatives in detail.

6 D. French, *Strategy of the Lloyd George Coalition,* is an excellent study, in particular see pp. 53–61.

7 Blake (ed.), *Private Papers,* p. 184. Blake's treatment of these critical months is more detailed than that of Sheffield and Bourne.

8 Blake (ed.), op. cit., pp. 193–4.

9 See Wiest, *Passchendaele and the Royal Navy,* summarized by Wiest in his chapter 'The Planned Amphibious Assault' in Liddle (ed.), *Passchendaele in Perspective,* pp. 201–14.

10 The fullest treatment of the Calais conference is in Blake (ed.), op. cit., pp. 198–212; see also Rose, *King George V,* pp. 200–203, and D. French, *Strategy of the Lloyd George Coalition,* pp. 56–7.

11 Woodward, *Lloyd George and the Generals,* pp. 150–51; D. French, ibid, p. 59.

12 Terraine, *Douglas Haig,* p. 336.

13 Sylvester in Arthur, *Forgotten Voices of the Great War,* p. 206; see also testimony of Private Haine of the HAC, p. 202. 'Web-feet', *The B.E.F. Times,* 5 March 1917, in Roberts and Pearson (eds), *The Wipers Times,* p. 171.

14 Kielmansegg, *Deutschland und der Erste Weltkrieg,* pp. 508–12; Heinz Hagenbücke, 'The German High Command' in Liddle (ed.), op. cit., pp. 45–56; Peter Oldham, *The Hindenburg Line.*

15 Thurlow's *The Pill Boxes of Flanders,* though essentially an early guide book, provides a detailed study of German bunkers and fortifications as well as of British blockhouses.

16 Morton and Granarstein, *Marching to Armageddon, passim.*

17 Wynne, *If Germany Attacks,* pp. 166–84.

18 Spears, *Prelude to Victory,* pp. 489–509, gives a characteristically vivid account of the battle.

19 Watt, *Dare Call It Treason,* pp. 175–213.

20 F. E. Vandiver in Liddle (ed.), op. cit., p. 33; Blake (ed.), op. cit., p. 229.

21 Oldham, *Messines Ridge,* p. 86. For full treatment of Messines, Passingham, *Pillars of Fire.* For good contemporary reports see *The Times,* 8 and 9 June 1917.

22 Harrington, *Plumer of Messines,* p. 104. Haig at Cassel: Blake (ed.), op. cit., p. 236. In fairness to Haig, it should be added that he was in Cassel for a meeting with Pétain. This was the occasion when he heard of the mutinous state of the French army.

23 Fr van Walleghem's account is in Macdonald, *Voices and Images of the Great War,* p. 214.

24 Liddle (ed.), op. cit., p. 482, and Prior and Wilson, *Passchendaele, passim.*

25 Blake, op. cit., pp. 236 and 239.

26 Callwell, *Sir Henry Wilson,* vol. 1, p. 359.

27 J. Bruce and K. Kelly, 'The Royal Flying Corps and the Struggle for Supremacy in the Air over the Salient' in Liddle (ed.), op. cit., pp. 159–73. For a full account of air operations in 1917 see Jones, *The War in the Air.*

28 B. Green (ed.), *Wisden Anthology, 1900–1940* (London, 1980), pp. 436–8, 488–91. Quotations are from *Wisden's* report of the match and obituary of Blythe.

29 Blake (ed.), op. cit., p. 246. Terraine, *The Road to Passchendaele* is a useful source book for all aspects of Third Ypres, accompanied by trenchant judgements.

12 Passchendaele, 1917

1 My narrative of the battles is based largely on: the official history (Edmonds, *Military Operations, France and Belgium, 1917,* vol. 2, especially pp. 130–233 and 250–98); Wolf, *In Flanders Fields,* pp. 113–31, 143–56; Macdonald, *They Called it Passchendaele;* the several contributions to Liddle (ed.), *Passchendaele in Perspective;* Prior and Wilson, *Passchendaele;* Warner, *Passchendaele.*

2 Blake, *The Private Papers,* p. 248.

3 Ibid, p. 249.

4 Brown, *The Imperial War Museum Book of the Western Front,* p. 252.

5 A facsimile of Chapman's diary entry is reproduced in Liddle, op. cit., p. 427. For Haig's diary comments, Blake, op. cit., p. 250; for Crown Prince Rupprecht, *Mein Kriegstagebuch,* vol. 2, p. 232. The stretcher-bearer photograph was taken by J. W. Brooke: see Carmichael, *First World War Photographers,* p. 64.

6 Sheffield and Bourne, *Douglas Haig*, p. 313. Arthur, *Forgotten Voices*, pp. 218–46, includes graphic accounts of the horrors of death in the mud by men who never expected to survive the ordeal.

7 The planning and preparations for the landing are fully examined in Wiest's invaluable *Passchendaele and the Royal Navy* and summarized in his chapter in Liddle (ed.), *Passchendaele in Perspective*, pp. 201–10.

8 Edmonds, *Military Operations, France and Belgium, 1917*, vol. 2, pp. 189–90.

9 See the division histories cited by John Lee in Liddle (ed.), op. cit., p. 218, including Inglefield, *History of the 20th (Light) Division*, from which the quotation is taken.

10 Halpern, *A Naval History of World War I*, pp. 408–10.

11 Vaughan, *Some Desperate Glory*, p. 230; Vaughan's book is a tragic minor classic.

12 D. French, *The Strategy of the Lloyd George Coalition*, pp. 137–40. For the course of events in Italy and the influence of 'sideshows' on Lloyd George see Palmer, *Victory 1918*, pp. 119–46.

13 Terraine, *The Road to Passchendaele*, p. 339. The incident was told by Edmonds to Liddell Hart in 1927.

14 Sheffield and Bourne, *Douglas Haig*, p. 362.

15 Rupprecht, *Mein Kriegstagebuch*, vol. 2, p. 260.

16 Liddle (ed.), *Passchendaele in Perspective*, pp. 52, 53, 228, 233, 235.

17 Ibid, pp. 295, 299.

18 Stand-by order to Rawlinson: ibid, p. 209. Polygon Wood and Broodseinde: ibid, pp. 53, 107–8, 235, 278–82.

19 Ibid, p. 281.

20 Sheffield and Bourne, op. cit., p. 335.

21 See the account by Private Vincent of the 2nd Australian Division in Liddle (ed.), op. cit., p. 240.

22 Rupprecht, *Mein Kriegstagebuch*, vol. 2, p. 271.

23 Wiest in Liddle (ed.), op. cit., p. 210, citing WO/158/239 NA/PRO.

24 For Canadian Corps and Second Passchendaele in general see Liddle (ed.), op. cit., pp. 244, 258–9, supplemented by Cave, *Passchendaele*, passim.

25 On the dispute, Liddle (ed.), op. cit., pp. 486–8.

26 Terraine, *Road to Passchendaele*, pp. 336–47.

13 'Everyone into Battle'

1 Falls, *Caporetto*, pp. 31–62, 76–108.

2 Hankey, *Supreme Command*, vol. 2, pp. 719–26; D. French, *Strategy of the Lloyd George Coalition*, pp. 162–6.

3 Samuel letter in Brown, *Western Front*, p. 278. For the tanks see Cooper, *Ironclads of Cambrai*.

4 D. French, *Strategy . . . Lloyd George*, pp. 164–8.

5 Gilmour, *Curzon,* p. 495; Shepherd and Bourne, *Douglas Haig*, p. 370.

6 Hankey, op. cit., vol. 2, pp. 756–60; Roskill, *Hankey*, p. 485.

7 Passingham, *All the Kaiser's Men*, pp. 179–80; Keegan, *First World War*, pp. 422–3.

8 D. French, *Strategy . . . Lloyd George*, pp. 219–21.

9 Blake (ed.), *Private Papers*, p. 291.

10 Cruttwell, *History of the Great War*, pp. 501–3. Cruttwell's summary of the ensuing battle remains superb.

11 D. J. Polley papers in the Imperial War Museum, cited in Johnson, *1918*, p. 43. For these events see also Terraine, *To Win a War*, pp. 59–64, and Middlebrook, *The Kaiser's Battle*.

12 Sulzbach, *With the German Guns*, p. 150.

13 Görlitz (ed.), *The Kaiser and his Court*, pp. 343–5.

14 Blake (ed.), op. cit., p. 298; Foch, *Memoirs*, p. 300.

15 Palmer, *Victory 1918*, pp. 170, 174, 177.

16 Keegan, op. cit., p. 434.

17 See the diary of Captain Dartford, a member of the British military mission to the Portuguese, cited in Brown, *Western Front*, pp. 304–5.

18 Hammerson (ed.), *No Easy Hopes or Lies*, p. 251

19 Cruttwell, op. cit., pp. 514–20

20 Sheffield and Bourne, *Douglas Haig*, p. 399–400.

21 Churchill, *World Crisis*, vol. 2, p. 1302, includes a facsimile of Haig's original draft.

22 Lieutenant-Colonel Murray's letter in Brown, *Western Front*, p. 307. For the Hampshires see Freyberg, *Bernard Freyberg VC*, pp. 128–9.

23 Cruttwell, op. cit., p. 521.

24 Keyes, *Naval Memoirs*, vol. 1, pp. 249–56. The best account of the Zeebrugge Raid is in Pitt, *Zeebrugge*.

25 Palmer, *Victory 1918*, traces the course of these sideshows during 1918 in chs 12, 14,15 and 17.

26 Terraine, *To Win a War*, pp. 70–73; Cruttwell, op. cit., pp. 524–7.

27 Lieutenant-Colonel Murray in Brown, *Western Front*, p. 327. In general, Palmer, *Victory 1918*, pp. 204–5 and Terraine, *To Win a War*, pp. 110–15.

28 Jeffrey, *Military Correspondence . . . Wilson*, p. 56; Blake (ed.), op. cit., pp. 323–4.

29 Kossmann, *The Low Countries*, p. 544.

30 Palmer, *Victory 1918*, pp. 211–12, with fuller account in Terraine, *To Win a War*, p. 167.

31 Thielemans (ed.), *Albert Ier*, p. 498.

32 Wheeler-Bennett, *Hindenburg*, pp. 164–9, for events in Spa and Berlin, with the letter printed on pp. 166–7. This paragraph simplifies complex political problems analysed more fully in Palmer, *Victory 1918*, chs 13 and 18.

33 As well as the books cited above, on the American position see MacMillan's stimulating *Peacemakers*, pp. 21–8.

34 Sulzbach, op. cit., p. 237.

35 Dartford's diary entry (1 November) in Brown, *Western Front*, p. 342.

14 The Pilgrim Trail

1 Sulzbach, *With the German Guns*, pp. 250–54.
2 Wheeler-Bennett, *King George VI*, pp. 118–19, includes an extract from Prince Albert's report to his father. For King Albert's speech of 22 November: Kossmann, *The Low Countries*, p. 561; Thielemans, *Albert Ier*, p. 165. Kossmann's work provides the most detailed history of Belgium in English.
3 Roberts and Pearson (eds), *The Wipers Times*, 'Horrors of Peace', p. 326; editorial, p. 319.
4 The fullest account of post-war Ypres's problems is in Dendooven, *Menin Gate and the Last Post*. Beckles Willson publicized his views in his *Ypres: The Holy Ground of British Arms*, published as soon as he was demobilized. See also Beckett's *Ypres*, pp. 181–4, and Marc Derez's invaluable 'A Belgian Salient for Reconstruction' in Liddle (ed.), *Passchendaele in Perspective*, pp. 448–5.
5 Jacky Platteeuw's photographic record, *The Great War in Ypres*, pp. 74, 78 and 79, shows the use made of both Nissen huts and the Albert Houses.
6 *De Standaard*, 9 July 1919, cited by Marc Derez in Liddle (ed.), op. cit., p. 446.
7 *The Times*, 25 July 1927; for background, Dendooven, op. cit., pp. 12–36, 40–53, 88–90.
8 'On Passing the New Menin Gate', R. Hart-Davies (ed.), *Siegfried Sassoon: The War Poems*, p. 153. For 'cemeteries and poppies', see Gunner Harold Coulter's postcard, cited by Brown in his *Western Front*, p. 347.
9 Major T. and Mrs V. Holt's *Battlefield Guide to the Ypres Salient* is a compendium rich in details of war graves and memorials. An ingenious four-colour map to help locate them accompanies the guidebook.
10 Marc Derez in Liddle (ed.), op. cit., p. 451.
11 Holt, op. cit.: Langemarck, pp. 136–9; Vladslo, pp. 231–4.
12 See the illustrations in Platteeuw, op. cit., pp. 112–13.
13 MacMillan, *Peacemakers*, p. 285.
14 Danchev and Todman (eds), *War Diaries*, p. 61; Hamilton, *Monty*, vol. 1, p. 340. After the Second World War, van Overstraeten wrote a 750-page defence of his policies, *Albert I–Leopold III*.
15 Visscher and Vanlangenhove, *Documents diplomatiques belges*, vol. 4, pp. 323–5.

15 Epilogue: 'The war had never stopped'

1 Alexander, *The Republic in Danger*, and Horne, *To Lose a Battle*, pp. 149–52, 154, 157.
2 Hamilton, *Monty*, vol. 1, pp. 117–221 and 190; Danchev and Todman (eds), *War Diaries*, pp. 7 and 14.
3 In addition to Horne's *To Lose a Battle*, pp. 172–201, see Field Marshal Lord Carver's study of Manstein in Barnett, *Hitler's Generals*, pp. 221–44.

4 For the Mechelen episode and its consequences: Vanwelkenhuyzen, 'L'Alerte du 10 janvier 1940', pp. 33–54.

5 Danchev and Tolman (eds), op. cit., pp. 30–31. For German invasion, Horne, *To Lose a Battle*, pp. 247–75.

6 Guderian, *Panzer Leader,* pp. 98–113, remains the best account of the panzer lightning war.

7 Weygand, *Mémoires*, pp. 79–80.

8 Ibid, pp. 80–81.

9 Ibid, pp. 95–6.

10 The main participants' versions of the Ypres conference are given at length in Overstraeten, *Albert I–Leopold III*, pp. 642–63, and more succinctly in Weygand, ibid, pp. 98–101. For the British background see Churchill, *The Second World War*, vol. 2, pp. 51–65.

11 Overstraeten, op. cit., pp. 663 and 670.

12 Danchev and Tolman (eds), op. cit., pp. 67–73, are invaluable for the events of this momentous week.

13 General Montgomery's diary, quoted by Hamilton, *Monty*, vol. 1, p 356, another major source.

14 Churchill entitled his chapter on the evacuation 'The Deliverance of Dunkirk', in *The Second World War*, vol. 2, pp. 87–104. For a judicious reassessment, see Harman, *Dunkirk*.

15 Kershaw, *Hitler: Nemesis*, p. 299, and n. 98 on p. 922. The dates of the visits are uncertain: 4 June and 27 June seem probable. The Holts in their *Battlefield Guide* use local sources to give 1 June for the first visit but, allowing for the complexity of the battle on that day, this seems to me too early. The Holts also reproduce a photograph, p. 139, of Hitler leaving Langemarck cemetery.

16 Chapman, *A Haven in Hell*, p. 121.

17 David Rennie in the *Daily Telegraph*, 21 August 2006, p. 16, with editorial comment p. 23.

18 Holt, op. cit., pp. 245–8.

SELECT BIBLIOGRAPHY

Only works consulted in the preparation of *The Salient* are listed here.

Alexander, M. S., *The Republic in Danger: General Maurice Gamelin and the Politics of French Defence, 1933–1940* (Cambridge, 1992)

Anon, *History of The Times*, vol. 4 (London, 1954)

Anon, Ministère de la Guerre, État-Major de l'Armée, Service Historique, *Les Armées françaises dans la Grande Guerre,* vols 4–8 (Paris, 1925–34)

Anon, *Ypres, 1914: An Official Account Published by Order of the German General Staff* (London, 1919)

Arthur, G., *A Life of Lord Kitchener,* 3 vols (London, 1920)

——*The Story of the Household Cavalry,* vol. 3 (London, 1926)

Arthur, Max, *Forgotten Voices of the Great War* (London, 2002)

Atkinson, C. T., *The Seventh Division, 1914–1918* (London, 1927)

Baedeker, Karl (ed.), *Belgium and Holland* (12th English edn; Leipzig, 1911)

Banks, Arthur, *A Military Atlas of the First World War* (London, 1975)

Barker, Ralph, *The Royal Flying Corps in France,* 2 vols (London, 1995–6)

Barnett, Correlli, *The Swordbearers* (London, 1963)

——*Hitler's Generals* (London, 1993)

Beckett, Ian F. W. (ed.), *The Army and the Curragh Incident, 1914* (London, 1986)

——(ed.), *The Judgement of History: Sir Horace Smith-Dorrien, Lord French and 1914* (London, 1993)

——*Ypres: The First Battle, 1914* (Harlow, 2004)

Binding, Rudolf, *A Fatalist at War* (London, 1929)

Bitsch, Marie-Thérèse, *La Belgique entre la France et l'Allemagne, 1905–1914* (Paris, 1994)

Blake, R. (ed.), *The Private Papers of Douglas Haig, 1914–1918* (London, 1952)

Bloem, Walter, *The Advance from Mons, 1914* (London, 1930)

Blunden, Edmund, *Undertones of War* (London, 1928)

Bonham Carter, Victor, *Soldier True: The Life and Times of Field Marshal Sir William Robertson* (London, 1964)

Brittain, Vera, *Testament of Youth* (London 1933)

Brock, M. and E. (eds), *H. H. Asquith: Letters to Venetia Stanley* (Oxford, 1982)

Brown, Malcolm, *The Imperial War Museum Book of 1918: Year of Victory* (London, 1998)

——*The Imperial War Museum Book of the Western Front* (London, 2001)

——*1914: The Men Who Went to War* (London, 2004)

——With Shirley Seaton, *Christmas Truce* (London, 1994)

Bryan, B., *The Irish Nuns at Ypres* (London, 1915)

Bumpus, T. Francis, *The Cathedrals and Churches of Belgium* (London, 1908/9)

Callwell, C. E., *Field Marshal Sir Henry Wilson: His Life and Diaries*, 2 vols (London, 1927)

Cammaerts, E., *Albert of Belgium, Defender of the Right* (London, 1935)

Carmichael, J., *First World War Photographers* (London, 1989)

Cassar, G. H., *Kitchener: Architect of Victory* (London, 1977)

Cave, Nigel, *Sanctuary Wood and Hooge* (Barnsley 1993)

——*Polygon Wood* (Barnsley 1996)

——*Passchendaele, the Fight for the Village* (Barnsley, 1997)

——*Hill 60* (Barnsley, 1998)

Cecil, H. and Liddle, P. H. (eds), *Facing Armageddon: The First World War Experienced* (London, 1996)

Chandler, D. (ed.), *The Oxford Illustrated History of the British Army* (Oxford and New York, 1994)

Chaney, Lisa, *Hide and Seek with Angels* (London, 2005)

Chapman, Guy, *A Passionate Prodigality* (London, 1933)

Chapman, Paul (ed. Ted Smith), *A Haven in Hell: Talbot House, Poperinghe* (Barnsley, 2000)

Charteris, J., *At GHQ* (London, 1931)

Childs, Sir Wyndham, *Episodes and Reflections* (London, 1930)

Churchill, W. S, *Marlborough: His Life and Times*, 2 vols (London, 1934)

——*The World Crisis, 1911–1918*, 5 vols (London, 1923–9; 1939 edn)

——*The Second World War*, vol. 2 (London, 1949)

Clark, Alan, *The Donkeys* (London, 1961)

Colman, J. B., *Ronald Colman: A Very Private Person* (London 1975)

Coombs, R. E. B., *Before Endeavours Fade* (London, 1976)

Cooper, B., *Ironclads of Cambrai* (London, 1967)

Craig, Gordon, *Germany, 1866–1945* (Oxford, 1978)

Craster, J. M., *Fifteen Rounds a Minute* (London, 1976)

Cross, M., and Bothwell, R. (eds), *Policy by Other Means* (Oxford, 1992)

Cruttwell, C. R. M. F., *A History of the Great War* (Oxford, 1934)

Danchev A., and Todman, D., (eds), *War Diaries, 1939–1945: Field Marshal Lord Alanbrooke* (London, 2001)

Dauzet, P., *La Bataille de Flandres* (Paris, 1917)

David, E., *Inside Asquith's Cabinet: From the Diaries of Charles Hobhouse* (London, 1977)

Dendooven, Dominick, *Menin Gate and Last Post; Ypres as Holy Ground* (Koksijde, 2001)

——With Jan Dewilde, *The Reconstruction of Ieper: A Walk through History* (Ieper, 1999)

Dugdale, E. C. B., *Arthur James Balfour*, vol. 2 (London, 1936)

Edmonds, J. E., *History of the Great War: Military Operations, France and Belgium, 1914–1918*, 14 vols (London, 1922–48)

Essen, L. van der, *The Invasion and the War in Belgium from Liège to the Yser* (London, 1917)

Evans, R. J. W., and Strandmann, H. Pogge von (eds), *The Coming of the First World War* (Oxford, 1999).

Falkenhayn, E. von, *General Headquarters and its Crucial Decisions* (London, 1919)

——*Die Oberste Heeresleitung* (Berlin, 1920)

Falls, Cyril, *The First World War* (London, 1960)

——*Caporetto, 1917* (London, 1966)

Farrar-Hockley, Anthony, *Death of an Army: Ypres, 1914* (London, 1967)

Fischer, Fritz, *Germany's Aims in the First World War* (London, 1967)

Foch, F., *The Memoirs of Marshal Foch* (London, 1931)

Frankland, Noble, and Dowling, Christopher (eds), *Decisive Battles of the 20th Century* (London and New York, 1976)

Fraser, Pamela, and Thornton, L. H., *The Congreves: Father and Son* (London, 1930)

French, David, *British Strategy and War Aims, 1914–1916* (London, 1986)

——*The Strategy of the Lloyd George Coalition, 1916–1918* (Oxford, 1995)

French, John, Viscount, *1914* (London, 1919)

Freyberg, P., *Bernard Freyberg VC: Soldier of Two Nations* (London, 1991)

Galet, E. J., *Albert, King of the Belgians in the Great War* (London, 1931)

Gardner, N., *Trial by Fire: Command and the British Expeditionary Force in 1914* (Westport, Conn., 1995)

Gibbs, P., *Pageant of the Years* (London, ?1932)

Gilbert, Martin, *Winston S. Churchill, 1914–1916,* vol. 3 (1971); *Companion*, 2 pts (London 1973)

——*Winston S. Churchill, 1916–1922*, vol. 4 (1975); *Companion*, 3 pts (London, 1978)

The First World War (London, 1994)

——*Routledge Atlas of the First World War* (rev. edn; London, 1995)

——*Somme: The Heroism and Horror of War* (London, 2006)

Gilmour, David, *Curzon* (London, 1994)

Gliddon, Gerald, *VCs of the First World War, 1914* (Stroud, 1991)

Görlitz, W. (ed.), *The Kaiser and his Court: The First World War Diaries of Admiral Georg von Müller, Chief of the Naval Cabinet, 1914–1918* (2nd edn; London, 1961)

Gooch, G. P., and Temperley, H. W. V., *British Documents on the Origins of the First World War*, vols 3 and 7 (London, 1928–30)

Gough, H., *The Fifth Army* (London, 1931)

Grey of Fallodon, Viscount, *Twenty Five Years, 1892–1916*, 2 vols (London, 1925)

Griffith, P., *Battle Tactics of the Western Front* (London, 1994)

Grigg, J., *Lloyd George: From Peace to War, 1912–1916* (London, 1985)

Guderian, Heinz, *Panzer Leader* (London, 1952)

Halpern, P., *A Naval History of World War I* (London, 1994)

Hamilton, Nigel, *Monty: The Making of a General, 1887–1942* (London, 1981)

Hammerson, M. (ed.), *No Easy Hopes or Lies: The World War I Letters of Lt Arthur Preston White* (London, 1991)

Hankey, M., *The Supreme Command, 1914–1918*, 2 vols (London, 1961)

Harman, N. H., *Dunkirk: The Necessary Myth* (London, 2005)

Harrington, T., *Plumer of Messines* (London, 1935)

Hart-Davies, R. (ed.), *Siegfried Sassoon: The War Poems* (London, 1983)

Hassall, C., *Rupert Brooke* (London, 1964)

Hatcher, J., *Laurence Binyon* (London 1995)

Hazlehurst, Cameron, *Politicians at War, July 1914–May 1915* (London, 1971)

Hay, Ian, *The First Hundred Thousand* (London, 1916)

Heinz, Max, *Loretto: Sketches of a War* (New York, 1930)

Hindenburg, Paul von Beneckendorf und von, *Aus meinen Leben* (Berlin, 1920)

Holmes, Richard, *The Little Field Marshal: Sir John French* (rev. edn; London, 2004)

Holt, Tonie and Valmai, *Battlefield Guide to the Ypres Salient* (rev. edn; Barnsley, 2003)

Horne, Alistair, *The Price of Glory, Verdun, 1916* (London, 1962)

——*To Lose a Battle: France, 1940* (London, 1969)

Howard, Michael, *The Continental Commitment* (London, 1972)

Hyndson, J. G. W., *From Mons to the First Battle of Ypres* (London, 1933)

Inglefield, V., *History of the 20th (Light) Division* (London, 1921)

Isselin, Henri, *The Battle of the Marne* (London, 1965)

Jeffery, K. (ed.), *Military Correspondence of Field Marshal Sir Henry Wilson, 1918–20* (London, 1985)

Jenkins, R., *Asquith: Portrait of a Man and an Era* (London, 1964)

Joffre, J., *Mémoires du Maréchal Joffre* (Paris, 1932)

Johnson, J. H., *1918: The Unexpected Victory* (London, 1997)

Jones, H. A., *History of the Great War: The War in the Air*, vol 4 (London, 1976)

Keegan, John, *The First World War* (London, 1999)

Keith-Falconer, A. W., *The Oxfordshire Hussars in the Great War* (London, 1927)

Kennedy, Paul (ed.), *The War Plans of the Great Powers, 1880–1914* (London, 1979)

Kershaw, Ian, *Hitler, 1936–1943: Nemesis* (London, 1998)

——*Hitler, 1889–1936: Hubris* (London, 2000)

Keyes, Roger, *The Naval Memoirs*, 2 vols (London, 1934–5)

Kielmansegg, Peter, Graf, *Deutschland und der Erste Weltkrieg* (Stuttgart, 1980)

Kipling, Rudyard, *The Irish Guards in the Great War*, vol. 1 (London, 1923)

Kitchen, M., *The Silent Dictatorship: The Politics of the German High Command under Hindenburg and Ludendorff, 1916–1918* (London, 1976)

Kossmann, E. A., *The Low Countries, 1780–1940* (Oxford, 1978)

Liddell Hart, B. H., *History of the First World War* (2nd edn; London, 1972)

Liddle, Peter (ed.), *Passchendaele in Perspective: The Third Battle of Ypres* (London, 1997)

Lindsay, J. H., *The London Scottish in the Great War* (London, 1925)

Lloyd George, D., *War Memoirs*, 6 vols (London, 1933–6; new edn 1938)

Lucy, J., *There's a Devil in the Drum* (London, 1938)

Ludendorff, Erich, *My War Memoirs, 1914–1918* (London, 1929)

Macdonald, Lyn, *1914: The Days of Hope* (London, 1987)

——*They Called it Passchendaele* (London, 1987)

——*Voices and Images of the Great War* (London, 1988)

McKisack, M., *The Fourteenth Century, 1307–1399* (Oxford, 1959)

MacMillan, M., *Peacemakers* (London, 2001)

Marder, A. J., *From the Dreadnought to Scapa Flow*, 5 vols (Oxford, 1974)

Marshall-Cornwall, J., *Foch as Military Commander* (London, 1972)

Maze, Paul, *A Frenchman in Khaki* (London, 1934)

Middlebrook, Martin, *The First Day on the Somme, 1 July 1916* (London, 1971)

——*The Kaiser's Battle* (London, 1978)

Mockler-Ferryman, A. F. (ed.), *The Oxfordshire and Buckinghamshire Light Infantry Chronicle* (London, 1920)

Morton, D., and Granarstein, J. L., *Marching to Armageddon: Canadians and the Great War, 1914–1919* (Toronto, 1989)

Müller, W., *Die Sendung von Oberleutnant Hentsch* (Berlin, 1922)

Neame, Lieutenant-General Sir Philip, *Playing with Strife: The Autobiography of a Soldier* (London, 1947)

Nevin, T., *Ernst Jünger and Germany* (London, 1997)

Nicol, G., *Uncle George: Field Marshal Lord Milne of Salonika and Rubislaw* (London, 1976)

O'Connor, Mike, *Airfields and Airmen: Ypres* (Barnsley, 2001)

Oldham, Peter, *The Hindenburg Line* (Barnsley, 1997)

Messines Ridge (Barnsley, 1998)

Overstraeten, R. van, *Albert I–Leopold III, 1920–1940* (Bruges, 1949)

——*Oxford Dictionary of National Biography* (Oxford, 2004)

Palmer, Alan, *The Gardeners of Salonika* (London, 1965)

——*The Kaiser* (London, 1978)

——*The Banner of Battle* (London, 1987)

——*Victory 1918* (London, 1998)

——*The East End* (rev. edn; London, 2000)

Pardon, S. H. (ed.), *Wisden Cricketers' Almanack*, nos 51–55 (London, 1915–19)

Passingham, Ian, *Pillars of Fire: The Battle of Messines Ridge, June 1917* (Stroud, 1998)

——*All the Kaiser's Men* (Stroud, 2003)

Pitt, Barrie, *Zeebrugge: St George's Day, 1918* (London, 1958)

——*1918, The Last Act* (London, 1962)

Platteeuw, Jacky, *The Great War in Ypres* (Stroud, 2005)

Pollock, J., *Kitchener: Saviour of the World* (London, 2001)

Prior, R., and Wilson, T., *Command on the Western Front: The Military Career of Sir Henry Rawlinson, 1914–18* (Oxford, 1992)

——*Passchendaele: The Untold Story* (London, 1996)

——*The Somme* (London and New Haven, 2005)

Puaux, R., *Marshal Foch* (Paris, n.d.)

Putowski, J., and Sykes, J., *Shot at Dawn* (Barnsley, 1989)

Raleigh, Walter, *The War in the Air*, vol. 1 (London, 1922)

Reichsarchiv, *Der Weltkrieg, 1914 bis 1918*, vols 2–13 (Berlin, 1925–37)

Ritter, Gerhard, *The Schlieffen Plan* (London, 1956)

——*Staatskunst und Kriegshandwerk*, vol. 3 (Munich, 1956)

——*The Sword and the Sceptre*, vols 3 and 4 (London, 1972–3)

Roberts, Andrew, *Waterloo* (London, 2005)

Roberts, F. J., and Pearson, J. H. (eds), intro. Malcolm Brown, notes by Patrick Beaver, *The Wipers Times: The Complete Series* (London, 2006)

Robertson, W., *Soldiers and Statesmen, 1914–1918*, 2 vols (London, 1926)

Rose, Kenneth, *King George V* (London, 1983)

Roskill, S., *Hankey: Man of Secrets*, vol. 1 (London, 1970)

Roynon, Gavin (ed.), *The Massacre of the Innocents: The Crofton Diaries, Ypres 1914–15* (Stroud, 2004)

Rupprecht von Bayern, Kronprinz, *Mein Kriegstagebuch*, 3 vols (Munich, 1929)

Schofield, Victoria, *Wavell* (London, 2006)

Seaman, Owen (ed.), *Punch*, vols 147–56 (London, 1914–18)

Sheffield, G., and Bourne, K. (eds), *Douglas Haig: War Diaries and Letters* (London, 2005)

Simkins, Peter, *Kitchener's Army: The Raising of the New Armies, 1914–16* (Manchester, 1988)

Smith-Dorrien, General Sir Horace, *Forty-Eight Years' Service* (London, 1925)

Smithers, A. J., *The Man Who Disobeyed: Sir Horace Smith-Dorrien and his Enemies* (London, 1970)

Spears, E. L., *Liaison 1914* (London, 1930)

——*Prelude to Victory* (London, 1939)

——*Assignment to Catastrophe*, 2 vols (London, 1954)

Stacke, H. F., *The Worcestershire Regiment in the Great War* (Kidderminster, 1928)

Strachan, Hew, *The First World War: To Arms*, vol. 1 (Oxford, 2001)

Strange, L., *Recollections of an Airman* (London, 1933)

Sulzbach, H., *With the German Guns: Four Years on the Western Front* (London, 1973)

Taylor, A. J. P., *The First World War* (London, 1963)

——*English History, 1914–1945* (Oxford, 1965)

Terraine, J., *Mons: Retreat to Victory* (London, 1960)

——*Douglas Haig: The Educated Soldier* (London, 1963)

——*The Smoke and the Fire* (London, 1963)

——*The Road to Passchendaele* (London, 1977)

——*To Win a War: 1918, Year of Victory* (London, 1986)

Thielemans, Marie-Rose (ed.), *Albert 1er: Carnets et Correspondance de Guerre, 1914–1915* (Paris, 1992)

Thurlow, E. G. L., *The Pill Boxes of Flanders* (London, 1933)

Travers, Tim, *The Killing Ground: The British army, the Western Front and the emergence of modern warfare, 1900–1918* (London, 1987)

Tuchman, Barbara, *The Guns of August* (London, 1962)

Tyng, S., *The Campaign of the Marne, 1914* (London, 1935)

Unruh, Karl, *Langemarck: Legende und Wirklichkeit* (Koblenz, 1986)

Vaughan, E. Campion, *Some Desperate Glory* (London, 1981)

Visscher, Ch. de, and Vanlangenhove (eds), *Documents diplomatiques belges, 1920–1940*, 5 vols (Brussels, 1964–6)

Volkmann, E. O., *Am Tor der neuen Zeit* (Berlin, 1933)

Warner, Philip, *Passchendaele* (London, 1987)

Watt, Richard M., *Dare Call It Treason* (New York, 1963)

Weygand, M., *Foch* (Paris, 1947)

——*Mémoires: Rappelé au Service* (Paris, 1950)

——*Weygand, mon Père* (Paris, 1956)

Wheeler-Bennett, J. W., *King George VI: His Life and Reign* (London and New York, 1965)

——*Hindenburg: The Wooden Titan* (rev. edn; London, 1967)

Wiest, Andrew, *Passchendaele and the Royal Navy* (London and New York, 1995)

Williams, Charles, *Pétain* (London, 2005)

Williams, Ian (ed.), *Newspapers of the First World War* (Newton Abbot, 1976)

Williams, Jeffrey, *Byng of Vimy: General and Governor General* (London, 1983)

Williamson, Anne, *Henry Williamson: Tarka and the Last Romantic* (Stroud, 1995)

Williamson, Henry, *The Wet Flanders Plain* (London, 1929)

——*A Fox under my Cloak* (London, 1955)

Williamson, Samuel R., jnr, *The Politics of Grand Strategy, Britain and France Prepare for War, 1904–1914* (Cambridge, Mass., 1969)

Willson, Beckles, *Ypres: The Holy Ground of British Arms* (Bruges, 1920)

Wilson, K. (ed.), *Decisions for War 1914* (London, 1993)

Woodward, D. R., *Lloyd George and the Generals* (Newark, NJ, 1983)

——(ed.), *Military Correspondence of Field Marshal Sir William Robertson, December 1915–February 1918* (London, 1990)

Wolff, Leon, *In Flanders Fields* (London, 1958)

Wrench, E. E., *Alfred, Lord Milner: The Man of No Illusions* (London, 1958)

Wynne, G. C., *If Germany Attacks: The Battle in Depth in the West* (London, 1940)

Wyrall, E., *The History of the Second Division, 1914–1918* (London, 1921)

ARTICLES IN PERIODICALS

Duffy, C. 'The Siege of Antwerp', *Purnell's History of the First World War*, no. 14, 1969

Dutton, D, 'The Fall of General Joffre', *Journal of Strategic Studies*, 1, no. 3, 1978

Fox, Colin, 'The myths of Langemarck', *Imperial War Museum Review*, 10, 1995.

Goldsmith, R. F. K. 'Territorial vanguard: a London Scottish diary', *Army Quarterly* 103, no. 2, 1976

Hargreaves, J. D., 'The Origin of the Anglo-French Military Conversations', *History*, 36, October 1951

Helmreich, J. E., 'British concern over Neutrality and British Intervention', *Journal of Modern History*, 36, no. 4, 1964

Hussey, John, 'A hard day at First Ypres: the Allied Generals and their Problems, 31 October 1914', *British Army Review*, 107, August 1994

Mackintosh, J. P., 'The role of the Committee of Imperial Defence', *English Historical Review*, 304, 1962

Mason, D., ' The Aisne', *Purnell's History of the First World War*, vol. 1, no.11, 1970

Swinson, Arthur, 'The Second Battle of Ypres', *Purnell's History of the First World War*, vol. 2, no. 14, 1970

Thomas, M. E., 'Anglo-Belgian military relations and the Congo Question, 1911–13, *Journal of Modern History*, 25, no. 2, 1953

Vanwelkenhuyzen, J., 'L'Alerte du 10 janvier 1940', *Revue d'histoire de la deuxième guerre mondiale*, no. 12, 1953

INDEX